Introduction to Knitting

Marshall Cavendish

PICTURE CREDITS

Atlantic Press, page 93
Beta Pictures, pages 83 (no. 17), 89, 98, 102, 111 (no. 32), 118-9
Camera Press, pages 66, 67, 70-71, 74, 75, 99, 105, 108, 119
Conway Press, page 83 (no. 16)
Richard Dunkley, page 3
Maison de Marie Claire, pages 88-89
Leslie Shrivell/Studio Briggs, pages 12, 19, 21, 23, 25, 27, 29, 31, 33, 35, 37, 39, 41, 45, 47, 49, 51, 53, 57, 59, 61, 63
Simis Press, pages 70, 82 (nos. 11-13), 103, 104, 111 (nos. 33 and 34)
Templetons, page 82 (nos. 14 and 15)
Michael James Ward, pages 43, 55, 78-79, 95

Edited by Nicky Hayden

Published by Marshall Cavendish Books Limited
58 Old Compton Street
London W1V 5PA

This volume first published 1975

Printed and bound in Hong Kong
by Dai Nippon Printing Company

ISBN 0 85685 090 X

Introduction

This book is a complete introduction to the wonderful craft of knitting, from casting on to the finishing touches—and it's not only for the beginner; as well as basic knitting know-how, Part One has instructions for a whole range of attractive stitches for more experienced knitters to learn or perfect. These include cables, Aran, Fair Isle, lace, picot, jacquard, stripes, checks and motifs. There are instructions for adapting a pattern, using a chart or designing a garment. In Part Two there are 36 attractive patterns for all the family— bright and stylish designs which make full use of the techniques described. These are starred in order of difficulty—one star for beginners, two for those who have some experience, and three for the expert knitter who enjoys a challenge! There are jerseys for men and women, boys and girls; dresses for women and children down to toddlers' size; trouser suits, slip-ons and jackets; warm hats, scarves, and gloves; clothes for day and clothes for evening—in fact a wide selection to suit every occasion.

Contents

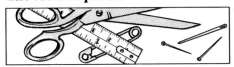

PART ONE

Knitting knowhow

With knitting, as with most things in life, there's always a best way to do a job. Even if you're an experienced knitter you can improve your skills by referring to the various methods of casting on, making buttonholes, hems and so on —and then choosing the exact method which gives a perfect finish to a particular pattern. For the creative knitter, there are dozens of beautiful stitches—with the added bonus of an attractive garment pattern which can be made up in a variety of styles with a wide range of decorative stitches. And an important chapter explains how to do your own designing and adapt existing patterns to fit you exactly. If you're a beginner, the next pages give all the basic know-how simply and clearly so you can soon catch up with the more exciting techniques.

The tools required

A rigid metal inch/centimetre rule
Scissors
Blunt-ended sewing needles
Rustless steel pins
Stitch holders to hold stitches not being worked

Knitting register for counting rows accurately
Knitting needle gauge to check needle sizes
Polythene bag in which to keep work clean
Iron and ironing pad or blanket
Cotton cloths suitable for use when pressing

Know your needles

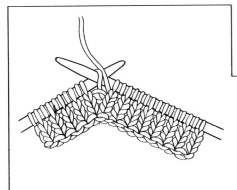

For 'flat' knitting—that is, working forwards and backwards on two needles in rows—needles are manufactured in pairs and each needle has a knob at one end to avoid the possibility of dropping stitches.
For 'circular' knitting—that is, working in rounds without a seam such as for socks or gloves —needles are manufactured in sets of four and each needle is pointed at both ends. A flexible, circular needle is also manufactured and is used for such designs as seamless, circular skirts. The effect is the same as dividing the work between three needles and working with the fourth, but a greater number of stitches may be used

Needle sizes

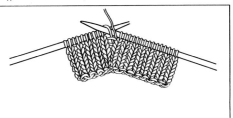

Here is a chart of comparable British, French and American needle sizes. With British needles, the higher the number the smaller the diameter of the needle, whereas the French and American system is the reverse. British needles are also manufactured in much larger sizes and are graded as sizes 0, 00 and 000.

KNITTING NEEDLE SIZES		
British	**French**	**American**
14	2	. 0
13	—	—
12	2.50	1
11	3.00	2
10	3.25	3
—	3.50	4
9	4.00	5
8	4.50	6
7	4.75	7
6	5.00	8
5	5.50	9
4	6.00	10
3	7.00	10¾
2	8.00	11
1	9.25	13

Know your yarns

'Yarn' is the word used to describe any spun thread, fine or thick, in natural fibres such as wool, cotton, linen, silk, angora or mohair, or in man-made fibres such as Acrilan, Orlon, Nylon or Courtelle.
The word 'ply' indicates the number of spun single threads which have been twisted together to produce a specific yarn. Each single thread may be spun to any thickness so that reference to the ply does not necessarily determine the thickness of the finished yarn, although the terms 2 ply, 3 ply and 4 ply are often used to mean yarn of a recognized thickness. The following ply classification is broadly applicable to the majority of hand-knitting yarns, whether made from natural fibres, man-made fibres or a blend of both.
Baby yarns are usually made from the highest quality yarns and are available in 2, 3 and 4 ply. Baby Quickerknit yarns are equivalent to a 4 ply but as they are very softly twisted, they are light in weight.

2, 3, and 4 ply yarns are available in natural fibres, man-made fibres or a blend of both usually made by twisting two spun single threads together, but there are exceptions to this.
Double Knitting yarns are usually made from four spun single threads—although there are exceptions to this—twisted together to produce hard-wearing yarns, virtually double the thickness of 4 ply yarns.
Chunky and Double-Double Knitting yarns are extra thick yarns which are ideal for heavier, outdoor garments such as childrens' anoraks. Some of these yarns are oiled to give greater warmth and protection.
Crepe yarns are usually available in 4 ply qualities—sometimes called 'single crepe'—and double knitting qualities—called 'double crepe'. They are more tightly twisted than normal yarns and produce a smooth, firm fabric which is particularly hardwearing.

Very important!

Since there is no official standardization, yarns marketed by various Spinners often vary in thickness and in yardage. As most yarns are marketed by weight, rather than yardage, even the density of dye used to produce certain colours in each range can result in more or less yarn in each ball, although the structure of the yarn is exactly the same.

If it is impossible to obtain the correct yarn quoted in the instructions, another comparable yarn may be used, provided the same tension as given in the pattern is achieved. There are many equivalent yarns which will knit up to the appropriate tension, but it is still essential to work a tension sample before beginning any design.

Always buy sufficient yarn at one time to ensure that all the yarn used is from the same dye lot. Yarn from a different dye lot may vary very slightly in colour.

Yarns and metrication

When purchasing yarns it is advisable to check on the weight of each ball, as they now vary considerably due to the introduction of the metric system. Metrication has already been adopted by some Spinners, while others are still in the process of changeover. Also, large stocks of yarns in standard ounces will take some time to run out, so this confused situation will be with us for some time. Here is a conversion table giving comparable weights in ounces and grams.

Measurements and metrication

The changeover from imperial to metric measurements of length—inches and yards to centimetres and metres—is bound to take time to adjust to. Of course it is best if you think only in metric measurements, but as some knitting patterns still give imperial measurements we have supplied a conversion table giving comparable measurements in inches and centimetres. You will find it on page 64. The metric equivalent sizes are also given on the patterns.

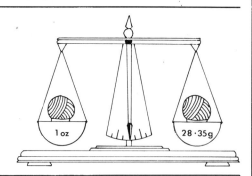

Useful weights—in grammes (g) and kilogrammes (kg)				Knitting yarn quantities (to convert either way)	
1oz	= 28·35g	25g	= 0·9oz	1oz = 25g + 3·35g For 3oz buy 4 balls of 25g	
4oz	= 113·4g	50g	= 1·8oz	7oz buy 8 balls of 25g	16oz buy 18 balls of 25g
8oz	= 226·8g	1kg/1000g	= 2·2lb	12oz buy 14 balls of 25g	20oz buy 23 balls of 25g
1lb	= 454g				

Success depends on tension

To make any design successfully it is essential to obtain the correct tension stated in the pattern. This means that the same number of stitches and rows to the inch—as originally obtained by the designer—must be achieved. As a beginner, it is vital to keep on practising and trying to obtain the correct tension. If it is impossible to hold both the yarn and needles comfortably and at the same time obtain the correct tension, then change the needle size. If there are too many stitches to the inch, try using one size larger needles; if there are too few stitches to the inch, try using one size smaller needles. Too many stitches to the inch means that the tension is too tight and too few stitches means that the tension is too loose.

This advice applies not only to the beginner but to all knitters beginning a new design. It is so often overlooked on the assumption that the knitter's tension is average and therefore accurate. The point to stress is that although all knitting patterns are carefully checked, the original designer of a garment may have produced a slightly tighter or looser tension than average. All the measurements of the garment will have been based on calculations obtained from this original tension.

Always test that the correct tension is being achieved by knitting at least a 2 inch square. A few minutes spent on this preparation lays the successful foundation for any garment. If it is overlooked, a great deal of work may be undertaken before the error in size is realized. Even half a stitch too many or too few can result in the completed garment being 2 inches too large or small.

Once the tension square has been worked, lay it on a flat surface and pin it down. Place a measure on the knitting and mark out 1 inch with pins. Count the number of stitches between the pins very carefully, then check the number of rows to one inch in the same way.

Opposite page: A superb example of knitting in random shapes, colours and stitches which will inspire you to explore the following pages Designed by Diane Chabot

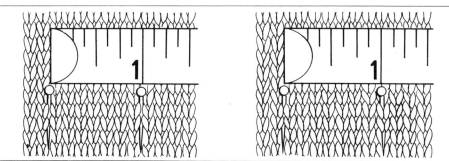

▲*Inches are marked out with pins, showing (a) 7 stitches to the inch, (b) 7½ stitches to the inch*

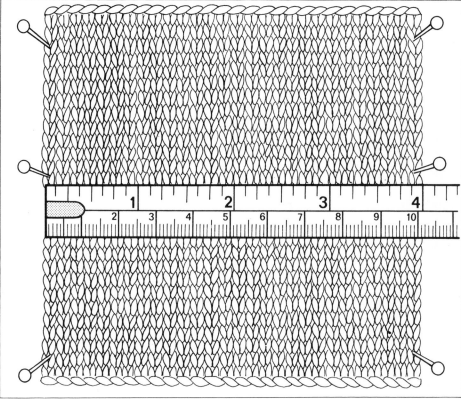

▲*Tension sample worked over 28 stitches, at 7 stitches per inch gives 10 centimetres (4 inches)*

The basic steps

Casting on is the first step in knitting as it provides the first row of loops on the needle. The next step is knitting and purling and these two methods form the basis of all stitches, however complicated they may appear. Casting off is the final stage and it securely binds off any stitches which remain after all the shaping has been completed, or at the end of the work.

Holding yarn and needles

Loop the end of the ball of yarn from the palm of the right hand between the fourth and third fingers, round the fourth finger and back between the fourth and third fingers, over the third finger, between the third and second fingers to the palm again, then back between the second and index fingers and over the index finger. Hold the needle which the stitches will be cast on to in the left hand; your right hand holds the needle which will be used to make the stitches.

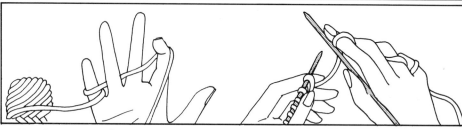

▲ *Holding the yarn and needles, looping round the fingers to control tension while casting on*

Two needle method of casting on

Make a slip loop in the end of the ball of yarn and put this loop on the left hand needle. Holding the yarn in the right hand, insert right hand needle point into the loop. Wind yarn under and over the point of the needle and draw a new loop through the first loop. Pass newly made loop on to the left hand needle. Place point of right hand needle between the two loops on the left hand needle and wind yarn under and over the point of the needle again and draw through a new loop. Pass newly made loop on to the left hand needle. Place point of right hand needle between the last two loops on the left hand needle and wind yarn under and over the point of the needle again and draw through a new loop. Pass newly made loop on to left hand needle. Continue in this way until the required number of stitches are formed. This method produces a firm edge and is also used as an intermediate stage in increasing.

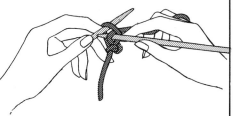

▲ *Making a slip loop*   ▲ *Left to right : three stages of the two-needle method of casting on*

Thumb method of casting on using one needle

Make a slip loop in the ball of yarn about a yard from the end—this length varies with the number of stitches to be cast on but one yard will be sufficient for about one hundred stitches. Put this loop on to the needle, which should be held in the right hand. Working with the short length of yarn in the left hand, pass this round the left thumb to the palm of the hand. Insert the point of the needle under the loop on the thumb and bring forward the long end of yarn from the ball. Wind long end of yarn under and over the point of the needle and draw through loop on thumb, leaving newly formed stitch on the needle. Tighten the stitch on the needle by pulling the short end, noting that the yarn is then wound round the left thumb ready for the next stitch. Continue in this way until the required number of stitches are formed. This method produces an elastic edge ideal for any garment which has to be pulled on over the head.

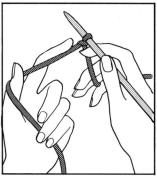
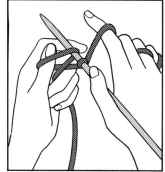
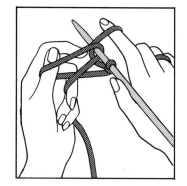
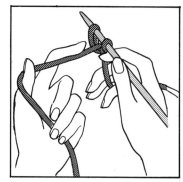

▲ *Left to right : four stages of the thumb method of casting on*

The basic stitches

To work knitted stitches Hold the needle with the cast on stitches in the left hand and the yarn and other needle in the right hand. Insert the point of the right hand needle into the first stitch on the left hand needle, from the front to the back. Keeping the yarn at the back of the work pass it under and over the top of the right hand needle and draw this loop through the stitch on the left hand needle. Keep this new stitch on the right hand needle and allow the stitch on the left hand needle to slip off. Repeat this action until all stitches are transferred to the right hand needle. To work the next row, change the needle holding the stitches to the left hand so that the yarn is again in position at the beginning of the row and knit to end.

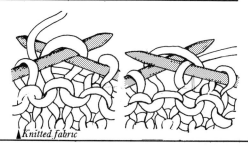

▲ *Knitted fabric*

To work purled stitches Hold the needle with the cast on stitches in the left hand and the yarn and other needle in the right hand. Insert the point of the right hand needle into the first stitch on the left hand needle from right to left. Keeping the yarn at the front of the work pass it over and round the top of the right hand needle and draw this loop through the stitch on the left hand needle. Keep this new stitch on the right hand needle and allow the stitch on the left hand needle to slip off. Repeat this action until all stitches are transferred to the right hand needle. To work the next row, change the needle holding the stitches to the left hand so that the yarn is again in position at the beginning of the row and purl to end.

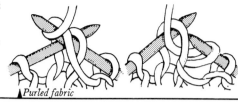
▲*Purled fabric*

Invisible method of casting on

Using a contrast length of yarn which is later removed and the 'thumb' method, cast on half the number of stitches required plus an extra one. Using the correct yarn and two needles, begin the ribbing which forms the invisible method.

1st row Holding the yarn in the right hand and the needle with the cast on stitches in the left hand, insert the point of the right hand needle into the first stitch from front to back, wind the yarn under and over the point of the needle and draw through a loop which is kept on the right hand needle—this is a knitted stitch and is called 'K1'—, *bring the yarn forward between the two needles and over the right hand needle to make a stitch on this row only—this is called 'yfwd'—, K1, repeat from the point marked with a * to the end of the row.

2nd row K1, *yfwd and keep at front of work without taking it back over the right hand needle, insert the point of the right hand needle into the front of the next stitch and lift it off the left hand needle on to the right

hand needle—this is a slipped stitch and is called 'sl 1'—, bring the yarn across in front of the sl 1 and back between the two needles again—this is called 'ybk'—, K1, repeat from the point marked with a * to the end of the row.

3rd row Sl 1, *ybk, K1, yfwd, sl 1, repeat from the point marked with a * to the end of the row. Repeat the 2nd and 3rd rows once more.

6th row K1, *bring the yarn forward between the two needles, insert the point of the right hand needle into the front of the next stitch, wind the yarn over the top of the needle and round to the front and draw through a loop which is kept

on the right hand needle—this is a purled stitch and is called 'P1'—, put the yarn back between the two needles, K1, repeat from the point marked with a * to the end of the row.

7th row P1, *put the yarn back between the needles, K1, bring the yarn forward between the needles, P1, repeat from the point marked with a * to the end of the row.

Continue repeating the 6th and 7th rows until the rib is the required length. Unpick the contrast yarn. This method gives the appearance of the ribbing running right round the edge with no visible cast on stitches.

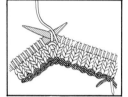  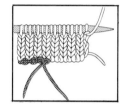
▲*Left to right: three stages in invisible casting on*

Circular method of casting on using four needles

When using a set of four needles, one is used for making the stitches and the total number of stitches required is divided between the remaining three needles. Using the 'two needle' method of casting on, cast on the required number of stitches on the first needle, then proceed to the second and third needles, taking care that the stitches do not become twisted. If preferred, all the stitches can be cast on to the first needle, then divided equally and slipped on to the second and third needles. These three needles are then formed into a circle and the spare needle is then ready to knit the first stitch on the first needle. This method produces a circular fabric without seams, such as socks or gloves.

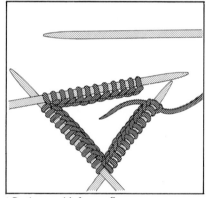
▲*Casting on with four needles*

▲*Joining stitches cast on with four needles*

Two needle method of casting off

To cast off on a knit row, knit the first two stitches in the usual way and leave on the right hand needle, *with the point of the left hand needle lift the first stitch on the right hand needle over the top of the second stitch and off the needle, leaving one stitch on the right hand needle, knit the next stitch and leave on the right hand needle, repeat from the point marked with a * until all stitches are cast off and one stitch remains on the right hand needle. Break off the yarn, draw through the last stitch and pull up tight. This method is also used as an intermediate stage in decreasing.

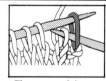 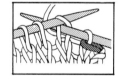
▲*Two stages of the two-needle method of casting off*

Invisible method of casting off

These instructions are for casting off in K1, P1 rib when an odd number of stitches has been used and right side rows begin with K1. Work in ribbing until only two more rows are required to give the finished depth, ending with a wrong side row.

1st row K1, *yfwd, sl 1, ybk, K1, rep from * to end.

2nd row Sl 1, *ybk, K1, yfwd, sl 1, rep from * to end.

Break off yarn, leaving an end three times the length of the edge to be cast off, and thread this into a blunt-ended needle. Hold the sewing needle

in the right hand and the stitches in the left hand, working throughout from right to left along the stitches to be cast off.

1 Insert the sewing needle into the first knit stitch as if to purl it and pull the yarn through, then into the next purl stitch as if to knit it and pull the yarn through, leaving both of these stitches on the left hand needle.

2 *First work two of the knit stitches. Go back and insert the sewing needle into the first knit stitch as if to knit it, pull the yarn through it and slip off the needle, pass the sewing needle in front of the next purl stitch and into the following knit stitch as if to purl it, pull the yarn through.

3 Now work two of the purl stitches. Go back and insert the sewing needle into the first purl stitch at the end of the row as if to purl it and slip it off the needle, pass the sewing needle behind the next stitch and into the following purl stitch as if to knit it, pull the yarn through.

Repeat from the point marked with a * until all the stitches have been worked off. Fasten off the yarn.

Circular method of casting off using four needles

Cast off the stitches on each needle as given for the 'two needle' method of casting off.

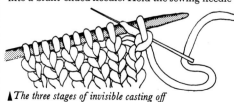  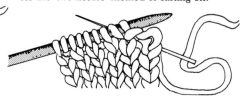
▲*The three stages of invisible casting off*

Shaping up to knitting

Knitting may be perfectly straight, as in a scarf, or intricately shaped as in a tailored jacket. This shaping is achieved by means of increasing the number of stitches in a row to make it wider, or decreasing the stitches in a row to make it narrower. Various methods may be used and some produce a decorative effect.

In the same way, beautiful stitches are produced by making stitches in a given sequence and compensating for the made stitches by decreasing later on in the row.

How to increase
The simplest way is to make an extra stitch at the beginning or the ending of the row, depending on the shape required. To do this, knit or purl the first stitch in the usual way but do not slip it off the needle. Instead, place the point of the right hand needle into the back of the same stitch and stitch and purl or knit into the stitch again. One stitch has been increased. To increase at the end of a row, knit until two stitches remain on the left hand needle, then increase into the next stitch and knit the last stitch.

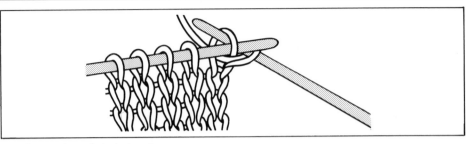

▲*Simple increasing at the beginning of a row*

Invisible increasing
Insert the right hand needle into the front of the stitch on the row below the next stitch on the left hand needle and knit a new stitch in the usual way. If the increase is on a purl row, then purl the new stitch.

Picking up the loop for invisible ►
increasing

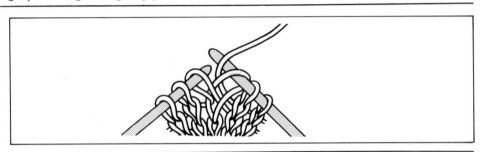

Increasing between stitches
With the right hand needle, pick up the yarn which lies between the stitch just worked and the next stitch on the left hand needle, and place it on the left hand needle. Knit into the back of this loop so that the new stitch is twisted and does not form a hole and place the new stitch on the right hand needle. If the increase is on a purl row, pick up the yarn between the stitches in the same way and purl into it from the back.

►

1. *Picking up the loop between stitches*
2. *Knitting into the back of the loop*
3. *The increased stitch placed on the right hand needle*

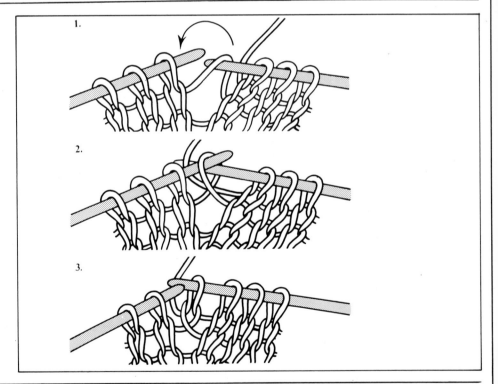

Multiple increasing
This technique is used when the sleeves of a garment are worked in one with the bodice. Cast on the required number of stitches at the beginning of the row, using the two needle method, and at the end of the row, reverse the work and again cast on the required number of stitches.

Casting on for multiple increasing ►

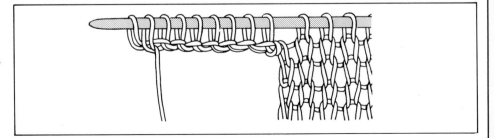

Decorative increasing

These techniques may be used to shape a garment but they also form the basis for lace patterns where a decorative eyelet hole is required.

To make a stitch between two knit stitches Bring the yarn forward between the needle then back over the right hand needle ready to knit the next stitch. The abbreviation for this is 'yfwd'.

To make a stitch between a purl and a knit stitch The yarn is already at the front of the work and is carried over the top of the right hand needle ready to knit the next stitch. The abbreviation for this is 'yon'.

To make a stitch between two purl stitches Take the yarn over the top of the right hand needle and round between the two needles to the front again ready to purl the next stitch. The abbreviation for this is 'yrn'.

To make a stitch between a knit and a purl stitch Bring the yarn forward between the two needles and over the top of the right hand needle and round between the two needles to the front again ready to purl the next stitch. The abbreviation for this is also 'yrn'.

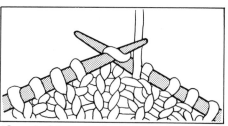
▲ *Increasing between 2 knit stitches*

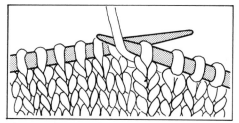
▲ *Increasing between a purl and a knit stitch*

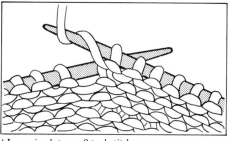
▲ *Increasing between 2 purl stitches*

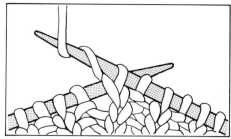
▲ *Increasing between a knit and a purl stitch*

How to decrease

The way to make a simple decrease is by working two stitches together, either at the ends of the row or at any given point. To do this on a knit row, insert the point of the right hand needle through two stitches instead of one and knit them together in the usual way. This stitch will slant to the right and the abbreviation is 'K2 tog'. If the decrease is on a purl row, purl two stitches together in the same way. This stitch will slant to the left and the abbreviation is 'P2 tog'.

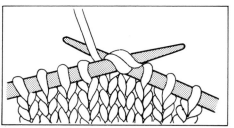
▲ *Decreasing by knitting two together*

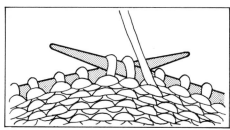
▲ *Decreasing by purling two together*

Decreasing by means of a slipped stitch

This method is most commonly used where decreases are paired, one slanting to the left and one to the right as on a raglan sleeve. Slip the first stitch on the left hand needle on to the right hand needle, then knit the next stitch. With the point of the left hand needle lift the slipped stitch over the knit stitch and off the needle. This stitch will slant to the left and the abbreviation is 'sl 1, K1, psso'. If the decrease is on a purl row, purl two stitches together through the back of the stitches. This stitch will slant to the right and the abbreviation is 'P2 tog tbl'.

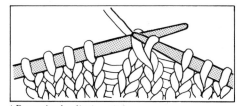
▲ *Decreasing by slipping stitch over*

Multiple decreasing

This method is used where a number of stitches need to be decreased in the centre of a row, such as neck shaping.

Work to the position in the row where the decreasing is required, knit the next two stitches then cast off the required number of stitches in the usual way, noting that the one stitch left on the right hand needle after casting off will be counted as part of the stitches worked to the end of the row. The work is now divided and each section is worked separately.

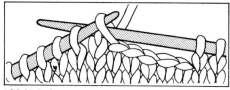
▲ *Multiple decrease by casting off*

Decorative decreasing

Sometimes the decorative use of decreasing is accentuated by twisting the stitches round the decrease to give them emphasis. This example shows a decrease which has been twisted and lies in the opposite direction to the line of the seam. The decrease is worked at the end of a knit row for the left hand side, and at the end of a purl row for the right hand side.

Knit to the last six stitches, pass the right hand needle behind the first stitch on the left hand needle and knit the next two stitches together through the back of the loops, then knit the first missed stitch and slip both stitches off the left hand needle and knit the last three stitches in the usual way. On a purl row, purl to the last six stitches, pass the right hand needle across the front of the stitch on the left hand needle and purl the next two stitches together, then purl the first missed stitch and slip both stitches off the left hand needle and purl the last three stitches in the usual way.

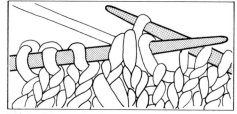
▲ *Twisted decrease in a knit row*

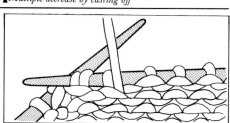
▲ *Purling two together in a purl row*

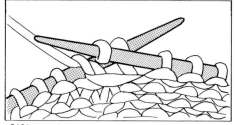
▲ *Lifting stitch over stitch already purled*

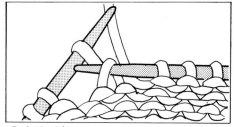
▲ *Purl side of decorative decrease*

7

Reading & adapting patterns

A finished garment should look just as attractive and well-fitting as in an illustration and a great deal of care is taken in compiling knitting patterns to ensure that this is possible. The secret lies in reading right through all the instructions before putting needle to yarn. Beginners and experts alike should pay particular attention to the making up section—a deceptively simple stitch or shape may require a crochet edging to give it that couture touch, or an unusual trimming effect. Make sure that all the necessary implements are to hand and that the instructions are completely clear, from buying the yarn right through to the final pressing.

Knitting publication styles vary but, basically, instructions fall into three sections.
1 Materials required, tension and finished sizes.
2 Working instructions for each piece.
3 Making up details, edgings, trimmings, etc.

Sizes
Check that the size range provides the size required. If the skirt or sleeve lengths need altering, read through the working instructions to see if the design allows for this adjustment. After the actual measurements of the design are given, take note that the instructions for the smallest size are given as the first set of figures and that the figures for the other sizes follow in order, sometimes in brackets. Go through the instructions and underline any figures applicable to the size required. Where only one set of figures is given it applies to all sizes.

Tension
This section must not be overlooked as it is the vital key to success. If the correct number of stitches and rows to the inch are not obtained then no amount of careful knitting and making up will produce a perfect garment. If a different needle size is required to achieve an accurate tension, it is of no importance at all—what is important is to obtain the correct number of stitches to the inch. If it is impossible to obtain the correct number of rows to the inch, check through the pattern and make sure that the design is not based on an exact number of rows. If it is measured in inches then the row tension is not so essential.

Materials
Each design has been worked out for the knitting yarn which is quoted and this should be obtained if possible. If for any reason it is quite impossible to obtain the correct yarn, select a substitute by referring to the Great Yarn Chart. The quantity given will only apply to the correct yarn and if a substitute is used, the quantity may vary slightly.

Working instructions
Each section will be given separately under an appropriate heading, such as 'back', 'front', 'sleeves', etc., and each section should be worked in the correct order. When measuring knitting it is necessary to lay it on a flat surface and use a rigid rule. Never measure round a curve—on an armhole or sleeve, measure the depth in a straight line. Where an asterisk, *, is used it means 'repeat'. It may be used in a pattern row where it means repeat from that point as directed. It is also used at the beginning of a section, sometimes as a double asterisk, **, to show a part which is to be repeated later on in the instructions.

Making up
Details are always given in the order in which the sections are to be assembled, together with instructions for any edgings or trimmings. Pressing instructions will also be given in this section and if a substitute yarn is being used, it is essential to check whether it requires pressing, or not.

Adapting or creating designs
Once the basic techniques of knitting have been mastered, it is a comparatively simple step to adapting existing designs or creating new ones. Using a basic, stocking stitch pattern, try and experiment by using one of the stitches given in this book, but make sure that the multiples of stitches given for any pattern can be divided into the original number of stitches given.
To create an original design, first decide on one of the following planning methods.
Graph paper planning method This method is most widely used by professional designers and involves planning on graph paper every stitch to be knitted—casting on and off, increasing, decreasing and openings—and shows in diagram form what the written instructions say in words. It is not worked to scale—one small square represents one stitch and each line of squares represents one row.

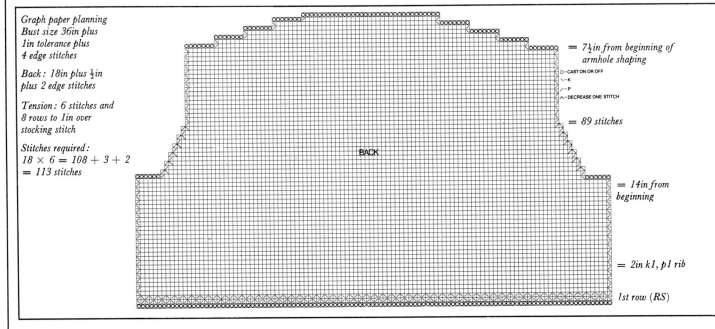

Graph paper planning
Bust size 36in plus
1in tolerance plus
4 edge stitches

Back: 18in plus ½in
plus 2 edge stitches

Tension: 6 stitches and
8 rows to 1in over
stocking stitch

Stitches required:
18 × 6 = 108 + 3 + 2
= 113 stitches

BACK

= 7½in from beginning of armhole shaping

○—CAST ON OR OFF
\—K
/—P
∧—DECREASE ONE STITCH

= 89 stitches

= 14in from beginning

= 2in k1, p1 rib

1st row (RS)

Choosing a yarn

Decide on a simple shape or pattern for a first attempt, then consider the yarn which will be most suitable for the stitch selected. If trying to adapt an existing pattern which uses a 4 ply and stocking stitch don't try and substitute a Double Knitting yarn and lace stitch—the two just won't combine. When creating a design, choose a firm, smooth yarn and experiment with some of the interesting stitches in this book until a suitable fabric has been achieved.

Tension

Make a sample 4 inches square, using the yarn and stitch selected and the needle size required to give a firm fabric, to find out exactly how many stitches and rows there are to 1 inch. Measure these very accurately and make a note of the figures, as all further caclulations will be based on these.

Paper pattern planning method This method may be most suitable for someone who has some dressmaking knowledge and involves making a paper shape from an existing garment.
For both methods the first stages are the same. The yarn, stitch and tension required must be decided.

Don't over-complicate what you're trying to do ►

Taking measurements

Make an accurate note of all measurements required—bust, underarm length, sleeve length, neck opening, shoulder seams, skirt length, waist and hips. Remember that on all garments an allowance must be made for movement, which is called 'tolerance'. For a bust measurement the tolerance is between 1 and 2 inches, depending on personal taste.

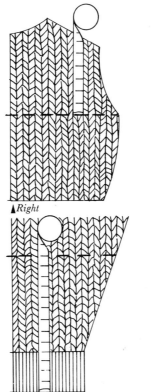

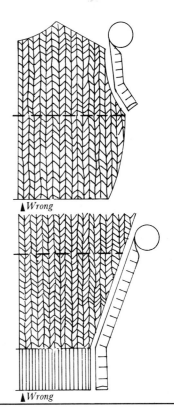

▲*Right*   ▲*Wrong*

▲*Right*   ▲*Wrong*

Casting on the right number of stitches

Take as an example a simple jersey in Old Shale stitch which, on a sample using No.10 needles and 4 ply yarn, gives a tension of 7 stitches and 9 rows to 1 inch. The back and the front will each represent half of the garment and the number of stitches required for the back will be based on half the bust measurement plus half the tolerance allowance, plus one stitch at each side to allow for seaming. Using the tension given, the stitches required for a 36 inch bust will be calculated as follows:— 18 inches at 7 stitches per inch = 126, plus 1 inch tolerance, 7 stitches = 133, plus one stitch at each end for seaming = 135 stitches. Now check that the stitch selected will divide evenly into this total, or whether it will be necessary to add or subtract a few stitches and alter the overall width slightly. In this case, Old Shale stitch requires multiples of 11 stitches plus 2 edge stitches. The nearest number to the required total of 135 is 134 stitches, and one stitch less will not greatly affect the measurements.

Where an existing pattern is being adapted, it is necessary to check the original figures given to see if they will give the correct multiples of 11 stitches plus 2 edge stitches. As an example, say that No.10 needles and 4 ply have been used to obtain a tension of 7½ stitches and 9½ rows to one inch worked over stocking stitch, the original figures for the 36 inch bust size will have been calculated as follows:— 18 inches at 7½ stitches per inch = 135, plus 7 stitches tolerance, to the nearest stitch, plus one stitch at each end for seaming = 144 stitches. The correct total required based on the new tension of 7 stitches to one inch, is 134 stitches. The easiest answer to this problem would be to change to No.11 needles and try and obtain the original 7½ stitches quoted and add one stitch to the original 144 given, making 145 stitches, or 13 multiples of 11 stitches plus 2 edge stitches.

The finishing touches

The making up and finishing touches on a garment can make or mar the results. First check whether the yarn used requires pressing or not—certain man-made fibres can be ruined by contact with heat.

Blocking and pressing

If pressing is required, place each piece of knitting on an ironing pad, right side down, and pin evenly round the edges. Once the piece is pinned out to shape, making sure that the knitting is never stretched, check with a rule that the width and length are the same as those given in the instructions. Using a clean, damp or dry cloth, as quoted, press the piece evenly with a warm or cool iron, taking great care not to press too heavily, and putting the iron down and lifting it up again without moving along the surface. As a general rule, it is not advisable to press garter stitch or ribbing.

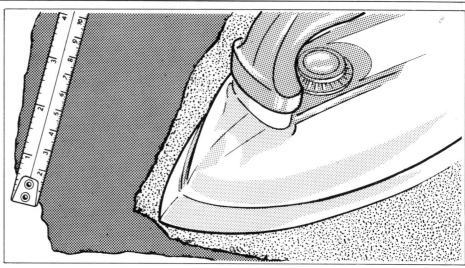

▲When pressing, keep a check on the measurements

Seaming

To seam the pieces together use a blunt-ended sewing needle which will not split the stitches.
Back stitch seam Begin seaming by working two or more small stitches, one on top of the other to secure the yarn, *with the needle at the back of the work move along to the left, bring the needle through to the front of the work the width of one stitch away from the last stitch, take the needle along to the right and back to the end of the previous stitch, put the needle through to the back of the work, repeat from * until the seam is completed.
Invisible seam This seam is worked with the right sides of the pieces facing. Begin by securing the yarn to one side. Pass the needle directly across to the other side of the work, picking up one stitch, then pass the needle directly back to the first side of the work, picking up one stitch. Continue working in this way as though making rungs of a ladder but pull the stitches tight so that they are invisible on the right side when the seam is finished.
Flat seam This is the best seam to use on ribbing. Secure the yarn as for invisible seams. Pass the needle through the edge stitch on the right hand side, directly across to the edge stitch on the left hand side and pull the yarn through. Then turn the needle and work through the next stitch on the left hand side directly across to the edge stitch on the right hand side, again pulling the yarn through. Continue along the seam in this way.

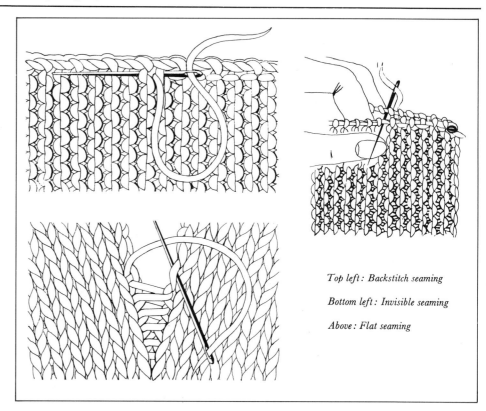

Top left: Backstitch seaming

Bottom left: Invisible seaming

Above: Flat seaming

Picking up stitches

This method is widely used for finishing necklines and borders. It is usual to pick up the stitches with the right side of the work facing in the case of a neckline, after one shoulder has been seamed to avoid using four needles. Hold the yarn and the needle in the right hand and insert the point of the needle through the fabric from the front to the back, loop the yarn over the needle and draw through a loop to the front of the work. Continue in this way until the required number of stitches are on the needle. To ensure that the stitches are picked up evenly and are well spaced, mark each section with pins at regular intervals and pick up the same number of stitches between the pins.

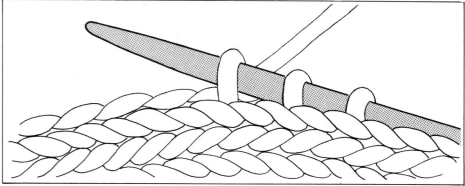

▲Knitting up stitches for a border

Grafting

Grafting is a method of joining two rows of stitches invisibly, such as the toes of socks where the edge formed by a sewn seam would be uncomfortable.

To graft two stocking stitch edges together have the stitches on two needles, one behind the other, with the same number of stitches on each needle. Break off the yarn from the last piece worked and thread this into a blunt-ended needle. Have the wrong sides of each piece facing each other, with the knitting needle points facing to the right. *Insert the sewing needle through the first stitch on the front needle as if to knit it, draw yarn through and slip stitch off knitting needle. Insert the sewing needle through the next stitch on the front needle as if to purl it, draw yarn through and leave stitch on knitting needle. Insert sewing needle through the first stitch on the back needle as if to purl it, draw yarn through and slip stitch off knitting needle, insert sewing needle through the next stitch on the back needle as if to knit it, draw yarn through and leave stitch on knitting needle. Repeat from * until all stitches have been worked off both needles.

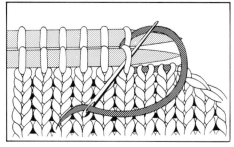

▲*Grafting stitches together*

Finishing touches

Many designs are trimmed with pompons or tassels or finished with the addition of embroidery and twisted cords.

Casing or herringbone stitch This method is used to finish a skirt waist, or trousers. Cut the elastic to the size required and join into a circle. Mark off the waistband of the shirt or trousers into quarters, also the elastic, and pin the elastic into position on the wrong side of the work. Taking care to distribute the knitting evenly, hold the waistband over the fingers of the left hand. Thread a blunt-ended needle and secure to the fabric. Take the yarn over the elastic and insert the sewing needle lightly through the fabric from right to left, draw the yarn through, take the yarn back over the elastic to the top edge about two stitches along, insert the sewing needle lightly through the fabric from right to left again, draw the yarn through.
Continue in this way all round waistband.

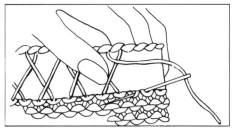

▲*Casing or herringbone stitch*

Twisted cords The number of strands of yarn required will vary according to the thickness of the cord and the yarn being used. Take the required number of strands and cut them into lengths three times the length of the finished cord. Enlist the aid of another person, but if this is not possible, then one end of the strands may be fastened over a hook. If working with another person, each should take one end of the strands and knot them together, then insert a pencil into the knot. Each person should twist the strands to the right until they are tightly twisted. Holding the strands taut, fold them in half at the centre and knot the two ends together. Holding the knot, give the cord a sharp shake, then smooth it from the knot to the folded end, to even out the twists. Make another knot at the folded end, cut through the folded loops and tease out the ends.

▲*A twisted cord*

Pompons Cut the two circles of cardboard the size required for the finishing pompon, then cut a circle from the centre of each. Place the two pieces of card together and wind the yarn evenly round until the centre hole is nearly filled, then thread the yarn into a blunt-ended needle to completely fill the centre. Cut through the yarn round the outer edge, working between the two pieces of card. Take a length of yarn and tie very securely round the centre of the pompon and between the two pieces of card, leaving an end long enough to secure the pompon to the garment. Cut away the two pieces of card and trim pompon to shape.

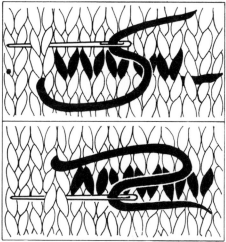

▲*Cutting a pompon*

Tassels Cut a length of card about 2 inches wide or the width of the required length of the tassel. Wind the yarn round and round the card until the desired thickness is obtained. Using a blunt-ended needle threaded with yarn, insert the needle at one edge of the card, under the strands, taking them all together and fasten off securely. Cut through the strands of yarn at the other untied edge of the card. Finish the tassel by winding an end of yarn several times round the top, folded ends and fasten off securely, leaving an end long enough to secure the tassel to the garment.

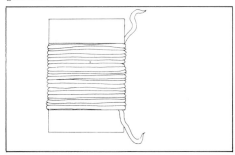

▲*Preparing a tassel*

Swiss darning For this embroidery use a yarn of the same thickness as the knitted fabric. Thread the yarn into a blunt-ended needle and begin at the lower right hand corner of the design to be embroidered, bring the needle up at the base of the first stitch to be embroidered from back to front and draw yarn through, insert the needle from right to left under the two loops of the same stitch one row above and draw yarn through, insert needle back into the base of this first stitch and up in the base of the next stitch to the left and draw yarn through. Continue along the row for as many stitches as are required. At the end of the row, insert the needle into the base of the last stitch worked then up in the centre of this same stitch, which will be the base of the same stitch on the next row above, now insert needle from left to right behind the two loops of this stitch on the row above and continue working as before but from left to right.

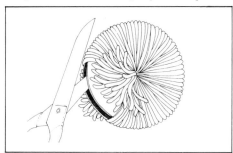

▲*Swiss darning*

Knitting in sequins The pattern will state the number and size of sequins required. To thread the sequins on to a ball of yarn before beginning to knit with it, fold a 10 inch strand of sewing cotton in half and thread a fine sewing needle with both cut ends, leaving a loop of cotton. Pass 6 inches of the ball of yarn to be used through the loop of cotton and slide sequins on to the needle, down the cotton and on to the yarn. When knitting with this yarn, slip sequin up close to the work, knit the next stitch through the back of the loop pushing the sequin through the stitch to the front of the work with the loop of the stitch.

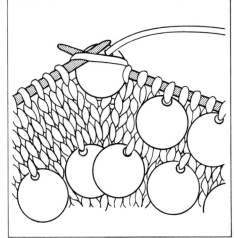

▲*Knitting in sequins*

All buttoned up

Neatly finished buttonholes and interesting buttons add the professional touch to any garment. Depending on the size of the button and the width of the buttonhole border, different methods may be applied.

Layette buttonholes

Work the front of the garment or the buttonhole band until the position for the first buttonhole is reached, ending with a wrong side row. On the next row, work a few stitches in the row, then pass the yarn forward, over or round the right hand needle to make an eyelet hole, then work the next two stitches together to compensate for this made stitch. On the next row, work across all the stitches in the usual way, including the made stitch. Repeat this action for the number of buttonholes required.

Layette buttonholes are neat and unobtrusive
▼ *A completed horizontal buttonhole*   ►

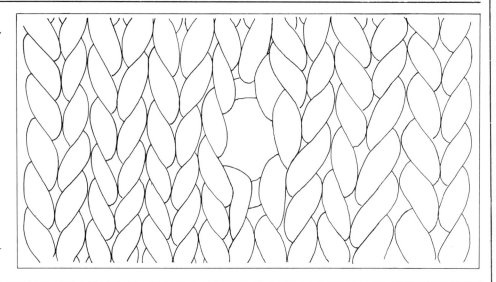

Horizontal buttonholes

When the buttonhole is to be made as part of the main fabric of a cardigan, finish at the centre front edge when the position for the buttonhole has been reached. On the next row, work a few stitches in the row, cast off the number of stitches required by the two needle method, then continue to the end of the row. On the next row, to avoid spoiling the buttonhole by a loose loop of yarn at one end, work to the last stitch before the cast off stitches and increase in this stitch by working into the front and back of it, then cast on one stitch less than was cast off in the previous row. Repeat this action for the number of buttonholes required.

▲*Six attractive variations of knitted buttons for the perfect finishing touch*

Vertical buttonholes

Work until the position for the buttonhole is reached, ending with a wrong side row. On the next row work across a few stitches to the position for the buttonhole, then turn the work and continue across these stitches only for the required number of rows to take the size of button, ending with a right side row. Break off the yarn and leave these stitches for the time being. Rejoin the yarn to the remaining stitches and work the same number of rows over these stitches again ending with a right side row. On the next row work across all the stitches in the usual way. Repeat this action for the number of buttonholes required.

For a vertical buttonhole, each side must be worked separately ►

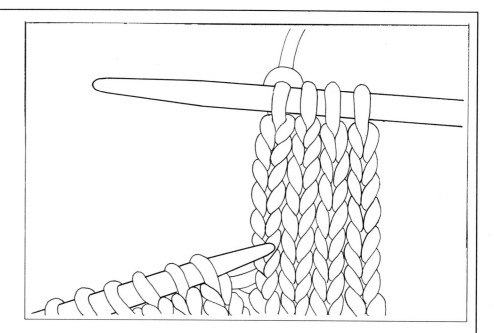

Reinforcing buttonholes

All buttonholes may be neatly reinforced by working round them in buttonhole stitch, using a matching silk thread. Take care not to work too many stitches round the hole so that the edges become stretched, or too few stitches which will make the hole smaller than intended. Horizontal and vertical buttonholes may also be neatened by means of a matching ribbon facing. The ribbon should be wide enough to cover the buttonholes with an extra ½ inch on either side and at each end. Take care not to stretch the knitting when measuring the ribbon length, and cut the button and buttonhole facing together so that they match exactly. Fold in the turnings on the ribbon and pin in place on the wrong side of the knitting, easing the fabric evenly and checking that the buttonholes are correctly spaced, then pin the ribbon on each side of every buttonhole to hold it in place. Slip stitch neatly round the edges of the ribbon. Cut the buttonholes in the ribbon making sure they are exactly the same size as the knitted buttonholes. Oversew the edges together, then work round each buttonhole with buttonhole stitch.

Neaten the ends of the buttonhole to avoid stretching ►

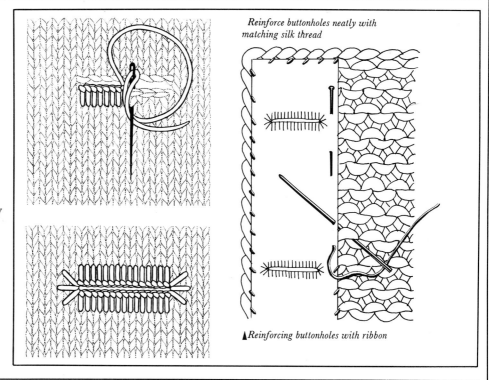

Reinforce buttonholes neatly with matching silk thread

▲ *Reinforcing buttonholes with ribbon*

Buttons

It is sometimes impossible to find buttons which exactly match or tone in with the yarn used for a garment. To overcome this problem, many patterns make provision for covering button moulds with crochet but it is just as simple to cover ready-made moulds, such as Trims, with knitting to achieve an exact match.

Blue stocking stitch button

Use 4 ply yarn and No.14 needles to cover a 1 inch Trim.
Cast on 4 stitches. Work in stocking stitch, increasing one stitch at each end of 2nd and every row until there are 12 stitches. Work 6 rows without shaping. Decrease one stitch at each end of every row until 4 stitches remain. Cast off. Cover Trim, following instructions.

Embroidered button

Work as given for stocking stitch button. Before covering the Trim, work initial or motif in the centre of the fabric, using Swiss darning.

Red moss stitch button

Use same materials and cast on as given for stocking stitch button.
1st row *K1, P1, rep from * to end.
Repeat this row to form moss stitch and complete as given for stocking stitch button.

Yellow moss stitch button

Use Double Knitting yarn and No.13 needles. Work as given for red moss stitch button. Place over a wooden button mould, work a row of running stitch round the outside edge of the fabric, draw up and fasten off, leaving an end of yarn long enough to sew on the button. If preferred, this button can be stuffed with cotton wool.

Green bobble button

Use Double Knitting yarn and No.13 needles.

Cast on 3 stitches. Beginning with a purl row, work in reversed stocking stitch, increasing one stitch at each end of 2nd and every row until there are 11 stitches. Work 2 rows without shaping. **Next row** P5 sts, (K1, P1, K1, P1, K1) all into next st, turn and P across these 5 sts, turn and K5, turn and P5, turn and K5 then lift the 2nd, 3rd, 4th and 5th sts over the first st. P5 sts.
Work 2 more rows in stocking stitch. Decrease one stitch at each end of every row until 3 stitches remain. Cast off. Complete as given for yellow moss stitch button.

Pink buttonhole stitch button

Use Double Knitting yarn to cover a ¾ inch diameter ring. Use yarn double and work in buttonhole stitch all round ring, keeping the edge of the buttonhole stitch always to the inside of the ring. When ring is completely covered, run the thread round the inside edge of the ring and draw up as tightly as required, leaving an end of yarn long enough to sew on the button.

Ways with hems

A neatly finished hem can give a swing to any skirt and the couture touch to a jersey or jacket. If the hem is to be worked in one with the main fabric of the garment, it is advisable to use one size smaller needles for the underside of the hem at the lower edge but this does not apply to any vertical edges.

Stocking stitch hem

Cast on the required number of stitches and beginning with a knit row, work an odd number of rows to give the required depth. Knit the next row through the back of all the stitches, instead of purling it, to mark the fold line. Beginning with a knit row again work the same number of rows as were worked at the beginning plus one extra row to end with a purl row. When the garment is completed, turn the hem to the wrong side of the work at the fold line and slip stitch in place.

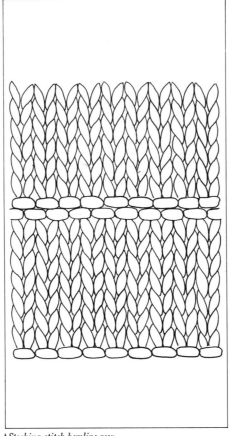

▲Stocking stitch hemline row

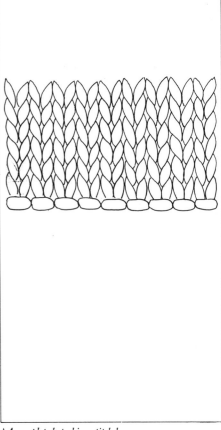

▲A completed stocking stitch hem

Knitted-in hem

Cast on and work as given for the stocking stitch hem, working two rows less after the fold line but again ending with a purl row. Before continuing with the garment, pick up the stitches of the cast on row with an extra needle and hold these stitches behind the stitches already on the left hand needle, with both points of the needles at the right hand side. Knit to the end of the next row, working one stitch together from each needle.

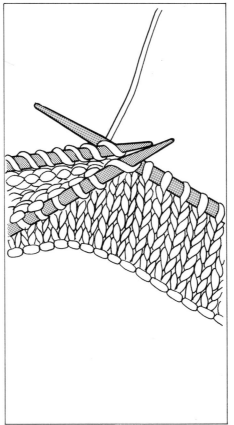

▲Knitting stitches together for a hem

▲A completed knitted-in hem

Picot hem

Cast on an odd number of stitches and beginning with a knit row work an even number of rows in stocking stitch to give the required depth. On the next row K1, *yfwd, K2 tog, repeat from * to the end. Beginning with a purl row work one row more than was worked at the beginning to end with a purl row. When the garment is completed, turn the hem to the wrong side of the work at the picot eyelet hole row and slip stitch in place.

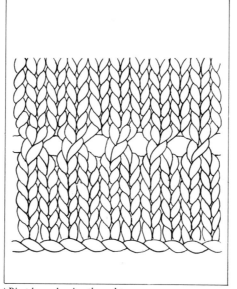

▲Picot hem, showing the eyelet row   ▲A completed picot hem

Ribbon faced hem

Cut the ribbon to the required length allowing extra for an overlap. Take care not to stretch the knitting when measuring the ribbon. Pin the ribbon to the wrong side of the work, turning in two rows of knitting at the lower edge. Slip stitch the ribbon in place along the top and bottom edges.

When facing with ribbon on two edges at right angles to each other, slip stitch the outside edge in place first. At the corner where the edges meet, fold the ribbon under to form a mitred corner before seaming the inside edge.

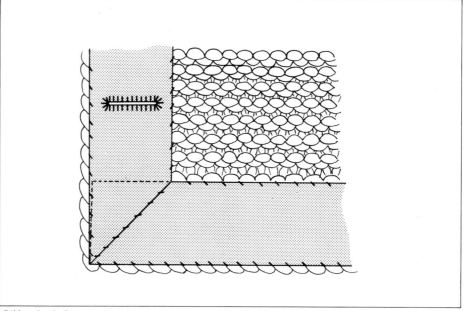

▲Ribbon-faced edges, showing a mitred corner

Vertical hem

Cast on the required number of stitches plus the extra stitches required to give the correct width for the turn in of the hem and allowing for double buttonholes to made if necessary. Work in stocking stitch across the full width of the stitches but on every knit row slip the last stitch of the extra hem stitches without working into it, to form a fold line. If the main fabric is worked in a patterned stitch, it is advisable to keep the extra hem stitches in stocking stitch throughout to avoid unnecessary bulk. When the garment is completed, turn in the hem to the wrong side of the work at the fold line and slip stitch in place.

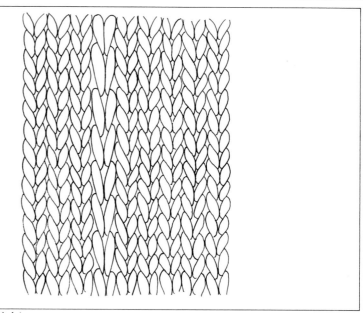

▲A finished vertical slip stitch hem

Into pocket

A basic design can quite easily be adapted to include either inserted pockets or patch pockets. Inserted pockets are worked in one with the main fabric of the garment and the pocket tops may be completed with a border in a contrasting stitch, such as garter stitch or single ribbing. Patch pockets can be added to any garment to give it an individual touch and look most effective when worked in a stitch which contrasts with the main fabric of the garment.

Inserted pockets

First check on the total number of stitches given for the section where the pocket is to be inserted. Work out the width and depth of the pocket and calculate how many stitches will be needed. As a guide, on one front of a cardigan, the pocket should begin 2 or 3 inches in from the side edge and should measure 4 or 5 square inches. Begin by making the inside flap first, casting on 2 extra stitches for seaming, and working in stocking stitch to avoid unnecessary bulk. Continue until the inside flap is the required depth, noting that if a welt is worked on the main part, the pocket should begin at the top of this, then leave these stitches on a holder. Work the main part of the garment until it is ½ to 1 inch less than the required pocket depth. Work a further ½ to 1 inch across all stitches but work the pocket top stitches in garter stitch or ribbing, ending with a right side row. On the next row, work to the pocket top stitches, cast off these stitches then continue to the end of the row. On the next row, work to within one stitch of the cast off stitches, place the right side of the inside flap stitches against the wrong side of the main fabric, work the next stitch together with the first stitch of the inside flap, continue across the inside flap stitches working the last stitch together with the first stitch of the other part of the main fabric. Continue across all stitches in the usual way. When the garment is completed, slip stitch the inside flap in place.

Working across the lining of an inserted pocket ▲

Sewing down the pocket lining ►

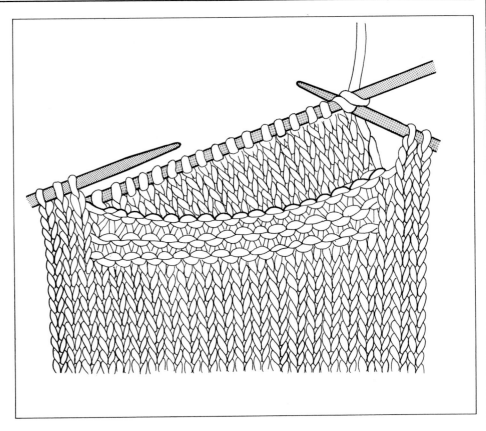

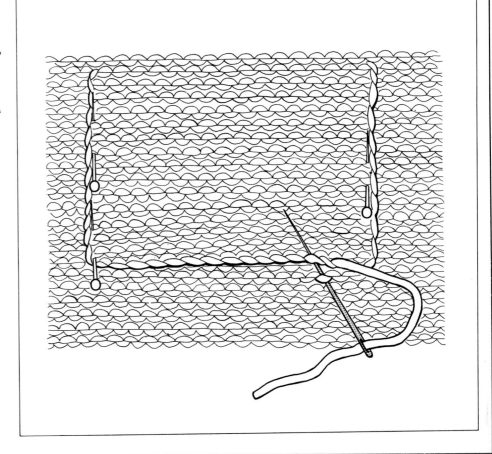

Patch pockets

Calculate the size and positioning of the pocket as given for inserted pockets. Work a square in the chosen stitch and then cast off. If a turned down flap is required, work a further 1 to 1½ inches before casting off but remember to check whether the stitch being used is reversible. As an example, if the pocket is in stocking stitch the flap will have to be reversed. End with a knit row before commencing the flap, then knit the following row as well to reverse the work. When the garment is completed, neatly stitch the pocket in place.

A completed patch pocket ▶

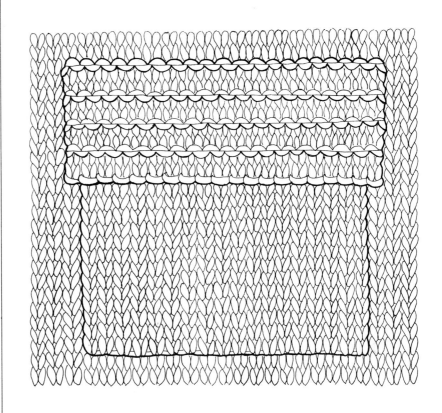

Flap pockets

Calculate and work the inside flap as given for inserted pockets but cast off these stitches instead of leaving them on a holder. Work the pocket flap in a contrasting stitch, casting on 2 stitches less than for the inside flap, and leave these stitches on a holder. Continue with the main part of the garment until the required depth is reached and cast off the pocket stitches as given for the inserted pockets. On the next row, work to the cast off stitches, place the wrong side of the pocket flap against the right side of the main fabric and work across the flap stitches, then continue across the other part of the main fabric. Continue across all the stitches in the usual way. When the garment is completed, slip stitch the inside flap in place.

A completed flap pocket, showing the front of the work ▶

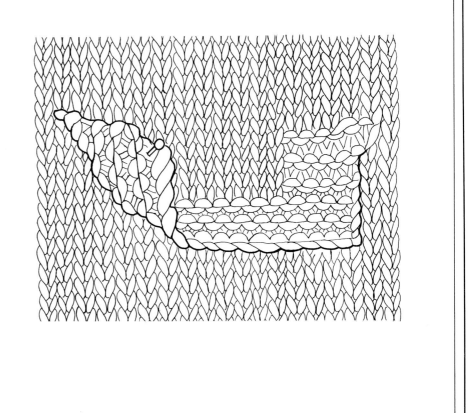

Cable & aran patterns

Cable stitches and Aran patterns are quite easy to knit and give an interesting texture to any fabric, whether fine or thick, Probably the most difficult aspect of these techniques to master is the long instructions which have to be given for a quite simple working method and which is then subsequently abbreviated in the pattern rows.

Cable stitches
All cable patterns are based on stitches which are moved from one position to another in a row, either crossing in front of, or behind, the following stitches to give the effect of twists in a rope. Where only 2 stitches are used, it is possible to avoid the use of a separate cable needle and knit the 2nd stitch on the left hand needle by passing the right hand needle in front of, or behind, the first stitch then going back to work this first stitch. When altering the position of more than 2 stitches, a special cable needle must be employed, This type of needle is very short and easy to handle, and is pointed at both ends.

Simple cable twist from right to left
Try a simple cable of 6 knit stitches against a background of purl stitches. Cast on 24 stitches.
1st row P9 sts, K6 sts, P9 sts.

2nd row K9 sts, P6 sts, K9 sts.
Repeat the 1st and 2nd rows twice more.
7th row P9 sts, slip the next 3 knit stitches onto the cable needle and hold them at the front of the work, with the right hand needle knit the next 3 stitches from the left hand needle, then knit the 3 stitches from the cable needle—called C6F —, P9 sts.
8th row As 2nd.
Repeat these 8 rows 3 times more. Cast off.

Simple cable twist from left to right
To twist the stitches the opposite way, again try a simple cable of 6 knit stitches against a background of purl stitches. Cast on 24 stitches.
1st row P9 sts, K6 sts, P9 sts.

2nd row K9 sts, P6 sts, K9 sts.
Rep the 1st and 2nd rows twice more.
7th row P9 sts, slip the next 3 knit stitches onto the cable needle and hold them at the back of the work, with the right hand needle knit the next 3 stitches from the left hand needle, then knit the 3 stitches from the cable needle — called C6B —, P9 sts.
8th row As 2nd.
Repeat these 8 rows 3 times more. Cast off.

Link cable
Dividing the number of stitches in the knit panel and taking half to the right and half to the left gives the effect of chain links. Cast on 24 stitches.
1st row P6 sts, K12 sts, P6 sts.
2nd row K6 sts, P12 sts, K6 sts.
Repeat the 1st and 2nd rows twice more.

7th row P6 sts, C6B, C6F, P6 sts.
8th row As 2nd.
Repeat these 8 rows 3 times more than 1st row again. Cast off.

Aran patterns
In common with all folk crafts, traditional Aran designs derive their meanings from the daily life of the Aran islanders. Rocks and cliffs are depicted in zigzag patterns and the fishermen's ropes are represented by numerous variations in cable stitches. Every stitch has a name and meaning and the history of Aran knitting makes fascinating reading.

Honeycomb stitch
Depicting the contribution made to life by the industrious bee! Cast on a number of stitches divisible by 8, i.e., 24 stitches.
1st row *Slip 2 sts on to the cable needle and hold at the back of the work, K2 sts from the left hand needle then K2 sts from the cable needle — called C4B —, slip 2 sts on to the cable needle and hold at the front of the work, K2 sts from the left hand needle then K2 sts from the cable needle — called C4F —, repeat from * to the end of the row.
2nd row P to end.
3rd row K to end.
4th row P to end.

5th row *C4F, C4B, repeat from * to the end of the row.
6th row P to end.
7th row K to end.
8th row P to end.
Repeat these 8 rows 3 times more then 1st row again. Cast off.

Ladder of life
Depicting man's desire to climb towards Heaven. Cast on a number of stitches divisible by 6 plus 1, i.e., 25 stitches.

1st row (right side of work) P1, *K5, P1, rep from * to end.
2nd row K1, *P5, K1, rep from * to end.
3rd row P to end. This row forms the rungs of a ladder.
4th row K1, *P5, K1, rep from * to end.
Repeat these 4 rows 7 times more. Cast off.

Trinity stitch
This stitch derives its name from the working method of making '3 in 1 and 1 in 3'. It is also known as blackberry stitch in England and bramble stitch in Scotland. Cast on a number of stitches divisible by 4, i.e., 24 stitches.
1st row P to end.
2nd row *K1, P1 and K1 all into the same st making 3 from 1, P3 together to make 1 from 3, repeat from * to end.

3rd row P to end.
4th row *P3 together to make 1 from 3, K1, P1, K1 all into the same st making 3 from 1, repeat from * to end.
Repeat these 4 rows 7 times more. Cast off.

Lobster claw stitch
Depicting the rich bounty of the seas. Cast on a number of stitches divisible by 9 plus 2, i.e., 29 stitches.
1st row P2, *K7, P2, repeat from * to end.

2nd row K2, *P7, K2, repeat from * to end.
3rd row P2, *slip 2 sts on to cable needle and hold at back of work, K1 from left hand needle then K2 from cable needle, K1, slip 1 st on to cable needle and hold at front of work, K2 sts from left hand needle then K1 from cable needle — called Cr7 —, P2, repeat from * to end.
4th row P2, *P7, K2, repeat from * to end.
Repeat these 4 rows 7 times more. Cast off.

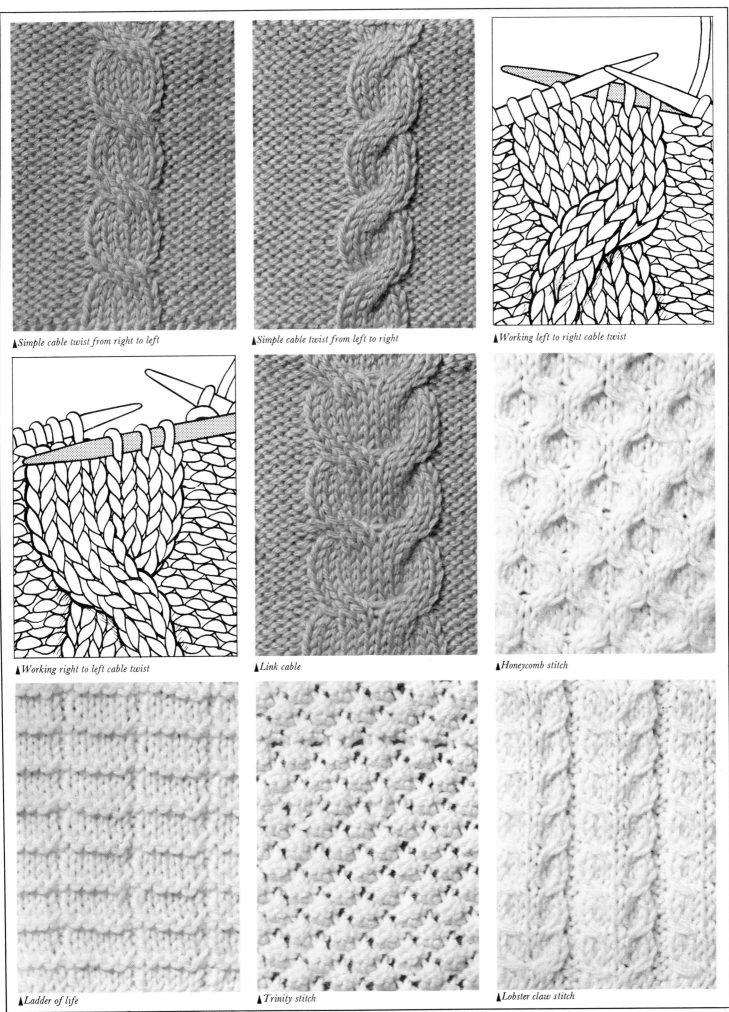

▲*Simple cable twist from right to left*

▲*Simple cable twist from left to right*

▲*Working left to right cable twist*

▲*Working right to left cable twist*

▲*Link cable*

▲*Honeycomb stitch*

▲*Ladder of life*

▲*Trinity stitch*

▲*Lobster claw stitch*

Lace knitting

Knitted lace is simple to work and beautiful to look at. The most gossamer and finest examples of lace knitting come from Unst, the most northerly of the Shetland islands. These stitches are seen at their best if a fine cotton or 2 ply yarn is used and needles not larger than size 10. They can be worked in rounds, either from the outside edge and decreasing to the centre, or from the centre and increasing to the outside edge, to produce exquisite table mats. Worked in rows and panels of contrasting stitches they make a delicate shawl, or a simple stitch can be used as a dainty edging for a handkerchief.

Casting on and off

All lace edges should be kept as open as possible, as any hard, thick lines caused by casting on, casting off or seaming will immediately spoil the beauty of the lace. The ideal method of casting on when working in rounds or in rows is a simplified 2 needle method. Cast on the first 2 stitches in the usual way but insert the right hand needle into the second stitch, instead of between the 2 stitches, draw a loop through and transfer it to the left hand needle, then continue in this way for the required number of stitches. Casting off should be worked very loosely, using a size larger needle.

Where a seam is required, it is better to graft the 2 edges together. To do this, cast on using spare yarn which can later be withdrawn, so that the first and last rows can be grafted together for an invisible finish.

Bead stitch

Cast on a number of stitches divisible by 7.
1st row (RS) *K1, K2 tog, yfwd, K1, yfwd, sl 1 knitwise, K1, psso, K1, rep from * to end.
2nd row *P2 tog tbl, yrn, P3, yrn, P2 tog, rep from * to end.
3rd row *K1, yfwd, sl 1 knitwise, K1, psso, K1, K2 tog, yfwd, K1, rep from * to end.
4th row *P2, yrn, P3 tog, yrn, P2, rep from * to end.
These 4 rows form the pattern.

Old Shale stitch variation

Cast on a number of stitches divisible by 11 plus 2.
1st row K to end.
2nd row P to end.
3rd row K1, *(K2 tog) twice, yfwd, (K1, yfwd) 3 times, (K2 tog) twice, rep from * to last st, K1.
4th row P to end.
These 4 rows form the pattern.

Horseshoe stitch

Cast on a number of stitches divisible by 10 plus 1.
1st row (WS) P to end.
2nd row K1, *yfwd, K3, sl 1, K2 tog, psso, K3, yfwd, K1, rep from * to end.
3rd row P to end.
4th row P1, *K1, yfwd, K2, sl 1, K2 tog, psso, K2, yfwd, K1, P1, rep from * to end.
5th row K1, *P9, K1, rep from * to end.
6th row P1, *K2, yfwd, K1, sl 1, K2 tog, psso, K1, yfwd, K2, P1, rep from * to end.
7ht row As 5th.
8th row P1, *K3, yfwd, sl 1, K2 tog, psso, yfwd, K3, P1, rep from * to end.
These 8 rows form the pattern.

Faggotting cable stitch

Cast on a number of stitches divisible by 12 plus 8.
1st row (RS) P2, *K2, yfwd, sl 1, K1, psso, P2, rep from * to end.
2nd row K2, *P2, yrn, P2 tog, K2, rep from * to end.
Repeat these 2 rows twice more.
7th row P2, K2, yfwd, sl 1, K1, psso, P2, *slip next 2 sts on to cable needle and hold at front of work, K2 from left hand needle then K2 from cable needle — called C4F —, P2, K2, yfwd, sl 1, K1, psso, P2, rep from * to end.
8th row As 2nd.
Repeat the 1st and 2nd rows 3 times more.
15th row P2, C4F, P2, *K2, yfwd, sl 1, K1, psso, P2, C4F, P2, rep from * to end.
16th row As 2nd.
These 16 rows form the pattern.

Leaf edging

Cast on 10 stitches.
1st row K3, (yfwd, K2 tog) twice, bring yarn forward and over the needle, then forward and over the needle again to make 2 sts — called y2rn —, K2 tog, K1.
2nd row K3, P1, K2, (yfwd, K2 tog) twice, K1.
3rd row K3, (yfwd, K2 tog) twice, K1, y2rn, K2 tog, K1.
4th row K3, P1, K3, (yfwd, K2 tog) twice, K1.
5th row K3, (yfwd, K2 tog) twice, K2, y2rn, K2 tog, K1.
6th row K3, P1, K4, (yfwd, K2 tog) twice, K1.
7th row K3, (yfwd, K2 tog) twice, K6.
8th row Cast off 3 sts, K5, (yfwd, K2 tog) twice, K1.
These 8 rows form the pattern.

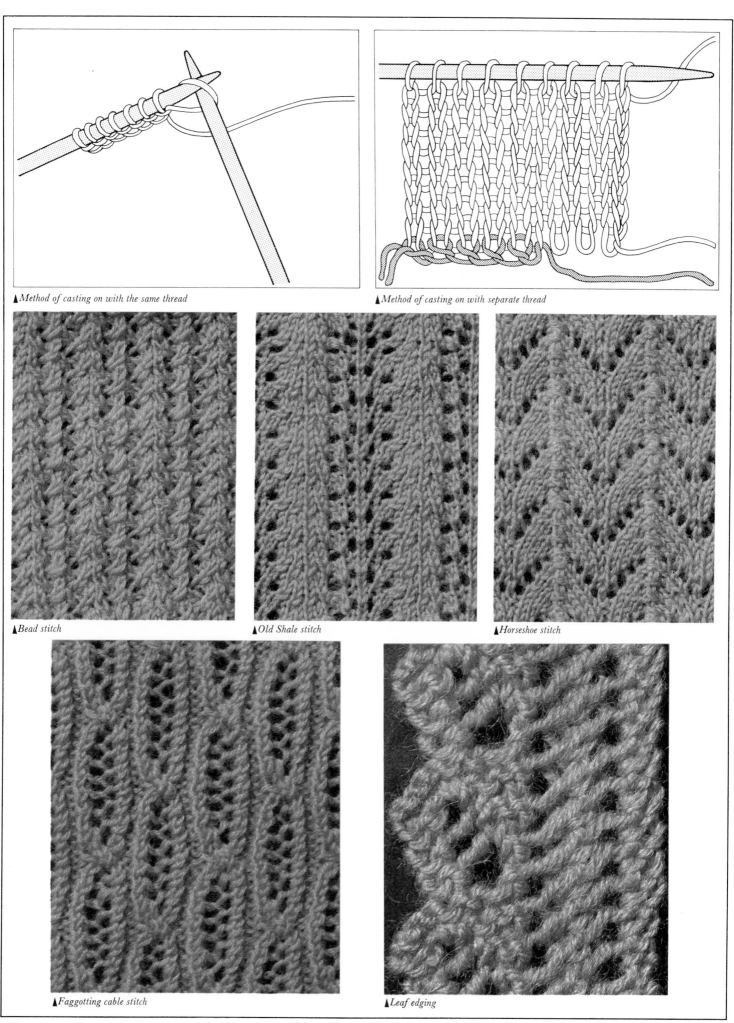

▲*Method of casting on with the same thread*

▲*Method of casting on with separate thread*

▲*Bead stitch*

▲*Old Shale stitch*

▲*Horseshoe stitch*

▲*Faggotting cable stitch*

▲*Leaf edging*

Simple stripes

Stripes using two or more contrasting shades are the simplest way of achieving a colourful effect in knitting. The most ordinary stitches and subtle combination of colours can produce the most interesting results.

Twisting yarns to change colour

When working any form of horizontal stripe, there is no problem about joining in a different ball of yarn. As one colour is finished at the end of a row, the new one is brought in at the beginning of the next row. As each new colour is brought into use, it is carried up the side of the work and when it is ready to come into use again it is merely twisted round the last colour used, before beginning to work.

Vertical or diagonal stripes, however, present something of a problem, as the colours must be changed at several points within the same row. When working narrow vertical or diagonal stripes it is quite simple to twist each yarn as it is brought into use with the last colour used, and carry the colour not in use across the back of the work. For wider stripes, it is not advisable to use this method as, apart from the waste, there is a tendency to pull the yarn too tightly which results in an unsightly bunching of the fabric and loss of tension. It is much better to divide each colour into small balls before beginning to work and use a separate ball of yarn for each stripe, twisting the colours together when a change is made.

It is important to remember that stripes worked by twisting the yarn on changing colour give a fabric of normal thickness, while stripes worked by carrying the yarn across the back produce a fabric of double thickness.

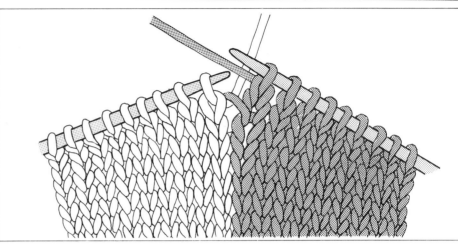
▲ *Working vertical stripes, seen from the right side*

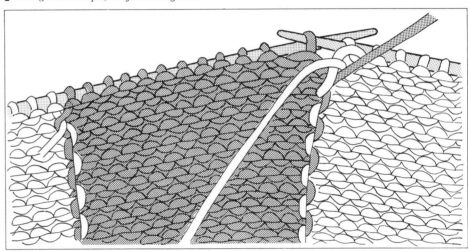
▲ *Wrong side of vertical stripes, showing yarns twisted to change colour*

Horizontal stripes

These are usually worked in stocking stitch and are achieved by changing colour at the beginning of a knit row. This gives an unbroken line of colour on the right side of the fabric. The number of rows can be the same in each colour or varied to give a random striped effect.

Ribbed stripes

Stripes in ribbing, if required to show an unbroken line of colour, need to have the colour change row knitted throughout although the other rows are worked in ribbing. An interesting effect is produced by working in rib, or fancy rib, irrespective of the colour change, to give a broken, random line in the pattern.

Cast on a number of stitches divisible by 10 plus 5.

1st row P5, *K1, yfwd, sl 1, ybk, K1, yfwd, sl 1, ybk, K1, P5, rep from * to end.

2nd row K1, yfwd, sl 1, ybk, K1, yfwd, sl 1, ybk, K1, *P5, K1, yfwd, sl 1, ybk, K1, yfwd, sl 1, ybk, K1, rep from * to end.

These 2 rows form the pattern and are repeated throughout, changing colour as required.

Chevron stripes

Cast on a number of stitches divisible by 13 plus 2.

1st row *K2, pick up loop between needles and place it on the left hand needle then K this loop through the back — called inc 1 —, K4, sl 1, P-wise, K2 tog, psso, K4, inc 1, rep from * to last 2 sts, K2.

2nd row P to end.

These 2 rows form the pattern and are repeated throughout, changing colour on a 1st row.

Vertical stripes

To work a wide stripe it is necessary to use a separate ball of yarn for each colour. Using 2 colours, the first colour would be referred to as A, and the second colour, B. Cast on 6 stitches with B, 6 with A, 6 with B and 6 with A, making a total of 24 stitches.

1st row *Using A, K6 sts, hold A to the left at the back of the work, take up B and bring it towards the right at the back of the work and under the A thread no longer in use, K6 B, hold B to the left at the back of the work, take up A and bring it towards the right at the back of the work and under the B thread no longer in use, rep from * to end, ending with K6 B.

2nd row (WS) *Using B, P6 sts, hold B to the left at the front of the work, take up A and bring it towards the right at the front of the work and over the B thread no longer in use, P6 A, hold A to the left at the front of the work, take up B and bring it towards the right at the front of the work and over the A thread no longer in use, rep from * to end, ending with P6 A.

These 2 rows form the pattern.

Diagonal stripes

Depending on the width of the stripes, the yarn can either be carried across the back of the work or separate balls of yarn used for each colour. To work a narrow diagonal stripe, cast on a number of stitches divisible by 5 plus 3, using 2 colours, A and B.

1st row K3 A, *K2 B, K3 A, rep from * to end.

2nd row P1 B, *P3 A, P2 B, rep from * to last 2 sts, P2 A.

3rd row K1 A, *K2 B, K3 A, rep from * to last 2 sts, K2 B.

4th row P1 A, P2 B, *P3 A, P2 B, rep from * to end.

Continue working in this way, moving the stripes one stitch to the right on K rows and one stitch to the left on P rows.

▲Ribbed stripes

▲Chevron stripes

▲Vertical stripes

▲Diagonal stripes

23

Jacquard

Jacquard knitting is the name given to patterned fabrics where more than one colour is used and where the pattern is knitted in at the same time as the background. It applies to the type of pattern which can be shown on a chart, in much the same way as cross stitch in embroidery is indicated. The usual feature is a bold, repeating design in large blocks of colour, where the yarn not in use is twisted regularly across the back of the work to carry it along, giving a thick, woven fabric.

Stranding method of carrying yarn not in use

Where the pattern is composed of small repeats with only a few stitches in any one colour, the colour not in use is carried loosely across the back of the work until it is required again, then twisted round the last colour used before beginning to knit with it again. It is essential not to drag the yarn from one group of stitches to the next, or the right side of the work will become puckered and uneven.

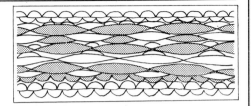

Stranding yarn ►
Weaving yarn ▼

Weaving method of carrying colour not in use

If there are more than three stitches in any group, it is advisable to twist the thread not in use at regular intervals with the yarn being used, to avoid long strands of yarn across the back of the work which can easily catch and distort the pattern.

To do this, using two colours classed as A and B, *knit the first stitch with A holding the yarn in the right hand in the usual way, insert the right hand needle into the next stitch then pick up B and carry it across the point of the right hand needle from right to left and knit the stitches with A in the usual way, repeat from * in this way, changing colours as required.

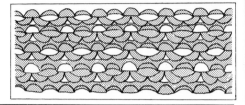

Using contrast colours over large areas

For collage knitting, where large, irregular blocks of colour are required, or in patterns such as large diamonds and checks, stranding or weaving the yarn across the back of the work will use a great deal of unnecessary yarn. For this type of pattern, it is best to use one separate ball of yarn for each area, twisting each new colour as it is brought into use with the last colour used before going on to the next area, as given for vertical stripes.

Working from a chart

Whether it is better to work from a chart showing each colour in a pattern as a separate symbol, or from row by row instructions where each separate colour is coded with a figure, such as A or B, is a matter of personal choice. The chart method is more often used in knitting publications, as it does not take up the amount of space required for row by row instructions. Both methods are given here for the rose motif.

Rose motif

For this motif, use on separate ball of yarn for each area of colour. Work out the exact position for placing the motif, such as on the left front shoulder of a plain jersey, or as a central motif on a pocket. It is worked over 34 stitches and 42 rows in 4 colours against the background colour. The background is coded A, the first contrast B, the second contrast C, the third contrast D and the fourth contrast E.
1st row Using A, K23, K2 B, K9 A.
2nd row P9 A, P2 B, P23 A.
3rd row K22 A, K2 B, K10 A.
4th row P10 A, P2 B, P5 A, P2 B, P15 A.
5th row K15 A, K4 B, K2 A, K1 B, K1 A, K2 B, K9 A.
6th row P12 A, P1 B, P2 A, P3 B, P1 C, P15 A.
7th row K15 A, K1 C, K3 B, K1 A, K1 B, K3 A, K3 B, K7 A.
8th row P7 A, P2 C, P3 B, P1 A, P1 B, P1 A, P2B, P1 C, P1 B, P15 A.
9th row K3 A, K1 B, K2 C, K9 A, K1 B, K1 C, K7 B, K2 C, K8 A.
10th row P8 A, P1 B, P2 C, P2 B, P1 A, P4 B P1 A, P1 B, P3 C, P4 A, P2 C, P1 B, P1 C, P3 A.
11th row K3 A, K2 C, K1 B, K2 C, K1 A, K2 B, K2 C, K2 B, K2 A, K1 B, K1 A, K1 B, K1 A, K1 B, K2 C, K1 B, K9 A.
12th row P12 A, P1 B, P1 A, P1 B, P3 A, P4 B, P1 C, P2 B, P1 A, P1 C, P1 B, P3 C, P3 A.
13th row K4 A, K3 C, K1 B, K1 A, K6 B, K2 A, K5 D, K2 A, K3 B, K7 A.
14th row P3 C, P1 B, P3 A, P4 B, P1 A, P2 D, P2 E, P2 D, P1 A, P6 B, P9 A.
15th row K6 A, K3 B, K2 A, K5 D, K5 E, K2 D, K3 B, K3 A, K1 B, K3 C, K1 A.
16th row P1 A, P2 C, P1 B, P1 C, P2 B, P2 A, P2 B, P1 D, P8 E, P3 D, P2 A, P4 B, P5 A.
17th row K5 A, K3 B, K1 C, K1 A, K3 E, K3 D, K7 E, K2 D, K2 A, K1 B, K1 C, K1 B, K2 C, K2 A.
18th row P3 A, P2 C, P1 B, P2 A, P3 D, P8 E, P3 D, P3 E, P2 C, P3 B, P4 A.
19th row K3 A, K3 B, K2 C, K1 A, K3 E, K7 D, K3 E, K2 D, K2 E, K1 D, K1 A, K2 C, K4 A.
20th row P7 A, P7 E, P1 D, P5 E, P3 D, P1 A, P2 E, P2 A, P1 C, P2 B, P3 A.
21st row K8 A, K6 D, K14 E, K6 A.
22nd row P7 A, P4 E, P2 D, P4 E, P4 A, P6 D, P7 A.
23rd row K4 A, K3 B, K5 D, K1 E, K5 D, K3 E, K3 D, K4 E, K3 B, K3 A.
24th row P1 A, P5 B, P2 E, P4 D, P2 E, P6 D, P3 E, P4 D, P4 B, P3 A.
25th row K7 A, K3 D, K3 E, K8 D, K2 E, K4 D, K1 A, K4 B, K2 A.
26th row P3 A, P3 B, P2 A, P3 D, P1 E, P1 D, P1 E, P6 D, P3 A, P1 E, P2 D, P2 A, P3 B, P3 A.
27th row K1 A, K6 B, K4 D, K3 E, K3 D, K1 E, K1 D, K1 E, K1 D, K1 E, K4 D, K2 E, K6 A.
28th row P6 A, P1 E, P2 D, P3 E, P3 D, P3 E, P2 A, P7 D, P1 B, P2 C, P4 B.
29th row K2 B, K3 C, K1 B, K2 A, K14 D, K5 E, K7A.
30th row P7 A, P4 E, P15 D, P3 A, P1 B, P3 C, P1 B.
31st row K9 A, K12 D, K1 E, K1 D, K4 E, K2 D, K1 C, K4 A.
32nd row P3 A, P4 C, P1 B, P5 E, P1 D, P1 E, P8 D, P11 A.
33rd row K7 A, K1 B, K4 A, K1 B, K5 D, K1 E, K1 A, K5 E, K1 A, K1 B, K4 C, K3 A.
34th row P2 A, P5 C, P1 B, P2 A, P3 E, P1 A, P1 B, P2 A, P2 D, P3 A, P1 B, P1 A, P2 B, P8 A.
35th row K9 A, K3 B, K6 A, K3 B, K6 A, K5 C, K2 A.
36th row P2 A, P3 C, P8 A, P3 B, P1 A, P1 C, P4 A, P1 B, P1 D, P2 B, P8 A.
37th row K7 A, K2 B, K1 D, K1 E, K3 A, K1 B, K1 C, K2 A, K3 B, K13 A.
38th row P14 A, P1 B, P4 A, P1 C, P1 B, P2 A, P1 E, P2 D, P1 B, P1 C, P6 A.
39th row K6 A, K1 B, K3 D, K24 A.
40th row P25 A, P2 D, P1 B, P6 A.
41st row K5 A, K1 B, K1 A, K1 D, K26 A.
42nd row P26 A, P1 E, P7 A.

Simple jacquard pattern

For this pattern, use the stranding method of carrying the colour not in use across the back of the work. Cast on a number of stitches divisible by 4 plus 1.
1st row (RS) Working from chart from right to left, *K1 A, K3 B, rep from * to last st, K1 A.
2nd row Working from chart from left to right, P2 A, *P1 B, P3 A, rep from * to last 3 sts, P1 B, P2 A.
Repeat 1st and 2nd rows once more.
5th row Using A, K to end.
6th row Using A, P to end.
These 6 rows form the pattern.

Large jacquard pattern

For this pattern, where more than 3 stitches are in any one colour, use the weaving method of carrying the yarn not in use across the back of the work. Cast on a number of stitches divisible by 10.
1st row (RS) Working from chart from right to left, *K1 B, K1 A, K2 B, K5 A, K1 B, rep from * to end.
2nd row Working from chart from left to right, *P2 B, P3 A, P5 B, rep from * to end.
3rd row *K5 B, K3 A, K2 B, rep from * to end.
4th row *P1 B, P2 A, P1 C, P2 A, P4 B, rep from * to end.
5th row *K4 B, K1 A, K3 C, K2 A, rep from * to end.
6th row *P1 A, P4 C, P1 A, P3 B, P1 A, rep from * to end.
7th row *K5 A, K5 C, rep from * to end.
8th row *P5 A, K5 C, rep from * to end.
9th row *K4 C, K2 A, K3 B, K1 A, rep from * to end.
10th row *P1 A, P4 B, P2 A, P3 C, rep from * to end.
11th row *K1 A, K1 C, K2 A, K5 B, K1 A, rep from * to end.
12th row *P7 B, P3 A, rep from * to end.
13th row *K3 A K7 B, rep from * to end.
14th row *P1 A, P2 B, P1 A, P2 B, P4 A, rep from * to end.
These 14 rows form the pattern.

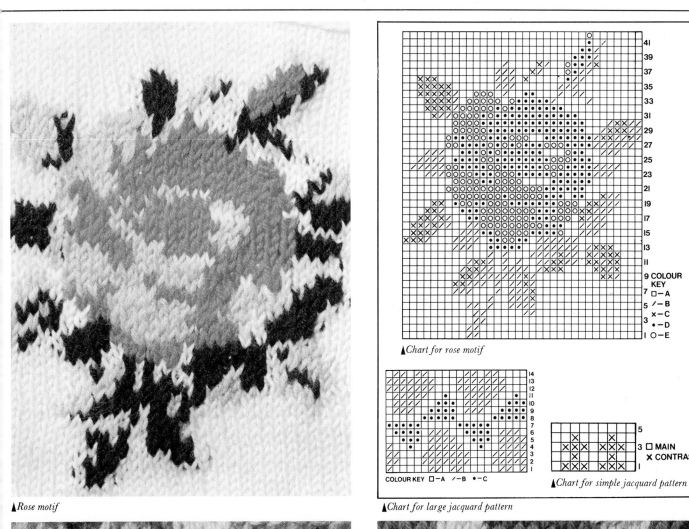

▲Rose motif

Chart for rose motif

9 COLOUR
KEY
7 □ – A
5 ╱ – B
  × – C
3 ● – D
1 ○ – E

▲Chart for rose motif

COLOUR KEY □ – A ╱ – B ● – C

▲Chart for large jacquard pattern

□ MAIN
× CONTRAST

▲Chart for simple jacquard pattern

▲Simple jacquard pattern

▲Large jacquard pattern

Fair Isle patterns

Traditional Fair Isle patterns are among the most beautiful designs in the world. If they are worked in the natural softly twisted yarns, which can vary in colour from white to a dark, blackish brown, they produce a fabric which is quite unique and highly treasured. The many brightly coloured patterns seen today have been introduced to cater for fashion demand.

Fair Isle designs do not need to have the yarns twisted on the wrong side of the fabric. Each area of colour is small, only two colours are used in any one row and they are carried directly from one stitch to the next to be worked in that colour.

Simple O and X design

A very old and often used design. Cast on a number of stitches divisible by 14 plus 1.

1st row (RS) Using A, K to end.

2nd row Working from chart from left to right P1 A, *P2 A, P2 B, P2 A, P1 B, P2 A, P2 B, P3 A, rep from * to end.

3rd row Working from chart from right to left, * K2 A, K2 B, K2 A, K3 B, K2 A, K2 B, K1 A, rep from * to last st, K1 A.

4th row P1 C, *P2 D, P2 C, P2 D, P1 C, P2 D, P2 C, P2 D, P1 C, rep from * to end.

5th row *K2 E, K2 F, K2 E, K3 F, K2 E, K2 F, K1 E, rep from * to last st, K1 E.

6th row As 4th.

7th row As 3rd.

8th row As 2nd.

9th row As 1st.

These 9 rows form the pattern.

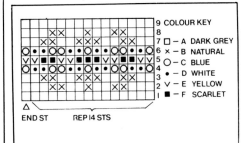

	COLOUR KEY
9	
8	
7	□ – A DARK GREY
6	× – B NATURAL
5	○ – C BLUE
4	• – D WHITE
3	
2	V – E YELLOW
1	■ – F SCARLET

END ST   REP 14 STS

▲*Chart for simple O and X design*

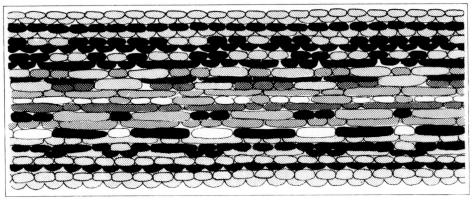

▲*Right side of simple O and X design*

▲*Wrong side of O and X design*

Flower motif

Cast on a number of stitches divisible by 28 plus 1.

1st row (RS) Working from chart from right to left, *K2 A, K1 B, K1 A, K1 B, K3 A, K4 B, K5 A, K4 B, K3 A, K1 B, K1 A, K1 B, K1 A, rep from * to last st, K1 A.

2nd row Working from chart from left to right, P1 A, *P2 A, P2 B, P1 A, P1 B, P1 A, P5 B, P3 A, P5 B, P1 A, P1 B, P1 A, P2 B, P3 A, rep from * to end.

Continue working from chart in this way until 25 rows have been worked.

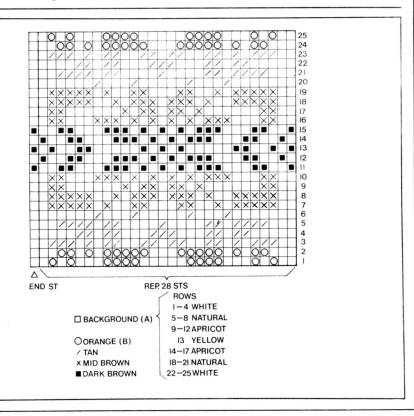

END ST   REP. 28 STS

□ BACKGROUND (A)

○ ORANGE (B)
／ TAN
× MID BROWN
■ DARK BROWN

ROWS	
1–4	WHITE
5–8	NATURAL
9–12	APRICOT
13	YELLOW
14–17	APRICOT
18–21	NATURAL
22–25	WHITE

Chart for flower motif ▶

▲*Flower motif*

▲*Star motif*

Star motif

Cast on a number of stitches divisible by 28 plus 1.

1st row (RS) Working from chart from right to left, *K2 A, K1 B, K5 A, K1 B, K4 A, K1 B, K1 A, K1 B, K4 A, K1 B, K5 A, K1 B, K1 A, rep from * to last st, K1 A.

2nd row Working from chart from left to right, P1 A, *P1 B, P6 A, P2 B, P4 A, P1 B, P4 A, P2 B, P6 A, P1 B, P1 A, rep from * to end.

Continue working from chart in this way until 25 rows have been worked.

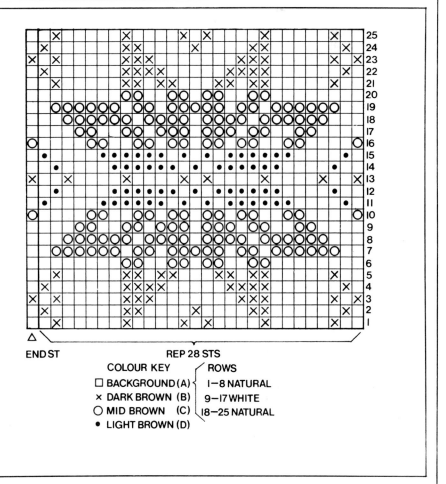

END ST

REP 28 STS

COLOUR KEY

		ROWS
□	BACKGROUND (A)	1–8 NATURAL
×	DARK BROWN (B)	9–17 WHITE
○	MID BROWN (C)	18–25 NATURAL
●	LIGHT BROWN (D)	

Chart for star motif ▶

Medallion shapes

Small or large medallion shapes can be knitted in rounds on four or more needles, flat in rows using two needles or circular, in rows, by means of turning a row at a given point to form wedge-shaped sections. Superb table mats, shawls, bedspreads and cushion covers may be made by using these techniques.

Medallion knitting in rounds

A medallion, when knitted on four or more needles can be square, pentagonal, hexagonal or circular. It can commence at the centre and increase to the outer edge, or commence at the outer edge and decrease to the centre. An example of this would be a beret, which combines both methods. On a small medallion it is easier to knit with no more than four needles and even on a six-sided shape, this can be achieved by working two sides on each of the three needles and using the fourth needle to knit the stitches Where a larger area is required, however, the total number of stitches needed to achieve this would entail three extra needles being brought into use. The method

of increasing and decreasing can be invisible, which would be most suitable for a stocking stitch beret, or decorative to give a lace effect for a shawl.

Simple pentagon medallion

There are five sides to a pentagon and this medallion begins at the centre by casting on 10 stitches, 2 for each side, on to one needle. Transfer 4 stitches on to the 2nd needle and 4 stitches on to the 3rd needle, leaving 2 stitches on the first needle. Join the needles into a round and knit all the stitches through the back of the loops to keep the centre flat.

1st round 1st needle — K into front then into back of first st — called inc 1 —, K1; 2nd needle — (inc 1, K1) twice; 3rd needle — (inc 1, K1) twice. 15 sts.
2nd round K to end.
3rd round 1st needle — (inc 1) twice, K1; 2nd needle — *(inc 1) twice, K1, rep from * once more; 3rd needle — *(inc 1) twice, K1, rep from k once more. 25 sts.
4th and 5th rounds K to end.

6th round 1st needle — inc 1, K2, inc 1, K1; 2nd needle — (inc 1, K2, inc 1, K1) twice; 3rd needle — (inc 1, K2, inc 1, K1) twice. 35 sts.
7th and 8th rounds K to end.
9th round 1st needle — inc 1, K4, inc 1, K1; 2nd needle — (inc 1, K4, inc 1, K1) twice; 3rd needle — (inc 1, K4, inc 1, K1) twice. 45 sts.
10th and 11th rounds K to end.
12th round 1st needle — inc 1, K6, inc 1, K1; 2nd needle — (inc 1, K6, inc 1, K1) twice; 3rd needle — (inc 1, K6, inc 1, K1) twice. 55 sts.
13th and 14th rounds K to end.
15th round 1st needle — inc 1, K8, inc 1, K1; 2nd needle — (inc 1, K8, inc 1, K1) twice; 3rd needle — (inc 1, K8, inc 1, K1) twice. 65 sts.
16th and 17th rounds K to end.
18th round 1st needle — inc 1, K10, inc 1, K1; 2nd needle — (inc 1, K10, inc 1, K1) twice; 3rd needle — (inc 1, K10, inc 1, K1) twice. 75 sts, 15 for each side.
19th and 20th rounds K to end.
Cast off loosely.

Medallion knitting in rows

A simple circular shape can be made by casting on a few stitches, then increasing at each end of every row, or alternate row, until a third of the length has been worked. Work without shaping until two-thirds has been completed, then decrease at each end of every row, or alternate row, until the original cast on number of stitches remain.
A simple square shape can commence at one

corner and increase outwards until a diagonal line is reached, then decrease again to the opposite corner. Even worked in a simple stitch, such as garter stitch, these squares look most effective when joined together with the garter stitch ridges of each square lying in opposite directions. Cast on 2 sts.
1st row K into front then into back of first st — called inc 1 —, inc 1. 4 sts.
2nd and every alt row K to end.

3rd row (Inc 1, K1) twice.
5th row Inc 1, K3, inc 1, K1.
7th row Inc 1, K5, inc 1, K1.
Continue increasing in this way until there are 50 sts.
Next row Sl 1, K1, psso, K to last 2 sts, K2 tog.
Next row K to end.
Rep last 2 rows until 2 sts rem. Cast off.

Circular medallions in rows

This technique, worked on 2 needles, forms wedge-shaped sections by means of turning at a given point in a row and leaving some stitches unworked. When turning in this way, say on a purl row, purl the given number of stitches then slip the next stitch from the left hand needle to the right hand needle without working it, take the yarn round this stitch to the back and return the slipped stitch to the left hand needle. Turn the work ready to knit the next row. Slipping the first unworked stitch in this way prevents a hole in the fabric being formed. When sections are made in this way, a seam is required to join the last section to the first sections. To avoid a hard line on this seam, cast on by the invisible method as given for lace knitting in Chapter 10 and join the seam by grafting the last row to the first row.

Circular table mat

Use a fine, cotton yarn and No.12 or No.11 needles. Cast on 25 sts.
1st row Sl 1, K19, yrn, P2 tog, K1, yfwd, K2.
2nd row K4, yrn, P2 tog, K18, turn, leaving 2 sts unworked.
3rd row Sl 1, K17, yrn, P2 tog, K2, yfwd, K2.
4th row K5, yrn, P2 tog, K16, turn, leaving 4 sts unworked.
5th row Sl 1, K15, yrn, P2 tog, K3, yfwd, K2.
6th row K6, yrn, P2 tog, K14, turn, leaving 6 sts unworked.
7th row Sl 1, K13, yrn, P2 tog, K2 tog, yfwd and over and round needle again — called y2rn —, K2, yfwd, K2.
8th row K6, P1, K1, yrn, P2 tog, K12, turn, leaving 8 sts unworked.
9th row Sl 1, K11, yrn, P2 tog, K8.
10th row Cast off 5 sts, K3, yrn, P2 tog, K10,

turn, leaving 10 sts unworked.
11th row Sl 1, K9, yrn, P2 tog, K1, yfwd, K2.
12th row K4, yrn, P2 tog, K8, turn, leaving 12 sts unworked.
13th row Sl 1, K7, yrn, P2 tog, K2, yfwd, K2.
14th row K5, yrn, P2 tog, K6, turn, leaving 14 sts unworked.
15th row Sl 1, K5, yrn, P2 tog, K3, yfwd, K2.
16th row K6, yrn, P2 tog, K4, turn, leaving 16 sts unworked.
17th row Sl 1, K3, yrn, P2 tog, K2 tog, y2rn, K2, yfwd, K2.
18th row K6, P1, K1, yrn, P2 tog, K2, turn, leaving 18 sts unworked.
19th row Sl 1, K1, yrn, P2 tog, K8.
20th row Cast off 5 sts, K3, yrn, P2 tog, K2, (yfwd, K2 tog) 8 times, K2.
These 20 rows form one selection. Repeat them 15 times more to complete mat. Graft sts.

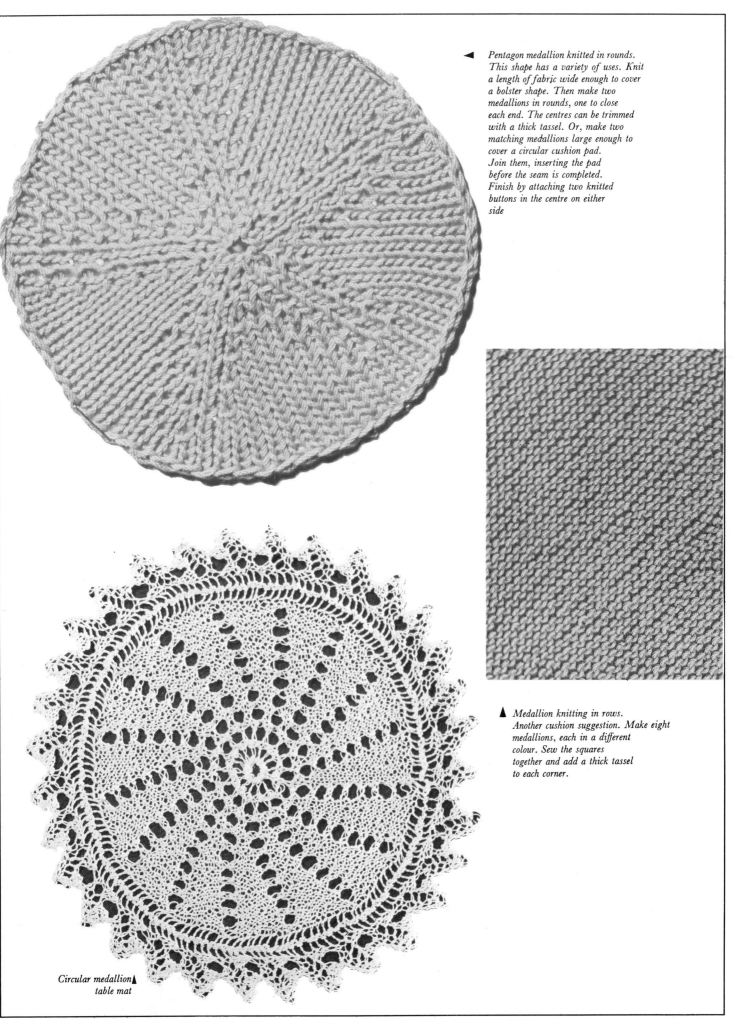

Pentagon medallion knitted in rounds. This shape has a variety of uses. Knit a length of fabric wide enough to cover a bolster shape. Then make two medallions in rounds, one to close each end. The centres can be trimmed with a thick tassel. Or, make two matching medallions large enough to cover a circular cushion pad. Join them, inserting the pad before the seam is completed. Finish by attaching two knitted buttons in the centre on either side

Medallion knitting in rows. Another cushion suggestion. Make eight medallions, each in a different colour. Sew the squares together and add a thick tassel to each corner.

Circular medallion table mat

Picot point & filet lace

Picot point knitting and filet lace knitting are both imitations of crochet techniques, worked on knitting needles. These methods form most decorative motifs and edgings and are best worked in a fine cotton to give a firm, crisp fabric.

Picot point knitting

This technique can be used to produce beautiful knitted flowers, lace edgings and insertions, decorative methods of casting off and strips of open lace fabric to any width.

Simple picot point

Using the 2 needle method, cast on 3 sts.

1st row K2 sts, lift the first st over the 2nd and off the right hand needle, K last st, lift the 2nd st over the 3rd st and off the right hand needle. Transfer remaining st to left hand needle. Cast on 2 sts, then rep the 1st row. Continue in this way until chain of picot points is the required length. Fasten off. The picot point can be made to any size by casting on and off 3, 4 or more stitches.

Picot point casting off

Work until position for casting off is reached.

Next row Insert right hand needle into the first st to be cast off, *cast on 2 sts, K and cast off 2 sts, K1 from left hand needle, cast off one st, transfer remaining st to left hand needle, rep from * across all sts to be cast off.

Picot point edging

Cast on a number of sts divisible by 5.

1st row K to end.

2nd row *(Insert right hand needle into first st, cast on 2 sts, K and cast off 2 sts, transfer remaining st to left hand needle) 4 times — called 4 picots —, K and cast off next 5 sts in usual way including st remaining after picots and returning last st to left hand needle, rep from * to end. Fasten off.

Picot point lace

Cast on and work first 2 rows as given for picot point edging, transferring last st to left hand needle. This forms the foundation row.

Next row *Make 4 picots as before keeping last st on right hand needle, join to centre of first 4 picots on foundation row by picking up and knitting a st between 2 centre picots, cast off one st, transfer remaining st to left hand needle, rep from * until one st remains, working into centre of each 4 picots of foundation row. Continue working in this way for required length.

Picot point flower

Work a simple picot of 5 points, casting on 3 sts for each point. Join into a circle by picking up and knitting lower st of first picot point, cast off one st, transfer remaining st to left hand needle. Commence petals.

1st row Cast on one st
2nd row K1, K into front and back of next st — called inc 1 —.
3rd row K3 sts.
4th row K2, inc 1.
5th row K4 sts.
6th row K3, inc 1.
7th, 8th, 9th and 10th rows K5 sts.
11th row Cast off one st, K3.
12th row K4 sts.

13th row Cast off one st, K2.
14th row K3 sts.
15th row Cast off one st, K1.
16th row K2 sts. Cast off one st.

Using right hand needle, pick up and knit a st between first and 2nd picot points, cast off one st, transfer remaining st to left hand needle. Rep these 16 rows 4 times more, joining each petal in same way. Fasten off.

Filet lace

This technique forms a fabric of solid squares of knitting, called blocks, and open mesh, called spaces, and garter stitch is used throughout.

Blocks

Each block consists of 3 knitted stitches in width and 4 rows in depth. Where the fabric gives alternating sections of blocks and spaces, the 3 block stitches are then treated as a space.

Spaces

Each space again consists of 3 stitches made by working y2rn, (sl 1 K-wise) twice, take the first slipped st over the 2nd to cast it off, K1, take the 2nd slipped st over the K1 to cast it off, and this method is repeated for each space. On the following row the 2nd made stitch of the y2rn is purled instead of knitted. Where the fabric gives alternating sections of spaces and blocks, these 3 space stitches are then treated as a block.

Simple filet lace insertion

Cast on 20 sts.

1st row K3 sts to form edge, work 2 spaces over next 6 sts, K3 sts for block, work 2 spaces over next 6 sts, K2 sts to form edge.
2nd row K4 sts, P1, K2, P1, K5, P1, K2, P1, K3.
3rd row As 1st.
4th row As 2nd.
5th row K3 edge sts, (work 1 space over next 3 sts, K3 sts for block) twice, work 1 space over next 3 sts, K2 edge sts.
6th row K4 sts, P1, (K5, P1) twice, K3.
7th row As 5th.
8th row As 6th.

Rep the 5th-8th rows twice more, 1st-4th rows once more then 5th-8th rows once more. These 24 rows form the pattern. Continue in pattern until work is required length.

▲Picot point lace

▲Picot point flower

▲Filet lace

31

Basic fabric stitches

Garter stitch
Cast on any number of stitches.
1st row K to end.
This row forms the pattern.

Stocking stitch
Cast on any number of stitches.
1st row K to end.
2nd row P to end.
These 2 rows form the pattern.

Twisted stocking stitch
This variation of stocking stitch has a twisted effect added on every knitted row by working into the back of every stitch.

Cast on any number of stitches.
1st row K into the back of each stitch to end.
2nd row P to end.
These 2 rows form the pattern.

Reversed stocking stitch
This variation of stocking stitch uses the wrong side, or purl side of the work to form the fabric.
Cast on any number of stitches.
1st row (right side) P to end.
2nd row K to end.
These 2 rows form the pattern.

Single rib
Cast on a number of stitches divisible by 2 + 1.
1st row K1, *P1, K1, rep from * to end.
2nd row P1, *K1, P1, rep from * to end.
These 2 rows form the pattern.
Where an even number of stitches are cast on, single rib is worked as follows:
1st row *K1, P1, rep from * to end.
This row forms the pattern.

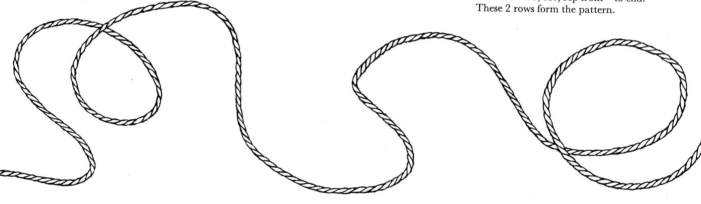

Rice stitch
Cast on a number of stitches divisible by 2 + 1.
1st row K to end.
2nd row P1, *K1, P1, rep from * to end.
These 2 rows form the pattern.

Broken rib
Cast on a number of stitches divisible by 2 + 1.
1st row K1, *P1, K1, rep from * to end.
2nd row P1, *K1, P1, rep from * to end.
3rd row K to end.
4th row As 3rd.
These 4 rows form the pattern.

Moss stitch
Cast on a number of stitches divisible by 2 + 1.
1st row K1, *P1, K1, rep from * to end.
This row forms the pattern.
Where an even number of stitches are cast on, moss stitch is worked as follows:
1st row *K1, P1, rep from * to end.
2nd row *P1, K1, rep from * to end.
These 2 rows form the pattern.

Irish moss stitch
Cast on a number of stitches divisible by 2 + 1.
1st row K1, *P1, K1, rep from * to end.
2nd row P1, *K1, P1, rep from * to end.
3rd row As 2nd.
4th row As 1st.
These 4 rows form the pattern.

Woven stitch
Cast on a number of stitches divisible by 2 + 1.
1st row K1, *yfwd, sl 1 P-wise, ybk, K1, rep from * to end.
2nd row P to end.
3rd row K2, *yfwd, sl 1 P-wise, ybk, K1, rep from * to last st, K1.
4th row As 2nd.
These 4 rows form the pattern.

Honeycomb slip stitch
Cast on a number of stitches divisible by 2 + 1.
1st row P1, *sl 1 P-wise, P1, rep from * to end.
2nd row P to end.
3rd row P2, *sl 1 P-wise, P1, rep from * to last st, P1.
4th row As 2nd.
These 4 rows form the pattern.

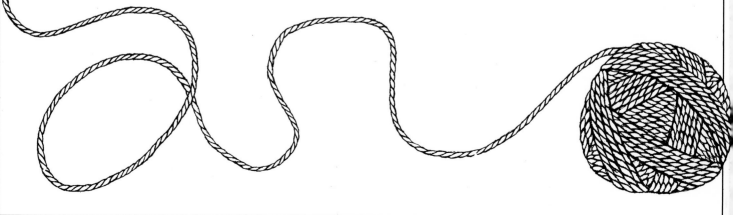

▲Garter stitch

▲Stocking stitch

▲Single rib

▲Rice stitch

▲Broken rib

▲Single moss stitch

▲Irish moss stitch

▲Woven stitch

▲Honeycomb slip stitch

33

Simple fabric stitches

Double rib
Cast on a number of stitches divisible by 4 + 2.
1st row K2, *P2, K2, rep from * to end.
2nd row P2, *K2, P2, rep from * to end.
These 2 rows form the pattern.

Double moss stitch
Cast on a number of stitches divisible by 4 + 2.
1st row K2, *P2, K2 rep from * to end.
2nd row P2, *K2, P2, rep from * to end.
3rd row As 2nd.
4th row As 1st.
These 4 rows form the pattern.

Seeded rib
Cast on a number of stitches divisible by 4 + 1.
1st row P1, *K3, P1, rep from * to end.
2nd row K2, P1, *K3, P1, rep from * to last 2 sts, K2.
These 2 rows form the pattern.

Broken basket stitch
Cast on a number of stitches divisible by 4 + 2.
1st row K to end.
2nd row P to end.
3rd row K2, *P2, K2, rep from * to end.
4th row P2, *K2, P2, rep from * to end.
These 4 rows form the pattern.

Twisted basket stitch
Cast on a number of stitches divisible by 4 + 2.
1st row K to end.
2nd row P to end.
3rd row K the second st, then the first st and sl both sts off the needle tog — called Tw2 —, *P2, Tw2, rep from * to end.
4th row P2, *K2, P2, rep from * to end.
5th row As 1st.
6th row As 2nd.
7th row P2, *Tw2, P2, rep from * to end.
8th row K2, *P2, rep from * to end.
These 8 rows form the pattern.

Wheat ear rib
Cast on a number of stitches divisible by 5 + 2.
1st row *P3, put the needle behind the first st and K into the back of the second st, then K the first st and sl both sts off the needle tog, rep from * to last 2 sts, P2.
2nd row *K3, P the second st, then the first st and sl both sts off the needle tog, rep from * to last 2 sts, K2.
These two rows form the pattern.

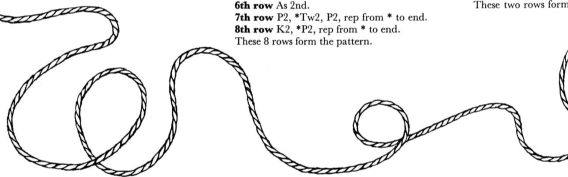

Crossed stitch pattern
Cast on a number of stitches divisible by 4.
1st row K1, *K the second st and lift it over the first st and off the needle, then K the first st — called Cr2R—, K2, rep from * to last 3 sts, Cr2R, K1.
2nd row P to end.
3rd row K3, *put the needle purlwise through the first st and draw the second st through, K this st and sl it off the needle, then K the first st — called Cr2L —, K2, rep from * to last st, K1.
4th row As 2nd.
These 4 rows form the pattern.

Lattice stitch
Cast on a number of stitches divisible by 2 + 1.
1st row K2, *put the needle behind the first st and K into the back of second st, then K the first st and sl both sts off the needle tog, rep from * to last st, K1.
2nd row P2, *P the second st, then the first st and sl both sts off the needle tog, rep from * to last st, P1.
These 2 rows form the pattern.

Diagonal slip stitch pattern
Cast on a number of stitches divisible by 5 + 2.
1st row P2, *sl 3, P2, rep from * to end.
2nd row P to end.
3rd row P3, *sl 3, P2, rep from * to last 4 sts, sl 3, P1.
4th row As 2nd.
5th row P1, sl 1, *P2, sl 3, rep from * to last 5 sts, P2, sl 2, P1.
6th row As 2nd.
7th row P1, sl 2, *P2, sl 3, rep from * to last 4 sts, P2, sl 1, P1.
8th row As 2nd.
9th row P1, sl 3, *P2, sl 3, rep from * to last 3 sts, P3.
10th row As 2nd.
These 10 rows form the pattern.

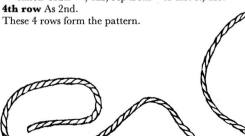

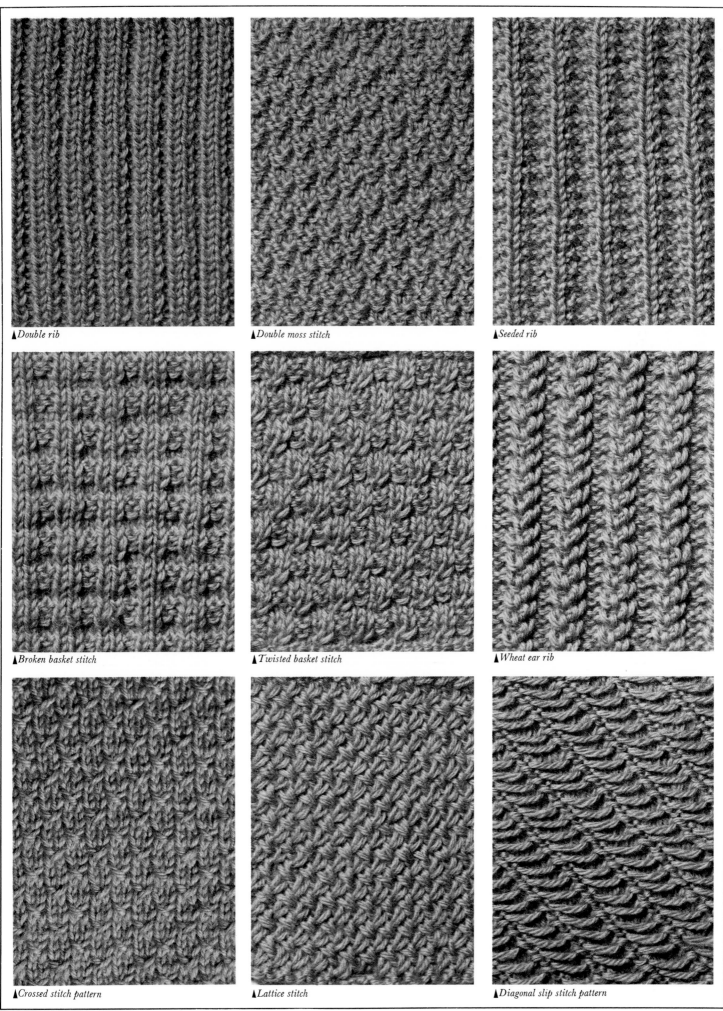

▲Double rib

▲Double moss stitch

▲Seeded rib

▲Broken basket stitch

▲Twisted basket stitch

▲Wheat ear rib

▲Crossed stitch pattern

▲Lattice stitch

▲Diagonal slip stitch pattern

More fabric stitches

Cane basket stitch
Cast on a number of stitches divisible by 6 + 2.
1st row K2, *P4, K2, rep from * to end.
2nd row P2, *K4, P2, rep from * to end.
3rd row As 1st.

4th row As 2nd.
5th row P3, *K2, P4, rep from * to last 5 sts, K2, P3.
6th row K3, *P2, K4, rep from * to last 5 sts,

P2, K3.
7th row As 5th.
8th row As 6th.
These 8 rows form the pattern.

Trellis stitch
Cast on a number of stitches divisible by 6 + 2.
1st row P3, *K2, P4, rep from * to last 5 sts, K2, P3.
2nd row K3, *P2, K4, rep from * to last 5 sts, P2, K3.
3rd row As 1st.
4th row As 2nd.
5th row P1, *sl next 2 sts on to a cable needle

and leave at back of work, K1, then P2 from cable needle — called C3B —, sl next st on to a cable needle and leave at front of work, P2, then K1 from cable needle — called C3F —, rep from * to last st, P1.
6th row K1, P1, *K4, P2, rep from * to last 6 sts, K4, P1, K1.
7th row P1, K1, *P4, K2, rep from * to last 6

sts, P4, K1, P1.
8th row As 6th.
9th row As 7th.
10th row As 6th.
11th row P1, *C3F, C3B, rep from * to last st, P1.
12th row As 2nd.
These 12 rows form the pattern.

Diamond quilting pattern
Cast on a number of stitches divisible by 6 + 2.
1st row K to end.
2nd row P1, P1 winding yarn twice round needle, *P4, P2 winding yarn twice round needle for each, rep from * to last 6 sts, P4, P1 winding yarn twice round needle, P1.
3rd row K1, sl 1 dropping the extra loop, *K4, sl 2 dropping the extra loops, rep from * to last 6 sts, K4, sl 1 dropping the extra loop, K1.
4th row P1, sl 1, *P4, sl 2, rep from * to last 6 sts, P4, sl 1, P1.

5th row K1, sl 1, *K4, sl 2, rep from * to last 6 sts, K4, sl 1, K1.
6th row As 4th.
7th row K1, *sl next st on to a cable needle and leave at front of work, K2, then K1 from cable needle — called C3F —, sl next 2 sts to a cable needle and leave at back of work, K1, then K2 from cable needle — called C3B —, rep from * to last st, K1.
8th row P3, *P2, winding yarn twice round needle for each, P4, rep from * to last 5 sts, P2 winding yarn twice round needle, P3.

9th row K3, *sl 2 dropping the extra loops, K4, rep from * to last 5 sts, sl 2 dropping the extra loops, K3.
10th row P3, *sl 2, P4, rep from * to last 5 sts, sl 2, P3.
11th row K3, *sl 2, K4, rep from * to last 5 sts, sl 2, K3.
12th row As 10th.
13th row K1, *C3B, C3F, rep from * to last st, K1.
14th row As 2nd.
The 3rd to 14th rows form the pattern.

Stepped stitch
Cast on a number of stitches divisible by 6 + 2.
1st row P2, *K4, P2, rep from * to end.
2nd row K2, *P4, K2, rep from * to end.
3rd row As 1st.

4th row As 2nd.
5th row P3, *K2, P4, rep from * to last 5 sts, K2, P3.
6th row K3, *P2, K4, rep from * to last 5 sts, P2, K3.

7th row As 5th.
8th row As 6th.
9th row P to end.
10th row K to end.
These 10 rows form the pattern.

Spiral rib
Cast on a number of stitches divisible by 6 + 2.
1st row P2, *K4, P2, rep from * to end.
2nd row K2, *P4, K2, rep from * to end.

3rd row P2, *K 2nd st, then 1st st and sl both sts off needle tog — called Tw2 —, Tw2, P2, rep from * to end.
4th row As 2nd.

5th row P2, *K1, Tw2, K1, P2, rep from * to end.
6th row As 2nd.
The 3rd to 6th rows form the pattern.

Corded rib
Cast on a number of stitches divisible by 6 + 2.
1st row P2, *K4, P2, rep from * to end.

2nd row P to end.
3rd row P2, *(sl 1, K1, yfwd, pass the sl st over the K1 and the yfwd) twice, P2, rep from *

to end.
4th row As 2nd.
The 3rd and 4th rows form the pattern.

Tassel stitch
Cast on a number of stitches divisible by 6 + 2.
1st row P2, *K4, P2, rep from * to end.
2nd row K2, *P4, K2, rep from * to end.
3rd row As 1st.
4th row As 2nd.
5th row K2, *insert needle between 4th and 5th stitches and draw through a loop, K1, P2, K3,

rep from * to end.
6th row *P3, K2, P2 tog, rep from * to last 2 sts, P2.
7th row K3, *P2, K4, rep from * to last 5 sts, P2, K3.
8th row P3, *K2, P4, rep from * to last 5 sts, K2, P3.
9th row As 7th.

10th row As 8th.
11th row P2, K3, *insert needle between 4th and 5th stitches and draw up a loop, K1, P2, K3, rep from * to last 3 sts, K1, P2.
12th row K2, P4, *K2, P2 tog, P3, rep from * to last 2 sts, K2.
These 12 rows form the pattern.

Mock smocking
Cast on a number of stitches divisible by 6 + 2.
1st row P2, *K4, P2, rep from * to end.
2nd row K2, *P4, K2, rep from * to end.
3rd row P2, *insert needle between 4th and 5th stitches and draw up a loop, K4, then pass the top thread of the loop over these 4 sts, P2, rep from * to end.

4th row As 2nd.
5th row K3, *P2, K4, rep from * to last 5 sts, P2, K3.
6th row P3, *K2, P4, rep from * to last 5 sts, K2, P3.
7th row Insert needle between 3rd and 4th stitches and draw up a loop, K3, then pass the top thread of the loop over these 3 sts, *P2,

insert needle between 4th and 5th stitches and draw up a loop, K4, then pass the top thread of the loop over these 4 sts, rep from * to last 5 sts, P2, insert needle after last st on left hand needle and draw up a loop, K3, then pass the top thread of the loop over these 3 sts.
8th row As 6th.
These 8 rows form the pattern.

Bobble rib
Cast on a number of stitches divisible by 6 + 2.
1st row P2, *K1, P2, rep from * to end.
2nd row K2, *P1, K2, rep from * to end.
3rd row P2, *K1, P2, (P1, K1, P1, K1) all into next st — called K4 from 1 —, P2, rep from * to end.
4th row K2, *P4, K2, P1, K2, rep from * to end.

5th row P2, *K1, P2, P4, turn and K4, turn again and P4, P2, rep from * to end.
6th row K2, *P4 tog, K2, P1, K2, rep from * to end.
7th row As 1st.
8th row As 2nd.
9th row P2, *K4 from 1, P2, K1, P2, rep from *

to end.
10th row K2, *P1, K2, P4, K2, rep from * to end.
11th row P2, *P4, turn and K4, turn again and P4, P2, K1, P2, rep from * to end.
12th row K2, *P1, K2, P4 tog, K2, rep from * to end.
These 12 rows form the pattern.

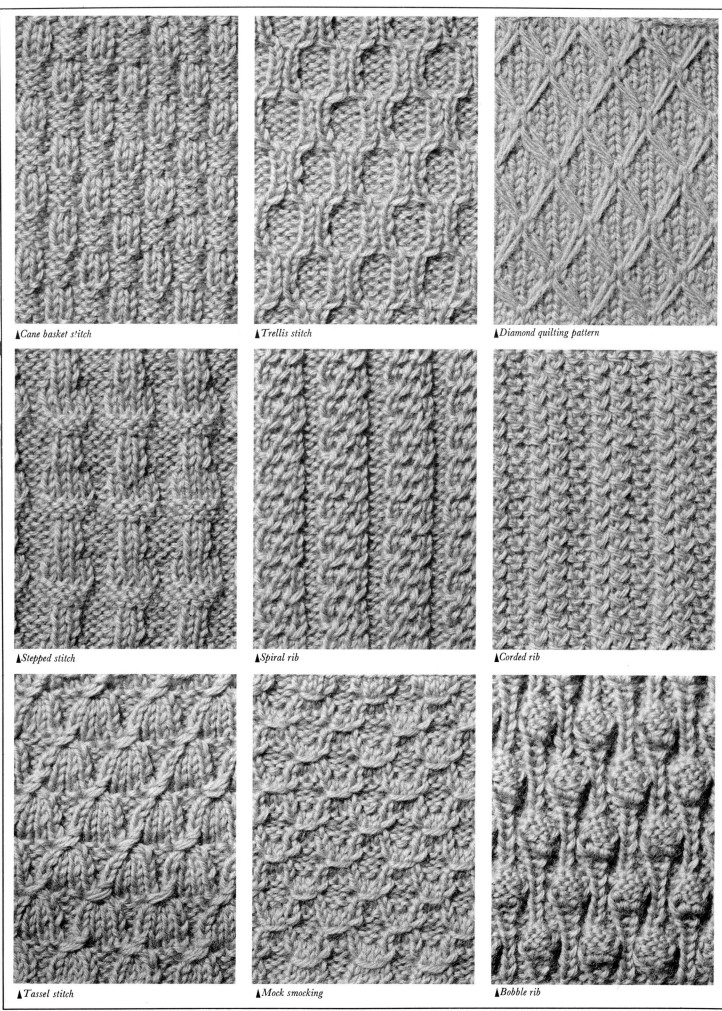

▲*Cane basket stitch*

▲*Trellis stitch*

▲*Diamond quilting pattern*

▲*Stepped stitch*

▲*Spiral rib*

▲*Corded rib*

▲*Tassel stitch*

▲*Mock smocking*

▲*Bobble rib*

Large patterns

Pyramid pattern
Cast on a number of stitches divisible by 15 + 1.

1st row K to end.
2nd row P4, *K8, P7, rep from * to last 12 sts, K8, P4.
3rd row K1, *K up 1, K2, sl 1, K1, psso, P6, K2 tog, K2, K up 1, K1, rep from * to end.
4th row P5, *K6, P9, rep from * to last 11 sts, K6, P5.
5th row K2, *K up 1, K2, sl 1, K1, psso, P4, K2 tog, K2, K up 1, K3, rep from * to last 14 sts, K up 1, K2, sl 1, K1, psso, P4, K2 tog, K2 K up 1, K2.
6th row P6, *K4, P11, rep from * to last 10 sts, K4, P6.
7th row K3, *K up 1, K2, sl 1, K1, psso, P2, K2 tog. K2, K up 1, K5, rep from * to last 13 13 sts, K up 1, K2, sl 1, K1, psso, P2, K2 tog, K2, K up 1, K3.
8th row P7, *K2, P13, rep from * to last 9 sts, K2, P7.
9th row K4, *K up 1, K2, sl 1, K1, psso, K2 tog, K2, K up 1, K7, rep from * to last 12 sts, K up 1, K2, sl 1, K1, psso, K2 tog, K2, K up 1, K4.
10th row P to end.
These 10 rows form the pattern.

Leaf pattern
Cast on a number of stitches divisible by 24 + 1.

1st row K1, *K up 1, sl 1, K1, psso, K4, K2 tog, K3, K up 1, K1, K up 1, K3, sl 1, psso, K4, K2 tog, K up 1 K1, rep from * to end.
2nd and every alt row P to end.
3rd row K1, *K up 1, K1, sl 1, K1, psso, K2, K2 tog, K4, K up 1, K1, K up 1, K4, sl 1, K1, psso,·

5th row K1, *K up 1, K2, sl 1, K1, psso, K2 tog, K5, K up 1, K1, K up 1, K5, sl 1, K1, psso, K2 tog, K2, K up 1, K1, rep from * to end.
7th row K1, *K up 1, K3, sl 1, K1, psso, K4, K2 tog, K up 1, K1, K up 1, sl 1, K1, psso, K4, K2 tog, K3, K up 1, K1, rep from * to end.
9th row K1, *K up 1, K4, sl 1, K1; psso, K2, K2

tog, K1, K up 1, K1, K up 1, K1, sl 1, K1, psso, K2, K2 tog, K4, K up 1, K1, rep from * to end.
11th row K1, *K up 1, K5, sl 1, K1, psso, K2 tog, K2, K up 1, K1, K up 1, K2, sl 1, K1, psso, K2 tog, K5, K up 1, K1, rep from * to end.
12th row As 2nd.
These 12 rows form the pattern.

Seeded chevron pattern
Cast on a number of stitches divisible by 14 + 2.

1st row K14, *K second st, then first st and sl both sts off the needles tog — called TwR —, K12, rep from * to last 2 sts, K2.
2nd row P1, *sl 1, P12, sl·1, rep from * to last st, P1.
3rd row K1, *put needle behind first st and K into the back of the second st, then K the first st and sl both sts off the needle tog — called TwL —, K10, TwR, rep from * to last st, K1.
4th row P1, K1, *sl 1, P10, sl 1, P1, K1, rep from * to end.
5th row K1, P1, *TwL, K8, TwR, K1, P1, rep from * to end.
6th row P1, K1, *P1, sl 1, P8, sl 1, K1, P1, K1, rep from * to end.
7th row K1, P1, *K1, TwL, K6, TwR, P1, K1, P1, rep from * to end.
8th row *(P1, K1) twice, sl 1, P6, sl 1, P1, K1, rep from * to last 2 sts, P1, K1.
9th row *(K1, P1) twice, TwL, K4, TwR, K1, P1, rep from * to last 2 sts, K1, P1.

10th row P1, *(K1, P1) twice, sl 1, P4, sl 1, (K1, P1) twice, rep from * to last st, K1.
11th row K1, *(P1, K1) twice, TwL, K2, TwR, (P1, K1) twice, rep from * to last st, P1.
12th row *(P1, K1) 3 times, sl 1, P2, sl 1, (P1, K1) twice, rep from * to last 2 sts, P1, K1.
13th row (K1, P1) 3 times, *TwL, TwR, (K1, P1) twice, TwR, (K1, P1) twice, rep from * to last 10 sts, TwL, TwR, (K1, P1) 3 times.
14th row P1, sl 1, *(P1, K1) 3 times, sl 1, K1, (P1, K1) twice, sl 2, rep from * to last 14 sts, (P1, K1) 3 times, sl 1, K1, (P1, K1) twice, sl 1, P1.
15th row K1 *TwL, (P1, K1) twice, TwL, (P1, K1) twice, TwR, rep from * to last st, K1.
16th row P2, *sl 1, (K1, P1) 5 times, sl 1, P2, rep from * to end.
17th row K2, *TwL, (K1, P1) 4 times, TwR, K2, rep from * to end.
18th row P3, *sl 1, (P1, K1) 4 times, sl 1, P4, rep from * to the last 13 sts, sl 1, (P1, K1) 4 times, sl 1, P3.
19th row K3, *TwL, (P1, K1) 3 times, TwR, K4,

rep from * to last 13 sts, TwL, (P1, K1) 3 times, TwR, K3.
20th row P4, *sl 1, (K1, P1) 3 times, sl 1, P6, rep from * to last 12 sts, sl 1, (K1, P1) 3 times. sl 1, P4.
21st row K4, *TwL, (K1, P1) twice, TwR, K6, rep from * to last 12 sts, TwL, (K1, P1) twice, TwR, K4.
22nd row P5, *sl 1, (P1, K1) twice, sl 1, P8, rep from * to last 11 sts, sl 1, (P1, K1) twice, sl 1, P5.
23rd row K5, *TwL, P1, K1, TwR, K8, rep from * to last 11 sts, TwL, P1 K1, TwR, K5.
24th row P6, *sl 1, K1, P1, sl 1, P10, rep from * to last 10 sts, sl 1, K1, P1, sl 1, P6.
25th row K6, *TwL, TwR, K10, rep from * to last 10 sts, TwL, TwR, K6.
26th row P8, *sl 1, P13, rep from * to last 8 sts, sl 1, P7.
27th row K7, *TwL, K12, rep from * to last 9 sts, TwL, K7.
28th row P to end.
These 28 rows form the pattern.

Travelling rib pattern
Cast on a number of stitches divisible by 12 + 2.

1st row P6, *K7, P5, rep from * to last 8 sts, K7, P1.
2nd row K1, *P7, K5, rep from * to last st, K1.
3rd row P5, *K second st, then first st and sl both sts off the needle tog — called TwR —, K4, TwR, P4, rep from * to last 9 sts, TwR, K4, TwR, P1.
4th row K2, *P7, K5, rep from * to end.
5th row P4, *TwR, K4, TwR, P4, rep from * to last 10 sts, TwR, K4, TwR, P2.
6th row K3, *P7, K5, rep from * to last 11 sts, P7, K4.
7th row P3 *TwR, K4, TwR, P4, rep from * to

last 11 sts, TwR, K4, TwR, P3.
8th row K4, *P7, K5, rep from * to last 10 sts. P7, K3.
9th row P2, *TwR. K4, TwR, P4, rep from * to end.
10th row K5, *P7, K5, rep from * to last 9 sts. P7, K2.
11th row P1, *TwR, K4, TwR, P4, rep from * to last st, P1.
12th row K6, *P7, K5, rep from * to last 8 sts, P7, K1.
13th row P1, *put needle behind first st and K into the back of second st, then K first st and sl both sts off the needle tog — called TwL —, K4, TwL, P4, rep from * to last st, P1.

14th row As 10th.
15th row P2, *TwL, K4, TwL, P4, rep from * to end.
16th row As 8th.
17th row P3, *TwL, K4, TwL, P4, rep from * to last 11 sts, TwL, K4, TwL, P3.
18th row As 6th.
19th row P4, *TwL, K4, TwL, P4, rep from * to last 10 sts, TwL, K4, TwL, P2.
20th row As 4th.
21st row P5, *TwL, K4, TwL, P4, rep from * to last 9 sts, TwL, K4, TwL, P1.
22nd row As 2nd.
The 3rd to 22nd rows form the pattern.

Medallion with bells
Cast on a number of stitches divisible by 16 + 3.

1st row P7, *K2, P1, K2, P11, rep from * to last 12 sts, K2, P1, K2, P7.
2nd row K7, *P2, K1, P2, K11, rep from * to last 12 sts, P2, K1, P2, K7.
3rd row P5, *P2 tog, K2, K up 1, P1, K up 1, K2, P2 tog, P7, rep from * to last 14 sts, P2 tog, K2, K up 1, P1, K up 1, K2, P2 tog, P5.
4th row K6, *P2, K3, P2, K9, rep from * to last 13 sts, P2, K3, P2, K6.
5th row P1, *(K1. P1, K1, P1, K1) all into next st — called K5 from 1 —, P2, P2 tog, K2, K up 1, P3, K up 1, K2, P2 tog, P2, rep from * to last 2 sts, K5 from 1, P1.
6th row K1, P5, turn and K5, turn again and P5, — called work 5x3—, *K3, P2, K5, P2, K3, work 5x3, rep from * to last st, K1.
7th row P1, sl 1, K1, psso, K1, K2 tog. *P1, P2 tog, K2, K up 1, P2, K5 from 1, P2, K up 1, K2,

P2 tog, P1, sl 1, K1, psso, K1, K2 tog, rep from * to last st, P1.
8th row K1, P3, *K2, P2, K3, work 5x3, K3, P2, K2, P3, rep from * to last st, K1.
9th row P1, sl 1, K2 tog, psso, *P2 tog, K2, K up 1, P3, sl 1, K1, psso, K1, K2 tog, P3, K up 1, K2, P2 tog, sl 1, K2 tog, psso, rep from * to last st, P1.
10th row K3, *P2, K4, P3, K4, P2, K3, rep from * to end.
11th row P1, P2 tog, *K2, K up 1, P2, K5 from 1, P1, sl 1, K2 tog, psso, P1, K5 from 1, P2, K up 1, K2, P3 tog, rep from * to end, ending last rep with P2 tog, P1 instead of P3 tog.
12th row K2, *P2, (K3, work 5x3) twice, K3, P2, K1, rep from * to last st, K1.
13th row P2, *K up 1, K2, P2 tog, P1, sl 1, K1, psso, K1, K2 tog, P3, sl 1, K1, psso, K1, K2 tog, P1, P2 tog, K2, K up 1, P1, rep from * to last st, P1.

14th row K3, *P2, K2, P3, K3, P3, K2, P2, K3, rep from * to end.
15th row P3, *K up 1, K2, P2 tog, sl 1, K2 tog, psso, P1, K5 from 1, P1, sl 1, K2 tog, psso, P2 tog, K2, K up 1, P3, rep from * to end.
16th row K4, *P2, K3, work 5x3, K3, P2, K5, rep from * to end, ending last rep with K4 instead of K5.
17th row P1, K5 from 1, *P2, K up 1, K2, P2 tog, P1, sl 1, K1, psso, K1, K2 tog, P1, P2 tog, K2, K up 1, P2, K5 from 1, rep from * to last st, P1.
18th row K1, work 5x3, *K3, P2, K2, P3, K2, K3, work 5x3, rep from * to last st, K1.
19th row P1, sl 1, K1, psso, K1, K2 tog, *P3, K up 1, K2, P2 tog, sl 1, K2 tog, psso, P2 tog, K2, K up 1, P3, sl 1, K1, psso, K1, K2 tog, rep from * to last st, P1.
20th row K1, P3, *K4, P2, K3, P2, K4, P3, rep from * to last st, K1.
continued overleaf

▲Pyramid pattern

▲Leaf pattern

▲Seeded chevron pattern

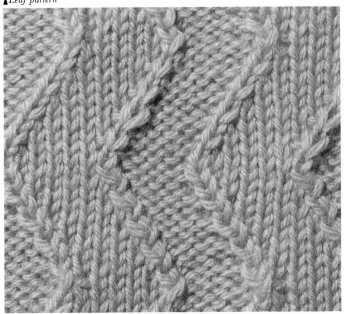

▲Travelling rib pattern

▲Medallion with bells

▲Butterfly stitch

continued from preceding page

21st row P1, sl 1, K2 tog, psso, P1, *K5 from 1, P2, K up 1, K2, P3 tog, K2, K up 1, P2, K5 from 1, P1, sl 1, K2 tog, psso, P1, rep from * to end.
22nd row K3, *work 5x3, K3, P2, K1, P2, K3,

work 5x3, K3, rep from * to end.
23rd row P3, *sl 1, K1, psso, K1, K2 tog, P1, P2 tog, K2, K up 1, P1, K up 1, K2, P2 tog, P1, sl 1, K1, psso, K1, K2 tog, P3, rep from * to end.
24th row K3, *P3, K2, P2, K3, P2, K2, P3, K3, rep from * to end.

25th row P1, K5 from 1, *P1, sl 1, K2 tog, psso, P2 tog, K2, K up 1, P3, K up 1, K2, P2 tog, sl 1, K2 tog, psso, P1, K5 from 1, rep from * to last st, P1.
26th row As 6th.
The 7th to 26th rows form the pattern.

Butterfly stitch

Cast on a number of stitches divisible by 10 + 7.
1st row K6, *yfwd, sl 5 P-wise, ybk, K5, rep from * to last st, K1.
2nd row P to end.
3rd-8th rows Rep 1st and 2nd rows 3 times more.
9th row K8, *insert the needle under the 4 long

threads, yrn and draw up a loop, keeping this loop on the right hand needle, K the next st, then sl the loop over this st — called butterfly 1 —, K9, rep from * to last 9 sts, butterfly 1, K8.
10th row As 2nd.
11th row K1, yfwd, sl 5 p-wise, ybk, *K5, yfwd, sl 5 P-wise, ybk, rep from * to last st, K1.

12th row As 2nd.
13th-18th rows Rep 11th and 12th rows 3 times more.
19th row K3, butterfly 1, *K9, butterfly 1, rep from * to last 3 sts, K3.
20th row As 2nd.
These 20 rows form the pattern.

More large patterns

Plaited cable

Cast on 13 sts.
1st row P2, K9, P2.
2nd row K2, P9, K2.
3rd row P2, sl next 3 sts on to cable needle and

leave at back of work, K3, then K3 from cable needle — called C6B —, K3, P2.
4th row As 2nd.
5th row As 1st.
6th row As 2nd.

7th row P2, K3, sl next 3 sts on to cable needle and leave at front of work, K3, then K3 from cable needle, — called C6F —, P2.
8th row As 2nd.
These 8 rows form the pattern.

Ribbed cable

Cast on 11 sts.
1st row P2, K into back of next st, — called KB1 —, *P1, KB1, rep from * twice more, P2.
2nd row K2, P into back of next st, — called

PB1 —, *K1, PB1, rep from * twice more, K2.
3rd-6th rows Rep the 1st and 2nd rows twice more.
7th row P2, sl the next 3 sts on to cable needle and leave at front of work, (KB1, P1) twice, then

KB1, P1, KB1 from cable needle, P2.
8th row As 2nd.
9th-12th rows Rep the 1st and 2nd rows twice more.
These 12 rows form the pattern.

Oxox cable

Cast on 12 sts.
1st row P2, K8, P2.
2nd row K2, P8, K2.
3rd row P2, sl next 2 sts on to cable needle and leave at back of work, K2, then K2 from cable

needle, — called C4B —, sl next 2 sts on to cable needle and leave at front of work, K2, then K2 from cable needle, —called C4F—, P2.
4th row As 2nd.
5th-8th rows As 1st-4th rows.
9th row As 1st.

10th row As 2nd.
11th row P2, C4F, C4B, P2.
12th row As 2nd.
13th-16th rows As 9th-12th rows.
These 16 rows form the pattern.

Aran diamond

Cast on 17 sts.
1st row P7, K1, P1, K1, P7.
2nd row K7, P1, K1, P1, K7.
3rd row P6, sl next st to cable needle and leave at back of work, K1, then P1 from cable needle, — called C2B —, K1, sl next st to cable needle and leave at front of work, P1, then K1 from cable needle, — called C2F —, P6.
4th row K6, (P1, K1) twice, P1, K6.
5th row P5, C2B, K1, P1, K1, C2F, P5.
6th row K5, (P1, K1) 3 times, P1, K5.

7th row P4, C2B, (K1, P1) twice, K1, C2F, P4.
8th row K4, (P1, K1) 4 times, P1, K4.
9th row P3, C2B, (K1, P1) 3 times, K1, C2F, P3.
10th row K3, (P1, K1) 5 times, P1, K3.
11th row P2, C2B; (K1, P1) 4 times, K1, C2F, P2.
12th row K2, (P1, K1) 6 times, P1, K2.
13th row P2, C2F, (P1, K1) 4 times, C2B, P2.
14th row As 10th.
15th row P3, C2F, (P1, K1) 3 times, P1, C2B, P3.
16th row As 8th.
17th row P4, C2F, (P1, K1) twice, P1, C2B, P4.
18th row As 6th.

19th row P5, C2F, P1, K1, P1, C2B, P5.
20th row As 4th.
21st row P6, C2F, P1, C2B, P6.
22nd row As 2nd.
23rd row P7, sl next 2 sts to cable needle and leave at front of work, K1, then K1, P1 from cable needle, P7.
24th row K8, P2, K7.
25th row P7, K1, C2F, P7.
26th row As 2nd.
The 3rd to 26th rows form the pattern.

Aran pattern with bobbles

Cast on 29 sts.
1st row K5, P7, K2 make bobble as follows (P1, K1, P1, K1, P1) all into the next st, turn, K5, turn, P5, sl 2nd, 3rd, 4th and 5th sts over the first st — called MB —, K2, P7, K5.
2nd row P5, K7, P2, P into the back of next st, —called PB1—, P2, K7, P5.
3rd row K5, P6, sl next st on to cable needle and leave at back of work, K2, then P1 from cable needle, —(called C3B)—, K into back of next st

— called KB1 —, sl next 2 sts on to cable needle and leave at front of work, P1, then K2 from cable needle, — called C3F —, P6, K5.
4th row P5, K6, P2, K1, PB1, K1, P2, K6, P5.
5th row K5, P5, C3B, P1, KB1, P1, C3F, P5, K5.
6th row P5, K5, P2, (PB1, K1) twice, PB1, P2, K5, P5.
7th row K2, MB, K2, P4, C3B, (KB1, P1) twice, KB1, C3F, P4, K2, MB, K2.
8th row P5, K4, P2, (K1, PB1) 3 times, K1, P2,

K4, P5.
9th row K1, (MB, K1) twice, P3, C3B, (P1, KB1) 3 times, P1, C3F, P3, (K1, MB) twice, K1.
10th row P5, K3, P2, (PB1, K1) 4 times, PB1, P2, K3, P5.
11th row K5, P2, C3B, (KB1, P1) 4 times, KB1, C3F, P2, K5.
12th row P5, K2, P2, (K1, PB1) 5 times, K1, P2, K2, P5.
These 12 rows form the pattern.

Lattice diamond

Cast on 18 sts.
1st row P6, K into back of next st, — called KB1 —, P1, K into back of next 2 sts, P1, KB1, P6.
2nd row K6, P into back of next st, — called PB1 —, K1, P into back of next 2 sts, K1, PB1, K6.
3rd row P5, sl next st on to cable needle and leave at back of work, KB1, then KB1 from cable needle, — called C2B—, C2B, sl next st on to cable needle and leave at front of work, P1, then KB1 from cable needle, — called C2F —, C2F, P5.
4th row K5, PB1, K1, PB1, K2, PB1, K1, PB1, K5.
5th row P4, (C2B) twice, P2, (C2F) twice, P4.
6th row K4, PB1, K1, PB1, K4, PB1, K1, PB1, K4.

7th row P3, C2B, sl next st on to cable needle and leave at back of work, KB1, then K1 from cable needle, P4, sl next st on to cable needle and leave at front of work, K1, then KB1 from cable needle, C2F, P3.
8th row K3, PB1, K1, (PB1) twice, K4, (PB1) twice, K1, PB1, K3.
9th row P2, (C2B) twice, C2F, P2, C2B, (C2F) twice, P2.
10th row K2, PB1, K1, (PB1, K2) 3 times, PB1, K1, PB1, K2.
11th row P1, (C2B) twice, P2, C2F, C2B, P2, (C2F) twice, P1.
12th row (K1, PB1) twice, K4, sl next st on to cable needle and leave at front of work, PB1, then PB1 from cable needle, K4, (PB1, K1) twice.

13th row P1, (C2F) twice, P2, C2B, C2F, P2, (C2B) twice, P1.
14th row As 10th.
15th row P2, (C2F) twice, C2B, P2, C2F, (C2B) twice, P2.
16th row As 8th.
17th row P3, (C2F) twice, P4, (C2B) twice, P3.
18th row As 6th.
19th row P4, (C2F) twice, P2, (C2B) twice, P4.
20th row As 4th.
21st row P5, (C2F) twice, (C2B) twice, P5.
22nd row K6, PB1, K1, sl next st on to cable needle and leave at front of work, PB1, then PB1 from cable needle, K1, PB1, K6.
The 3rd-22nd rows form the pattern.

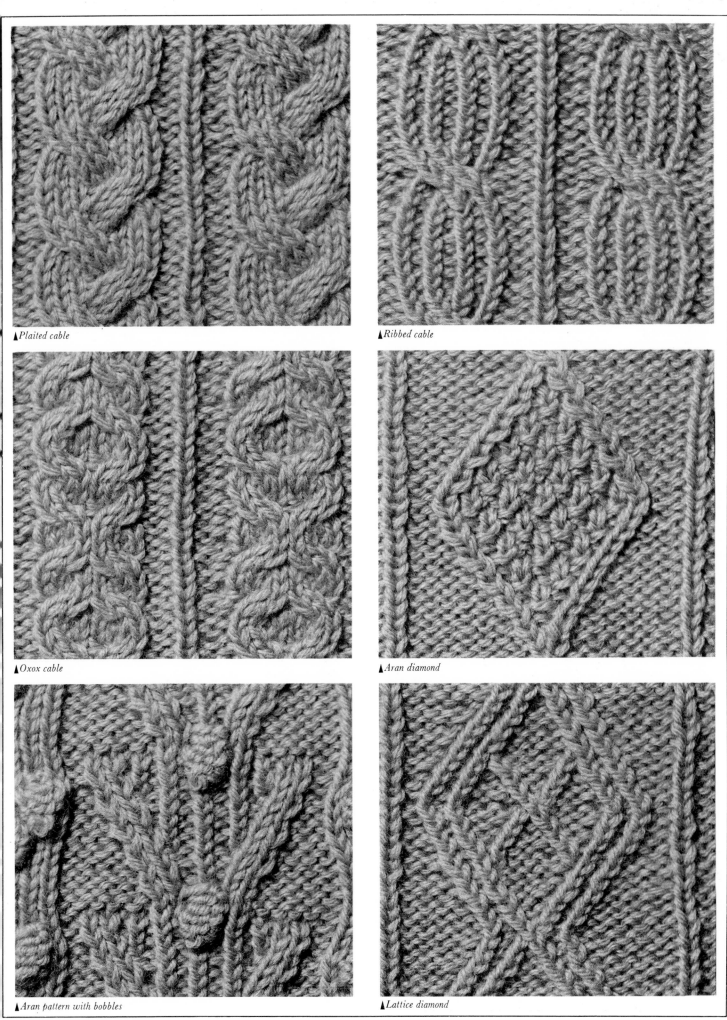

▲ Plaited cable

▲ Ribbed cable

▲ Oxox cable

▲ Aran diamond

▲ Aran pattern with bobbles

▲ Lattice diamond

41

▲Long sleeved crew neck version

▲Sleeveless V-neck version

▲Long-sleeved V-neck version

▲Short sleeved crew neck version

His/her jersey can be made in any stitch shown on pages 36 & 37 ►

basic jersey design

Sizes
To fit 34[36:38]in bust/chest
Length to shoulder, 22[22½:23]in, adjustable
Long sleeve seam, 17[17½:18]in, adjustable
Short sleeve seam, 4in
The figures in brackets [] refer to the 36 and
38in sizes respectively

Tension
6 sts and 8 rows to 1in over st st worked on No.9
needles

Materials
Long sleeved version 19[20:22] x 25gr balls
of Lee Target Motoravia Double Knitting
Short sleeved version 16[17:18] x 25gr balls
Sleeveless version 13[14:15] x 25gr balls
One pair No.9 needles; One pair No.11 needles
Set of 4 No.11 needles pointed at both ends

Back
Using No.11 needles cast on 109[115:121] sts.
1st row K1, *P1, K1, rep from * to end.
2nd row P1, *K1, P1, rep from * to end.
Rep these 2 rows for 1½in, ending with a 2nd
row and inc one st in centre of last row. 110[116:
122] sts. Change to No.9 needles. Beg with a K
row cont in st st, or any of the stitches given on
pages 36 and 37, until work measures 14½in from
beg, ending with a WS row.

Shape armholes
Keeping sequence of patt used correct, cast off
at beg of next and every row 4 sts twice and
2 sts twice. Dec one st at each end of next and
foll 5[6:7] alt rows. 86[90:94] sts. Cont without
shaping until armholes measure 7½[8:8½]in from
beg, ending with a WS row.

Shape neck and shoulders
Next row Cast off 6[7:7] sts, patt 25[25:26] sts,
turn and leave rem sts on holder.
Next row Cast off 2 sts, patt to end.
Next row Cast off 6 [7:7] sts, patt to end.
Rep last 2 rows once more, then first of them
again. Cast off rem 7[5:6] sts.
With RS of work facing, sl first 24[26:28] sts
on to holder for centre back neck, rejoin yarn to
rem sts and patt to end. Complete to match
first side, reversing shaping.

Front (crew neck)
Work as given for back until armhole shaping is
completed. Cont without shaping until armholes
measure 5½[6:6½]in from beg, ending with a WS row.

Shape neck
Next row Patt 35[36:37]sts, turn and leave rem
sts on holder.
Complete this side first. Cast off 2 sts at beg
of next and foll 2 alt rows, then dec one st at
neck edge on foll 4 alt rows. Cont without
shaping until armhole measures same as back
to shoulder, ending at armhole edge.

Shape shoulder
Cast off at beg of next and every alt row 6[7:7]
sts 3 times and 7[5:6] sts once.
With RS of work facing, sl first 16[18:20] sts
on to holder and leave for centre neck, rejoin
yarn to rem sts and patt to end. Complete to
match first side, reversing shaping.

Front (v-neck)
Work as given for back until front measures 12
rows less than back to underarm.

Divide for neck
Next row Patt 55[58:61] sts, turn and leave rem
sts on holder.
Next row Patt to end.
Next row Patt to last 3 sts, K2 tog, K1.
Next row P2 sts, patt to end.
Keeping 2 sts at neck edge in st st, cont to dec
one st at neck edge on every 4th row twice more,
then work 1 row ending with a WS row.

Shape armhole

Next row Cast off 4 sts, patt to last 2 sts, K2.

Next row P2 sts, patt to end.

Next row Cast off 2 sts, patt to last 3 sts, K2 tog, K1.

Dec one st at armhole edge on foll 6[7:8] alt rows, *at the same time* cont to dec one st at neck edge on every 4th row until 25[26:27] sts rem. Cont without shaping until armhole measures same as back to shoulder, ending at armhole edge.

Shape shoulder

Cast off at beg of next and every alt row 6[7:7] sts 3 times and 7[5:6] sts once.

With RS of work facing, rejoin yarn to rem sts and patt to end.

Next row Patt to end.

Next row K1, sl 1, K1, psso, patt to end.

Next row Patt to last 2 sts, P2.

Complete to match first side, reversing shaping.

Long sleeves

Using No.11 needles cast on 49[49:55] sts. Work 1½in K1, P1 rib as given for back, ending with a 2nd row and inc one st in centre of last row. 50[50:56] sts. Change to No.9 needles. Beg with a K row cont in st st, or patt as given for back, inc one st at each end of 7th[3rd:7th] and every foll 8th row until there are 78[82:86] sts. Cont without shaping until sleeve measures 17[17½:18]in from beg, or required length to underarm, ending with a WS row.

Shape top

Cast off 4 sts at beg of next 2 rows. Dec one st at each end of next and foll 11[12:13] alt rows ending with a WS row. Cast off at beg of next and every row 2 sts 8[8:10] times, 3 sts 4 times, 4 sts twice and 10[12:10] sts once.

Short sleeves

Using No.11 needles cast on 73[73:79] sts. Work 1in K1, P1 rib as given for back, ending with a 2nd row and inc one st in centre of last row. 74[74:80] sts. Change to No.9 needles. Beg with a K row cont in st st, or patt as given for back, inc one st at each end of 7th[3rd:7th] and every foll 8th[6th:6th] row until there are 78[82:86] sts. Cont without shaping until sleeve measures 4in from beg, ending with a WS row.

Shape top

Work as given for long sleeves.

Crew neckband

Join shoulder seams. Using set of 4 No.11 needles and with RS of work facing, K up 8 sts down right back neck, K across back neck sts inc one st in centre, K up 8 sts up left back neck, **, K up 24 sts down left front neck, K across front neck sts onc one st in centre and K up 24 sts up right front neck. 106[110:114] sts. Cont in rounds of K1, P1 rib for 2½in. Cast off loosely in rib. Fold neckband in half to WS and sl st down.

V-neckband

Work as given for crew neckband to **, K up 63 [66:69] sts down left front neck, pick up loops lying between sts at centre front and K tbl, marking this st with coloured thread, then K up 63 [66:69] sts up right front neck. 168[176:184] sts. Work in rounds of K1, P1 rib, as foll:

Next round Rib to 2 sts before centre front st, sl 1, K1, psso, P1, K2 tog, rib to end.

Rep last round for 1in. Cast off in rib, still dec at centre front.

Armbands for sleeveless version

Using No.11 needles and with RS of work facing, K up 107[113:119] sts round armholes. Beg with a 2nd row work 1in K1, P1 rib as given for back. Cast off in rib.

To make up

Press each piece under a damp cloth with a warm iron. Set in sleeves. Join side and sleeve seams. Press seams.

Basic lace stitches

Laburnum stitch

Cast on a number of stitches divisible by 5 + 2.
1st row P2, *K3, P2, rep from * to end.
2nd row K2, *P3, K2, rep from * to end.
3rd row P2, *keeping yarn at front of work, sl 1, ybk, K2 tog, psso, bring yarn over top of needle from back to front, then round needle again, P2, rep from * to end.
4th row K2, *P into the back of the first made st, then into the front of the second made st, P1, K2, rep from * to end.
These 4 rows form the pattern.

Indian pillar stitch

Cast on a number of stitches divisible by 4 + 3.
1st row (RS) P to end.
2nd row K2, *insert needle purlwise into the next 3 sts as if to P3 tog, but work (P1, K1, P1) into these 3 sts, K1, rep from * to last st, K1.
These 2 rows form the pattern.

Faggotting rib

Cast on a number of stitches divisible by 5 + 1.
1st row P1, *K2, yfwd, sl 1, K1, psso, P1, rep from * to end.
2nd row K1, *P2, yrn, P2 tog, K1, rep from * to end.
These 2 rows form the pattern.

Lace rib

Cast on a number of stitches divisible by 5 + 2.
1st row P2, *K1, yfwd, sl 1, K1, psso, P2, rep from * to end.
2nd row K2, *P3, K2, rep from * to end.
3rd row P2, *K2 tog, yfwd, K1, P2, rep from * to end.
4th row As 2nd.
These 4 rows form the pattern.

Eyelet cable rib

Cast on a number of stitches divisible by 5 + 2.
1st row P2, *K3, P2, rep from * to end.
2nd row K2, *P3, K2, rep from * to end.
3rd row P2, *sl 1, K2, psso the 2 sts, P2, rep from * to end.
4th row K2, *P1, yrn, P1, K2, rep from * to end. These 4 rows form the pattern.

Cat's eye pattern

Cast on a number of stitches divisible by 4.
1st row K4, *yfwd, yrn, K4, rep from * to end.
2nd row P2, *P2 tog, P the first made st, K the second made st, P2 tog, rep from * to last 2 sts, P2.
3rd row K2, yfwd, *K4, yfwd, yrn, rep from * to last 6 sts, K4, yfwd, K2.
4th row P3, *(P2 tog) twice, P the first made st, K the second made st, rep from * to last 7 sts, (P2 tog) twice, P3.
These 4 rows form the pattern.

Open star stitch

Cast on a number of stitches divisible by 3.
1st row K2, *yfwd, K3, pass the first of these 3 sts over the other two, rep from * to last st, K1.
2nd row P to end.
3rd row K1, *K3, pass the first of these 3 sts over the other two, yfwd, rep from * to last 2 sts, K2.
4th row As 2nd.
These 4 rows form the pattern.

Hyacinth stitch

Cast on a number of stitches divisible by 6 + 3.
1st row P to end.
2nd row K1, *(K1, P1, K1, P1, K1) into the next st, K5 tog, rep from * to last 2 sts, (K1, P1, K1, P1, K1) into the next st, K1.
3rd row As 1st.
4th row K1, *K5 tog, (K1, P1, K1, P1, K1) into the next st, rep from * to last 6 sts, K5 tog, K1.
5th row As 1st.
6th row K to end, winding yarn 3 times round needle for each st.
7th row P to end, dropping the extra loops.
The 2nd to 7th rows form the pattern.

Diagonal openwork stitch

Cast on a number of stitches divisible by 2 + 1.
1st row K1, *yfwd, K2 tog, rep from * to end.
2nd row P to end.
3rd row K2, *yfwd, K2 tog, rep from * to last st, K1.
4th row As 2nd.
These 4 rows form the pattern.

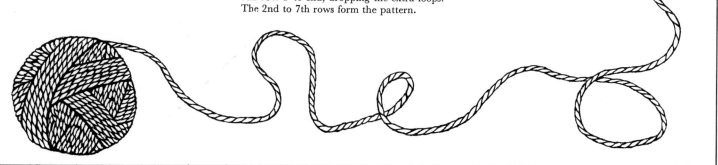

▲Laburnum stitch

▲Indian pillar stitch

▲Faggoting rib

▲Lace rib

▲Eyelet cable rib

▲Cat's eye pattern

▲Open star stitch

▲Hyacinth stitch

▲Diagonal openwork stitch

Simple lace stitches

Spider lace stitch
Cast on a number of stitches divisible by 6 + 1.
1st row K1, *K2 tog, yfwd, K1, yfwd, sl 1, K1, psso, K1, rep from * to end.
2nd and every alt row P to end.
3rd row K2 tog, *yfwd, K3, yfwd, sl 1, K2 tog, psso, rep from * to last 5 sts, yfwd, K3, yfwd, sl 1, K1, psso.
5th row K1, *yfwd, sl 1, K1, psso, K1, K2 tog, yfwd, K1, rep from * to end.
7th row As 5th.
9th row As 5th.
11th row K2, *yfwd, sl 1, K2 tog, psso, yfwd, K3, rep from * to last 5 sts, yfwd, sl 1, K2 tog, psso, yfwd, K2.
12th As 2nd.
These 12 rows form the pattern.

Alternating feather stitch
Cast on a number of stitches divisible by 6 + 1.
1st row K1, *K2 tog, yfwd, K1, yfwd, sl 1, K1, psso, K1, rep from * to end.
2nd row P to end.
Repeat these 2 rows 5 times more.
13th row K1, *yfwd, sl 1, K1, psso, K1, K2 tog, yfwd, K1, rep from * to end.
14th row P to end.
Repeat these 2 rows 5 times more.
These 24 rows form the pattern.

Lace arrow pattern
Cast on a number of stitches divisible by 6 + 1.
1st row K3, *yfwd, sl 1, K1, psso, K4, rep from * to last 4 sts, yfwd, sl 1, K1, psso, K2.
2nd and every alt row P to end.
3rd row K1, *K2 tog, yfwd, K1, yfwd, sl 1, K1, psso, K1, rep from * to end.
5th row K2 tog, *yfwd, K3, yfwd, sl 1, K2 tog, psso, yfwd, rep from * to last 5 sts, K3, yfwd, sl 1, K1, psso.
7th row K1, *yfwd, sl 1, K1, psso, K1, K2 tog, yfwd, K1, rep from * to end.
9th row As 7th.
10th row P to end.
These 10 rows form the pattern.

Mesh lace pattern
Cast on a number of stitches divisible by 6 + 1.
1st row K1, *yfwd, sl 1, K1, psso, K1, K2 tog, yfwd, K1, rep from * to end.
2nd and every alt row P to end.
3rd row K1, *yfwd, K1, sl 1, K2 tog, psso, K1, yfwd, K1, rep from * to end.
5th row K1, *K2 tog, yfwd, K1, yfwd, sl 1, K1, psso, K1, rep from * to end.
7th row K2 tog, *(K1, yfwd) twice, K1, sl 1, K2 tog, psso, rep from * to last 5 sts, (K1, yfwd) twice, K1, sl 1, K1, psso.
8th row As 2nd.
These 8 rows form the pattern.

Tortoise stitch
Cast on a number of stitches divisible by 6 + 1.
1st row K1, *yfwd, sl 1, K1, psso, K1, K2 tog, yfwd, K1, rep from * to end.
2nd and every alt row P to end.
3rd row K2, *yfwd, K3, rep from * to last 2 sts, yfwd, K2.
5th row K2 tog, *yfwd, sl 1, K1, psso, K1, K2 tog, yfwd, sl 1, K2 tog, psso, rep from * to last 7 sts, yfwd, sl 1, K1, psso, K1, K2 tog, yfwd, sl 1, K1, psso.
7th row K1, *K2 tog, yfwd, K1, yfwd, sl 1, K1, psso, K1, rep from * to end.
9th row As 3rd.
11th row K1, *K2 tog, yfwd, sl 1, K2 tog, psso, yfwd, sl 1, K1, psso, K1, rep from * to end.
12th row As 2nd.
These 12 rows form the pattern.

Miniature leaf pattern
Cast on a number of stitches divisible by 6 + 1.
1st row K1, *K2 tog, yfwd, K1, yfwd, sl 1, K1, psso, K1, rep from * to end.
2nd and every alt row P to end.
3rd row K2 tog, *yfwd, K3, yfwd, sl 2 tog knitwise, K1, pass the 2 sl sts over — called p2sso —, rep from * to last 5 sts, yfwd, K3, yfwd, sl 1, K1, psso.
5th row K1, *yfwd, sl 1, K1, psso, K1, K2 tog, yfwd, K1, rep from * to end.
7th row K2, *yfwd, sl 2 tog knitwise, K1, p2sso, yfwd, K3, rep from * to last 5 sts, yfwd, sl 2 tog knitwise, K1, p2sso, yfwd, K2.
8th row As 2nd.
These 8 rows form the pattern.

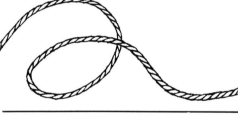

Arrowhead lace pattern
Cast on a number of stitches divisible by 6 + 1.
1st row K1, *yfwd, sl 1, K1, psso, K1, K2 tog, yfwd, K1, rep from * to end.
2nd row P to end.
3rd row K2, *yfwd, sl 2 tog knitwise, K1, pass the 2 sl sts over, yfwd, K3, rep from * to last 5 sts, yfwd, sl 2 tog knitwise, K2, p2sso, yfwd, K1.
4th row As 2nd.
These 4 rows form the pattern.

Chevron lace pattern
Cast on a number of stitches divisible by 6 + 1.
1st row K3, *yfwd, K2, K2 tog, K2, rep from * to last 4 sts, yfwd, K2, K2 tog.
2nd row P to end.
3rd row *K2 tog, K2, yfwd, K2, rep from * to last st, K1.
4th row As 2nd.
These 4 rows form the pattern.

Trefoil rib pattern
Cast on a number of stitches divisible by 6 + 1.
1st row P1, *K5, P1, rep from * to end.
2nd row K1, *P5, K1, rep from * to end.
3rd row P1, *K1, yfwd, sl 1, K2 tog, psso, yfwd, K1, P1, rep from * to end.
4th row As 2nd.
5th row P1, *K2, yfwd, sl 1, K1, psso, K1, P1, rep from * to end.
6th row As 2nd.
These 6 rows form the pattern.

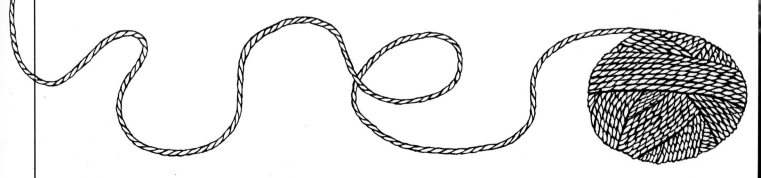

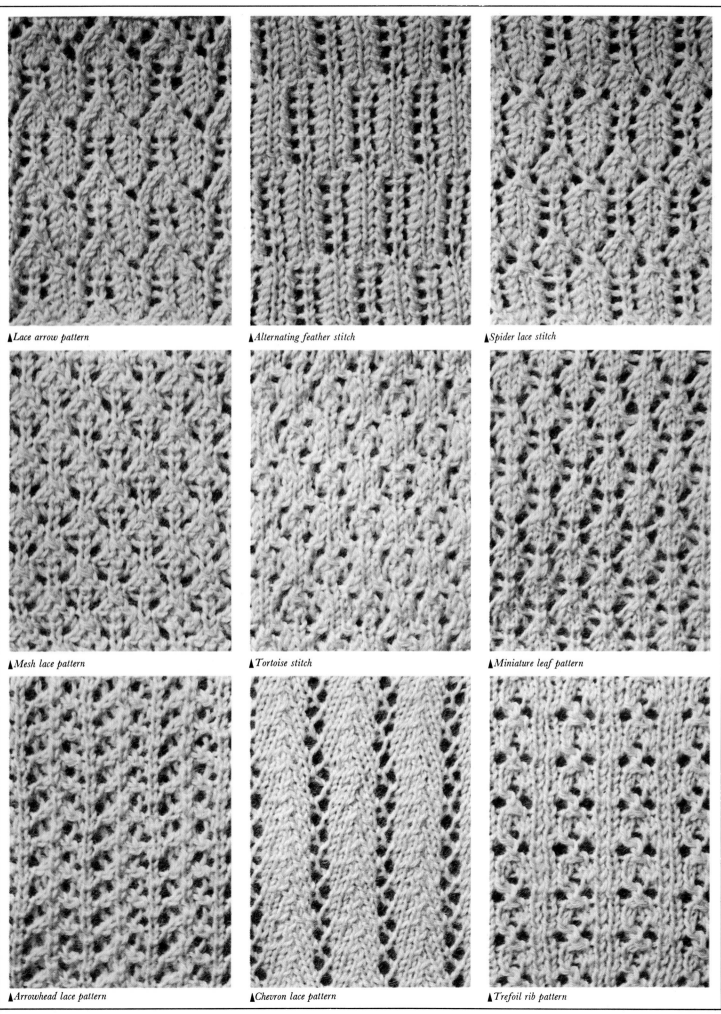

▲*Lace arrow pattern*

▲*Alternating feather stitch*

▲*Spider lace stitch*

▲*Mesh lace pattern*

▲*Tortoise stitch*

▲*Miniature leaf pattern*

▲*Arrowhead lace pattern*

▲*Chevron lace pattern*

▲*Trefoil rib pattern*

more simple lace stitches

Old shale variation
Cast on a number of stitches divisible by 11 + 2.
1st row K to end.

2nd row P to end.
3rd row K1, *(P2 tog) twice, yon, K1, (yfwd, K1) twice, yrn, (P2 tog) twice, rep from * to

last st, K1.
4th row P to end.
These 4 rows form the pattern.

Lace diamond pattern
Cast on a number of stitches divisible by 6 + 1.
1st row P1, *K5, P1, rep from * to end.
2nd row K1, *P5, K1, rep from * to end.
3rd row P1, *yon, sl 1, K1, psso, K1, K2 tog, yrn, P1, rep from * to end.
4th row K1, *K into back of next st — called

K1B —, P3, K1B, K1, rep from * to end.
5th row P2, *yon, sl 1, K2, psso the 2 sts, yrn, P3, rep from * to last 5 sts, yon, sl 1, K2, psso the 2 sts, yrn, P2.
6th row K2, *K1B, P2, K1B, K3, rep from * to last 6 sts, K1B, P2, K1B, K2.

7th row P2, *K2 tog, yfwd, sl 1, K1, psso, P3, rep from * to last 6 sts, K2 tog, yfwd, sl 1, K1, psso, P2.
8th row K1, *P2 tog tbl, yrn, P1, yrn, P2 tog, K1, rep from * to end.
These 8 rows form the pattern.

Embossed leaf pattern
Cast on a number of stitches divisible by 7.
1st row P to end.
2nd row K to end.
3rd row P3, *yon, K1, yrn, P6, rep from * to last 4 sts, yon, K1, yrn, P3.
4th row K3, *P3, K6, rep from * to last 6 sts, P3, K3.
5th row P3, *K1, (yfwd, K1) twice, P6, rep from * to last 6 sts, K1, (yfwd, K1) twice, P3.
6th row K3, *P5, K6, rep from * to last 8 sts, P5, K3.
7th row P3, *K2, yfwd, K1, yfwd, K2, P6, rep

from * to last 8 sts, K2, yfwd, K1, yfwd, K2, P3.
8th row K3, *P7, K6, rep from * to last 10 sts, P7, K3.
9th row P3, *K3, yfwd, K1, yfwd, K3, P6, rep from * to last 10 sts, K3, yfwd, K1, yfwd, K3, P3.
10th row K3, *P9, K6, rep from * to last 12 sts, P9, K3.
11th row P3, *sl 1, K1, psso, K5, K2 tog, P6, rep from * to last 12 sts, sl 1, K1, psso, K5, K2 tog, P3.
12th row As 8th.
13th row P3, *sl 1, K1, psso, K3, K2 tog, P6, rep from * to last 10 sts, sl 1, K1, psso, K3, K2

tog, P3.
14th row As 6th.
15th row P3, *sl 1, K1, psso, K1, K2 tog, P6, rep from * to last 8 sts, sl 1, K1, psso, K1, K2 tog, P3.
16th row As 4th.
17th row P3, *sl 1, K2 tog, psso, P6, rep from * to last 6 sts, sl 1, K2 tog, psso, P3.
18th row As 2nd.
19th row As 1st.
20th row As 2nd.
These 20 rows form the pattern.

Snowdrop lace pattern
Cast on a number of stitches divisible by 8 + 3.
1st row K1, K2 tog, yfwd, *K5, yfwd, sl 1, K2 tog, psso, yfwd, rep from * to last 8 sts, K5, yfwd, sl 1, K1, psso, K1.

2nd and every alt row P to end.
3rd row As 1st.
5th row K3, *yfwd, sl 1, K1, psso, K1, K2 tog, yfwd, K3, rep from * to end.
7th row K1, K2 tog, yfwd, *K1, yfwd, sl 1,

K2 tog, psso, yfwd, rep from * to last 4 sts, K1, yfwd, sl 1, K1, psso, K1.
8th row As 2nd.
These 8 rows form the pattern.

Falling leaf pattern
Cast on a number of stitches divisible by 10 + 1.
1st row K1, *yfwd, K3, sl 1, K2 tog, psso, K3, yfwd, K1, rep from * to end.
2nd and every alt row P to end.
3rd row K1, *K1, yfwd, K2, sl 1, K2 tog, psso, K2, yfwd, K2, rep from * to end.
5th row K1, *K2, yfwd, K1, sl 1, K2 tog, psso, K1, yfwd, K3, rep from * to end.

7th row K1, *K3, yfwd, sl 1, K2 tog, psso, yfwd, K4, rep from * to end.
9th row K2 tog, *K3, yfwd, K1, yfwd, K3, sl 1, K2 tog, psso, rep from * to last 9 sts, K3, yfwd, K1, yfwd, K3, sl 1, K1, psso.
11th row K2 tog, *K2, yfwd, K3, yfwd, K2, sl 1, K2 tog, psso, rep from * to last 9 sts, K2, yfwd, K3, yfwd, K2, sl 1, K1, psso.
13th row K2 tog, *K1, yfwd, K5, yfwd, K1,

sl 1, K2 tog, psso, rep from * to last 9 sts, K1, yfwd, K5, yfwd, K1, sl 1, K1, psso.
15th row K2 tog, *yfwd, K7, yfwd, sl 1, K2 tog, psso, rep from * to last 9 sts, yfwd, K7, yfwd, sl 1, K1, psso.
16th row As 2nd.
These 16 rows form the pattern.

Cat's paw pattern
Cast on a number of stitches divisible by 12 + 1.
1st row K5, *yfwd, sl 1, K2 tog, psso, yfwd, K9, rep from * to last 8 sts, yfwd, sl 1, K2 tog, psso, yfwd, K5.
2nd and every alt row P to end.
3rd row K3, *K2 tog, yfwd, K3, yfwd, sl 1, K1,

psso, K5, rep from * to last 10 sts, K2 tog, yfwd, K3, yfwd, sl 1, K1, psso, K3.
5th row As 1st.
7th row As 1st.
9th row K2 tog, *yfwd, K9, yfwd, sl 1, K2 tog, psso, rep from * to last 11 sts, yfwd, K9, yfwd, sl 1, K1, psso.

11th row K2, *yfwd, sl 1, K1, psso, K5, K2 tog, yfwd, K3, rep from * to last 11 sts, yfwd, sl 1, K1, psso, K5, K2 tog, yfwd, K2.
13th row As 9th.
15th row As 7th.
16th row As 2nd.
These 16 rows form the pattern.

Zig Zag lace pattern
Cast on a number of stitches divisible by 4 + 1.
1st row *K2, K2 tog, yfwd, rep from * to last st, K1.
2nd row K1, P2, *yrn, P2 tog, P2, rep from * to last 3 sts, yrn, P2 tog, P1.

3rd row *K2 tog, yfwd, K2, rep from * to last st, K1.
4th row P to end.
5th row K1, *yfwd, sl 1, K1, psso, K2, rep from * to end.
6th row P1, *P2 tog tbl, yrn, P2, rep from * to

end.
7th row K3, *yfwd, sl 1, K1, psso, K2, rep from * to last 2 sts, yfwd, sl 1, K1, psso.
8th row As 4th.
These 8 rows form the pattern.

Spiders web pattern
Cast on a number of stitches divisible by 6 + 3.
1st row K2, K2 tog, *yfwd, K1, yfwd, K2 tog, yfwd, sl 1, K2 tog, psso, rep from * to last 5 sts, yfwd, K1, yfwd, K2 tog, K2.

2nd and every alt row P to end.
3rd row K1, K2 tog, *yfwd, K3, yfwd, K3 tog, rep from * to last 6 sts, yfwd, K3, yfwd, K2 tog, K1.
5th row K2, *yfwd, K2 tog, yfwd, sl 1, K2 tog,

psso, yfwd, K1, rep from * to last st, K1.
7th row K3, *yfwd, K3 tog, yfwd, K3, rep from * to end.
8th row As 2nd.
These 8 rows form the pattern.

Gothic stitch
Cast on a number of stitches divisible by 10 + 1.
1st row K1, *yfwd, sl 1, K1, psso, K5, K2 tog, yfwd, K1, rep from * to end.
2nd and every alt row P to end.
3rd row K2, *yfwd, sl 1, K1, psso, K3, K2 tog, yfwd, K3, rep from * to last 9 sts, yfwd, sl 1, K1, psso, K3, K2 tog, yfwd, K2.
5th row K3, *yfwd, sl 1, K1, psso, K1, K2 tog, yfwd, K5, rep from * to last 8 sts, yfwd, sl 1,

K1, psso, K1, K2 tog, yfwd, K3.
7th row K4, *yfwd, sl 1, K2 tog, psso, yfwd, K7, rep from * to last 7 sts, yfwd, sl 1, K2 tog, psso, yfwd, K4.
9th row K1, *yfwd, sl 1, K1, K2 tog, yfwd, K1, rep from * to end.
10th row As 2nd.
11th-18th rows Rep the 9th and 10th rows 4 times.
19th row K2, *yfwd, sl 1, K1, psso, K3, K2

tog, yfwd, K3, rep from * to last 9 sts, yfwd, sl 1, K1, psso, K3, K2 tog, yfwd, K2.
21st row K3, *yfwd, sl 1, K1, psso, K1, K2 tog, yfwd, K5, rep from * to last 8 sts, yfwd, sl 1, K1, psso, K1, K2 tog, yfwd, K3.
23rd row K4, *yfwd, sl 1, K2 tog, psso, yfwd, K7, rep from * to last 7 sts, yfwd, sl 1, K2 tog, psso, yfwd, K4.
24th row As 2nd.
These 24 rows form the pattern.

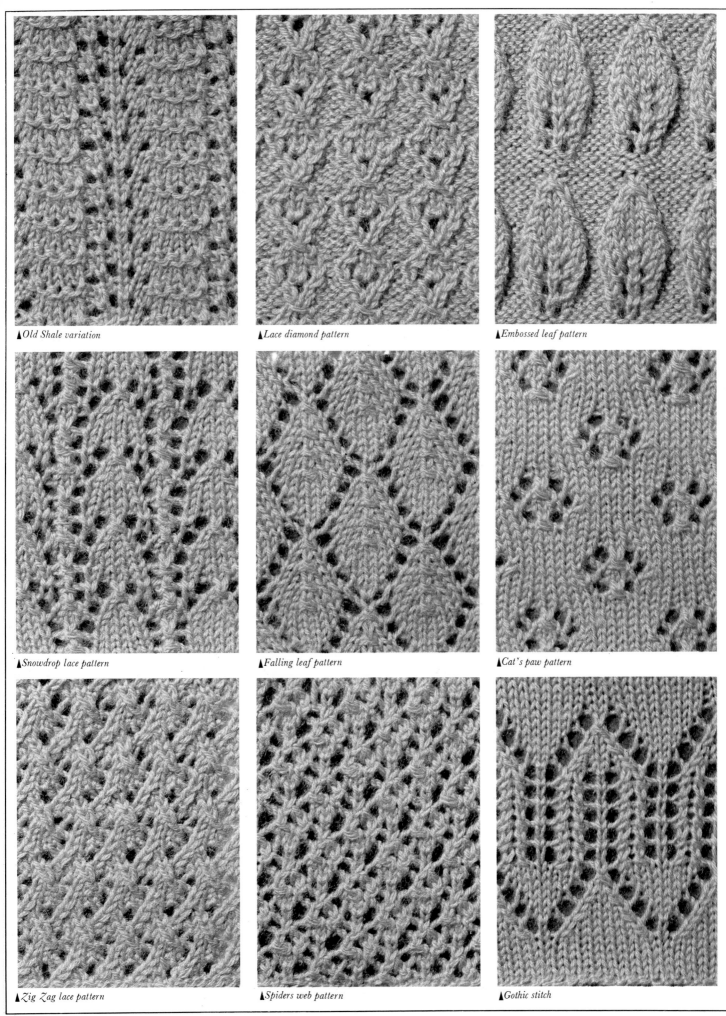

▲Old Shale variation

▲Lace diamond pattern

▲Embossed leaf pattern

▲Snowdrop lace pattern

▲Falling leaf pattern

▲Cat's paw pattern

▲Zig Zag lace pattern

▲Spiders web pattern

▲Gothic stitch

large lace patterns

Shell and shower pattern
Cast on a number of stitches divisible by 12 + 3
1st row K2, *yfwd, K4, sl 1, K2 tog, psso, K4, yfwd, K1, rep from * to last st, K1.
2nd and every alt row P to end.
3rd row K3, *yfwd, K3, sl 1, K2 tog, psso, K3, yfwd, K3, rep from * to end.

5th row K1, K2 tog, *yfwd, K1, yfwd, K2, sl 1, K2 tog, psso, K2, yfwd, K1, yfwd, sl 1, K2 tog, psso, rep from * to last 12 sts, yfwd, K1, yfwd, K2, sl 1, K2 tog, psso, K2, yfwd, K1, yfwd, sl 1 K1, psso, K1.
7th row K1, *yfwd, sl 1, K1, psso, K2, yfwd, sl 1, K2 tog, psso, K1, yfwd, K2, rep from * to last 2 sts, yfwd, K2 tog.
9th row K2, *yfwd, sl 1, K2 tog, psso, yfwd, K1, rep from * to last st, K1.
10th row As 2nd.
These 10 rows form the pattern.

Ogee lace
Cast on a number of stitches divisible by 24 + 1
1st row *K2, yfwd, K2 tog, K1, K2 tog, K3, yfwd, sl 1, K1, psso, yrn, P1, yon, K2, yfwd, sl 1, K1, psso, K1, sl 1, K1, psso, sl 1, K1, psso, yfwd, K1, rep from * to last st, K1.
2nd row P1, *P7, yrn, P2 tog, P5, yrn, P2 tog, P8, rep from * to end.
3rd row *K1, yfwd, K2 tog, K1, K2 tog, K3, yfwd, sl 1, K1, psso, K1, yfwd, K1, yfwd, K3, yfwd, sl 1, K1, psso, K1, sl 1, K1, psso, K1, sl 1, K1, psso, yfwd, rep from * to last st, K1.
4th row P1, *P6, yrn, P2 tog, P7, yrn, P2 tog, P7, rep from * to end.
5th row *K3, K2 tog, K3, yfwd, sl 1, K1, psso, K1, yfwd, K3, yfwd, K3, yfwd, sl 1, K1, psso, K1, sl 1, K1, psso, K2, rep from * to last st, K1.
6th row P1, *P5, yrn, P2 tog, P9, yrn, P2 tog, P6, rep from * to end.
7th row *K2, K2 tog, K3, yfwd, sl 1, K1, psso, K3, yfwd, K1, yfwd, K5, yfwd, sl 1, K1, psso, K1, sl 1, K1, psso, K1, rep from * to last st, K1.
8th row P1, *P4, yrn, P2 tog, P11, yrn, P2 tog, P5, rep from * to end.
9th row *K1, K2 tog, K3, yfwd, sl 1, K1, psso, K3, yfwd, K3, yfwd, K5, yfwd, sl 1, K1, psso, K1,

sl 1, K1, psso, rep from * to last st, K1.
10th row P1, *P3, yrn, P2 tog, P13, yrn, P2 tog, P4, rep from * to end.
11th row Sl 1, K1, psso, *K3, yfwd, sl 1, K1, psso, K1, sl 1, K1, psso, yfwd, K2, yfwd, K2 tog, K2 tog, K3, yfwd, sl 1, K1, psso, K1, sl 1, K2 tog, psso, rep from * to last 23 sts, K3, yfwd, sl 1, K1, psso, K1, sl 1, K1, psso, yfwd, K2, yfwd, K1, yfwd, K2, yfwd, K2 tog, K3, yfwd, sl 1, K1, psso, K1, sl 1, K1, psso.
12th row P1, *P2, yrn, P2 tog, P15, yrn, P2 tog, P3, rep from * to end.
13th row Sl 1, K1, psso, *K2, yfwd, sl 1, K1, psso, K5, yfwd, K3, yfwd, K7, yfwd, sl 1, K1, psso, sl 1, K2 tog, psso, rep from * to last 23 sts, K2, yfwd, sl 1, K1, psso, K5, yfwd, K3, yfwd, K7, yfwd, sl 1, K1, psso, sl 1, K1, psso.
14th row K1, *P1, yrn, P2 tog, P17, yrn, P2 tog, P1, K1, rep from * to end.
15th row *P1, yon, K2, yfwd, sl 1, K1, psso, K1, sl 1, K1, psso, K1, sl 1, K1, psso, yfwd, K3, yfwd, K2 tog, K1, K2 tog, K3, yfwd, sl 1, K1, psso, yrn, rep from * to last st, P1.
16th row As 12th.
17th row *K1, yfwd, K3, yfwd, sl 1, K1, psso, K1, sl 1, K1, psso, K1, sl 1, K1, psso, yfwd, K1,

yfwd, K2 tog, K1, K2 tog, K3, yfwd, sl 1, K1, psso, K1, yfwd, rep from * to last st, K1.
18th row As 10th.
19th row *K2, yfwd, K3, yfwd, sl 1, K1, psso, K1, sl 1, K1, psso, K5, K2 tog, K3, yfwd, sl 1, K1, psso, K1, yfwd, K1, rep from * to last st, K1.
20th row As 8th.
21st row *K1, yfwd, K5, yfwd, sl 1, K1, psso, K1, sl 1, K1, psso, K3, K2 tog, K3, yfwd, sl 1, K1, psso, K3, yfwd, rep from * to last st, K1.
22nd row As 6th.
23rd row *K2, yfwd, K5, yfwd, sl 1, K1, psso, K1, sl 1, K1, psso, K1, K2 tog, K3, yfwd, sl 1, K1, psso, K3, yfwd, K1, rep from * to last st, K1.
24th row As 4th.
25th row *K1, yfwd, K2, yfwd, K2 tog, K3, yfwd, sl 1, K1, psso, K1, sl 1, K2 tog, psso, K3, yfwd, sl 1, K1, psso, K1, sl 1, K1, psso, yfwd, K2, yfwd, rep from * to last st, K1.
26th row As 2nd.
27th row *K2, yfwd, K7, yfwd, sl 1, K1, psso, sl 1, K2 tog, psso, K2, yfwd, sl 1, K1, psso, K5, yfwd, K1, rep from * to last st, K1.
28th row P1, *P8, yrn, P2 tog, P1, K1, P1, yrn, P2 tog, P9, rep from * to end.
These 28 rows form the pattern.

Trailing leaf pattern
Cast on a number of stitches divisible by 13 + 6.
1st row K1, K2 tog, yfwd, *K5, yfwd, K1, sl 1, K1, psso, K2 tog, K1, yfwd, K2 tog, yfwd, rep from * to last 3 sts, K3.
2nd and every alt row P to end.
3rd row K1, yfwd, *sl 1, K1, psso, yfwd, K1, sl 1, K1, psso, K4, K2 tog, (K1, yfwd) twice, rep from

* to last 5 sts, sl 1, K1, psso, yfwd, K1, sl 1, K1, psso.
5th row K2, *yfwd, sl 1, K1, psso, yfwd, K1, sl 1, K1, psso, K2, K2 tog, K1, yfwd, K3, rep from * to last 4 sts, (yfwd, sl 1, K1, psso) twice.
7th row K3, *yfwd, sl 1, K1, psso, yfwd, K1, sl 1, K1, psso, K2 tog, K1, yfwd, K5, rep from * to last 3 sts, yfwd, sl 1, K1, psso, K1.

9th row *K2 tog, K1, yfwd, K2 tog, (yfwd, K1) twice, sl 1, K1, psso, K4, rep from * to last 6 sts, K2 tog, K1, yfwd, K2 tog, yfwd, K1.
11th row K2 tog, *yfwd, K2 tog, yfwd, K3, yfwd, K1, sl 1, K1, psso, K2, K2 tog, K1, rep from * to last 4 sts, yfwd, K2 tog, yfwd, K2.
12th row As 2nd.
These 12 rows form the pattern.

Spanish lace
Cast on a number of stitches divisible by 34 + 4.
1st row K2, *K3, K2 tog, K4, yrn, P2, (K2, yfwd, sl 1, K1, psso) 3 times, P2, yon, K4, sl 1, K1, psso, K3, rep from * to last 2 sts, K2.
2nd row P4, *P2 tog tbl, P4, yrn, P1, K2, (P2, yrn, P2 tog) 3 times, K2, P1, yrn, P4, P2 tog, P4, rep from * to end.
3rd row K3, *K2 tog, K4, yfwd, K2, P2, (K2, yfwd, sl 1, K1, psso) 3 times, P2, K2, yfwd, K4, sl 1, K1, psso, K2, rep from * to last st, K1.

4th row P2, *P2 tog tbl, P4, yrn, P3, K2, (P2, yrn, P2 tog) 3 times, K2, P3, yrn, P4, P2 tog, rep from * to last 2 sts, P2.
5th-12th rows Rep the 1st-4th rows twice more.
13th row *(K2, yfwd, sl 1, K1, psso) twice, P2, yon, K4, sl 1, K1, psso, K6, K2 tog, K4, yrn, P2, K2, yfwd, sl 1, K1, psso, rep from * to last 4 sts, K2, yfwd, sl 1, K1, psso.
14th row *(P2, yrn, P2 tog) twice, K2, P1, yrn, P4, P2 tog, P4, P2 tog tbl, P4, yrn, P1, K2, P2, yrn, P2 tog, rep from * to last 4 sts, P2, yrn,

P2 tog.
15th row *(K2, yfwd, sl 1, K1, psso) twice, P2, K2, yfwd, K4, sl 1, K1, psso, K2, K2 tog, K4, yfwd, K2, P2, K2, yfwd, sl 1, K1, psso, rep from * to last 4 sts, K2, yfwd, sl 1, K1, psso.
16th row *(P2, yrn, P2 tog) twice, K2, P3, yrn, P4, P2 tog, P2 tog tbl, P4, yrn, P3, K2, P2, yrn, P2 tog, rep from * to last 4 sts, P2, yrn, P2 tog.
17th-24th rows Rep the 13th-16th rows twice more.
These 24 rows form the pattern.

Cockle shell pattern
Cast on a number of stitches divisible by 19 + 2.
1st row K to end.
2nd row K to end.
3rd row K2, *yrn, P2 tog, K13, P2 tog, yon, K2, rep from * to end.
4th row K2, *(K1, P1) into next st, K15, (K1, P1) into next st, K2, rep from * to end.
5th row As 1st.
6th row As 1st.

7th row K2, *(yrn, P2 tog) twice, K11, P2 tog, yrn, P2 tog, yon, K2, rep from * to end.
8th row K2, *(K1, P1) into next st, K1, (K1, P1) into next st, K13, (K1, P1) into next st, K1, (K1, P1) into next st, K2, rep from * to end.
9th row As 1st.
10th row K7, *K14 winding the yarn 3 times round needle for each st, K11, rep from * to last 20 sts, K14 winding the yarn 3 times round needle for each st, K6.

11th row K2, *(yrn, P2 tog) twice, yrn, sl the next 14 sts on to right hand needle, dropping the extra loops, sl these 14 sts back on to left hand needle and P15 tog, (yrn, P2 tog) twice, yon, K2, rep from * to end.
12th row K1, *(K1, (K1, P1) into next st) 6 times, K1, rep from * to last st, K1.
These 12 rows form the pattern.

Diamond lace pattern
Cast on a number of stitches divisible by 26 + 3.
1st row K1, K2 tog, *yfwd, (K2 tog, yfwd) twice, K5, yfwd, sl 1, K1, psso, K1, K2 tog, yfwd, K5, (yfwd, sl 1, K1, psso) twice, yfwd, sl 1, K2 tog, psso, rep from * to end, but ending with sl 1, K1, psso, K1.
2nd and every alt row P to end.

3rd row K3, *yfwd, (K2 tog, yfwd) twice, sl 1, K1, K1, K2 tog, yfwd, K5, yfwd, sl 1, K1, psso, K1, K2 tog, (yfwd, sl 1, K1, psso) twice, yfwd, K3, rep from * to end.
5th row K3, *K1, yfwd, (K2 tog, yfwd) twice, sl 1, K2 tog, psso, yfwd, K7, yfwd, K3 tog, (yfwd, sl 1, K1, psso) twice, yfwd, K4, rep from * to end.

7th row K2, *K2 tog, yfwd, K1, yfwd, (K2 tog, yfwd) twice, sl 1, K1, psso, K2, yfwd, sl 1, K2 tog, psso, yfwd, K2, K2 tog, (yfwd, sl 1, K1, psso) twice, yfwd, K1, yfwd, sl 1, K1, psso, K1, rep from * to last st, K1.
9th row K1, K2 tog, *yfwd, K3, yfwd, (K2 tog, yfwd) twice, sl 1, K2 tog, psso, yfwd, K3, yfwd, *continued overleaf*

50

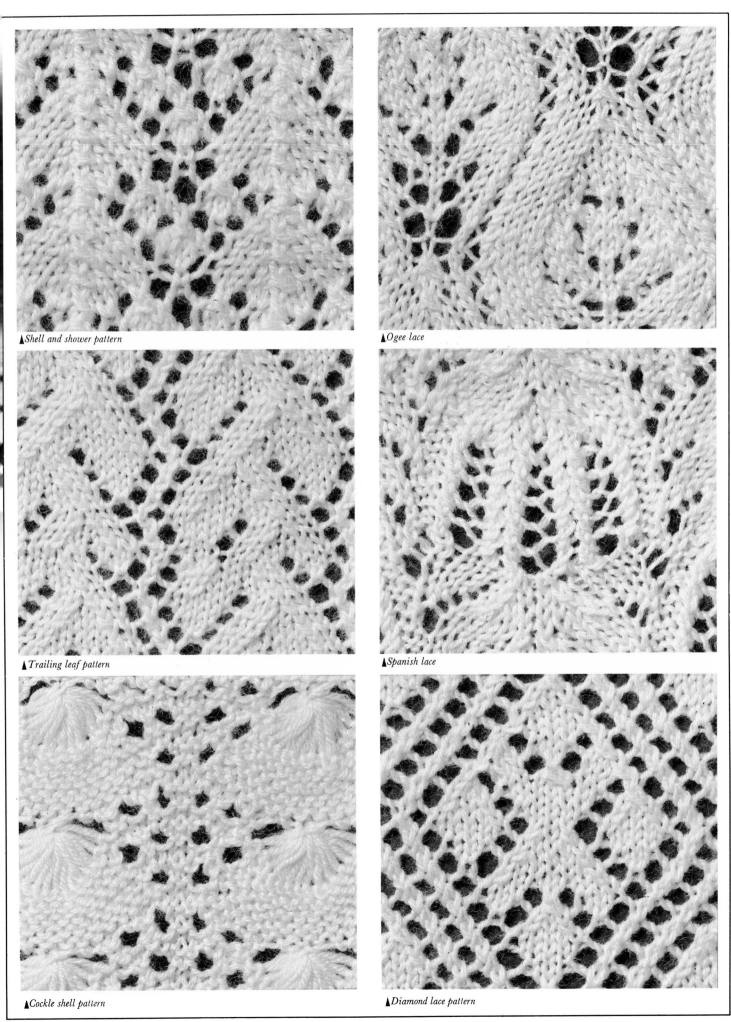

▲*Shell and shower pattern*

▲*Ogee lace*

▲*Trailing leaf pattern*

▲*Spanish lace*

▲*Cockle shell pattern*

▲*Diamond lace pattern*

continued from preceding page

K3 tog, (yfwd, sl 1, K1, psso) twice, yfwd, K3, yfwd, sl 1, K2 tog, psso, rep from * to end, but ending with sl 1, K1, psso, K1.

11th row K3, *K1, K2 tog, yfwd, K1, yfwd, (K2 tog, yfwd) twice, sl 1, K1, psso, K3, K2 tog, (yfwd, sl 1, K1, psso) twice, yfwd, K1, yfwd, sl 1, K1, psso, K4, rep from * to end.

13th row K3, *K2 tog, yfwd, K3, yfwd, (K2 tog, yfwd) twice, sl 1, K1, psso, K1, K2 tog, (yfwd, sl 1, K1, psso) twice, yfwd, K3, yfwd, sl 1, K1, psso, K3, rep from * to end.

15th row K2, *K2 tog, yfwd, K5, yfwd, (sl 1, K1, psso, yfwd) twice, sl 1, K2 tog, psso, (yfwd, K2 tog) twice, yfwd, K5, yfwd, sl 1, K1, psso, K1,

rep from * to last st, K1.

17th row K3, *K1, yfwd, sl 1, K1, psso, K1, K2 tog, yfwd, (sl 1, K1, psso, yfwd) twice, K3, (yfwd, K2 tog) twice, yfwd, sl 1, K1, psso. K1, K2 tog, yfwd, K4, rep from * to end.

19th row K3, *K2, yfwd, K3 tog, yfwd, (sl 1, K1, psso, yfwd) twice, K5, (yfwd, K2 tog) twice. yfwd, sl 1, K2 tog, psso, yfwd, K5, rep from * to end.

21st row K1, K2 tog, *yfwd, K2, K2 tog, yfwd, (sl 1, K1, psso, yfwd) twice, K1, yfwd, sl 1, K1, psso, K1, K2 tog. yfwd, K1, (yfwd, K2 tog) twice, yfwd, sl 1, K1, psso, K2, yfwd, sl 1, K2 tog, psso, rep from * to end, but ending with sl 1, K1, psso, K1.

23rd row K3, *yfwd, K3 tog, yfwd. (sl 1, K1, psso, yfwd) twice, K3, yfwd, sl 1, K2 tog, psso, yfwd, K3, (yfwd, K2 tog) twice, yfwd, sl 1, K2 tog, psso, yfwd, K3, rep from * to end.

25th row K3, *K2 tog, yfwd, (sl 1, K1, psso, yfwd) twice, K1, yfwd, sl 1, K1, psso, K5, K2 tog, yfwd, K1, (yfwd, K2 tog) twice, yfwd, sl 1, K1, psso, K3, rep from * to end.

27th row K2, *K2 tog, yfwd, (sl 1, K1, psso, yfwd) twice, K3, yfwd, sl 1, K1, psso, K3, K2 tog, yfwd, K3, (yfwd, K2 tog) twice, yfwd, sl 1, K1, psso, K1, rep from * to last st, K1.

28th row As 2nd row.

These 28 rows form the pattern.

large lace patterns

Alternated Old Shale pattern

Cast on a number of stitches divisible by 10 + 3.
1st row K to end.
2nd row P to end.
3rd row K1, (K2 tog) twice, *(yfwd, K1) 3 times, yfwd, sl 1, K1, psso, sl 1, K2 tog, psso, K2 tog, rep from * to last 8 sts, (yfwd, K1) 3 times, yfwd, (sl 1, K1, psso) twice, K1.
4th row K to end.
Rep these 4 rows twice more.
13th row As 1st.
14th row As 2nd.
15th row K2, yfwd, K1, yfwd, *sl 1, K1, psso, sl 1, K2 tog, psso, K2 tog, (yfwd, K1) 3 times, yfwd, rep from * to last 10 sts, sl 1, K1, psso, sl 1, K2 tog, psso, K2 tog, (yfwd, K1) twice, K1.
16th row As 4th.
Rep the last 4 rows twice more.
These 24 rows form the pattern.

Candlelight pattern

Cast on a number of stitches divisible by 12 + 1.
1st row K1, *yfwd, sl 1, K1, psso, K7, K2 tog, yfwd, K1, rep from * to end.
2nd and every alt row P to end.
3rd row K1, *yfwd, K1, sl 1, K1, psso, K5, K2 tog, K1, yfwd, K1, rep from * to end.
5th row K1, *yfwd, K2, sl 1, K1, psso, K3, K2 tog, K2, yfwd, K1, rep from * to end.
7th row K1, *yfwd, K3, sl 1, K1, psso, K1, K2 tog, K3, yfwd, K1, rep from * to end.
9th row K1, *yfwd, K4, sl 1, K2 tog, psso, K4, yfwd, K1, rep from * to end.
11th row *K4, K2 tog, yfwd, K1, yfwd, sl 1, K1, psso, K3, rep from * to last st, K1.
13th row *K3, K2 tog, K1, (yfwd, K1) twice, sl 1, K1, psso, K2, rep from * to last st, K1.
15th row *K2, K2 tog, K2, yfwd, K1, yfwd,

K2, sl 1, K1, psso, K1, rep from * to last st, K1.
17th row *K1, K2 tog, K3, yfwd, K1, yfwd, K3, sl 1, K1, psso, rep from * to last st, K1.
19th row K2 tog, *K4, yfwd, K1, yfwd, K4, sl 1, K2 tog, psso, rep from * to last 11 sts, K4, yfwd, K1, yfwd, K4, sl 1, K1, psso.
20th row As 2nd.
These 20 rows form the pattern.

Fern pattern

Cast on a number of stitches divisible by 30 + 2.
1st row P2, *sl 1, K2 tog, psso, K9, yfwd, K1, yrn, P2, yon, K1, yfwd, K9, K3 tog, P2, rep from * to end.
2nd and every alt row K2, *P13, K2, rep from * to end.
3rd row P2, *sl 1, K2 tog, psso, K8, (yfwd, K1) twice, P2, (K1, yfwd) twice, K8, K3 tog, P2, rep from * to end.
5th row P2, *sl 1, K2 tog, psso, K7, yfwd, K1, yfwd, K2, P2, K2, yfwd, K1, yfwd, K7, K3 tog, P2, rep from * to end.
7th row P2, *sl 1, K2 tog, psso, K6, yfwd, K1,

yfwd, K3, P2, K3, yfwd, K1, yfwd, K6, K3 tog, P2, rep from * to end.
9th row P2, *sl 1, K2 tog, psso, K5, yfwd K1, yfwd, K4, P2, K4, yfwd, K1, yfwd, K5, K3 tog, P2, rep from * to end.
10th row As 2nd.
These 10 rows form the pattern.

Drooping elm leaf pattern

Cast on a number of stitches divisible by 15 + 1.
1st row K1, *yfwd, K1, sl 1, K1, psso, P1, K2 tog, K1, yrn, P1, sl 1, K1, psso, P1, K2 tog, yfwd, K1, yfwd, K1, rep from * to end.
2nd row P1, *P4, K1, P1, K1, P3, K1, P4, rep from * to end.
3rd row K1, *yfwd, K1, sl 1, K1, psso, P1, K2 tog, K1, P1, sl 1, K2 tog, psso, yfwd, K3, yfwd, K1, rep from * to end.

4th row P1, *P6, K1, P2, K1, P4, rep from * to end.
5th row K1 *yfwd, K1, yfwd, sl 1, K1, psso, P1, (K2 tog) twice, yfwd, K5, yfwd, K1, rep from * to end.
6th row P1, *P7, K1, P1, K1, P5, rep from * to end.
7th row K1, *yfwd, K3, yfwd, sl 1, K2 tog, psso, P1, yon, K1, sl 1, K1, psso, P1, K2 tog,

K1, yfwd, K1, rep from * to end.
8th row P1, *P3, K1, P3, K1, P7, rep from * to end.
9th row K1, *yfwd, K5, yfwd, sl 1, K1, psso, K1, sl 1, K1, psso, P1, K2 tog, K1, yfwd, K1, rep from * to end.
10th row P1, *P3, K1, P2, K1, P8, rep from * to end.
These 10 rows form the pattern.

Madeira lace pattern

Cast on a number of stitches divisible by 6 + 1.
1st row K2, *yrn, P3 tog, yon, K3, rep from

* to last 5 sts, yrn, P3 tog, yon, K2.
Rep this row 5 times more.
7th row K5, *yrn, P3 tog, yon, K3, rep from

* to last 2 sts, K2.
Rep this row 5 times more.
These 12 rows form the pattern.

Flower pattern

Cast on a number of stitches divisible by 10 + 1.
1st row K3, *yfwd, sl 1, K1, psso, K8, rep from * to last 8 sts, yfwd, sl 1, K1, psso, K6.
2nd and every alt row P to end.
3rd row K4, *yfwd, sl 1, K1, psso, K8, rep from * to last 7 sts, yfwd, sl 1, K1, psso, K5.
5th row K5, *yfwd, sl 1, K1, psso, K8, rep from * to last 6 sts, yfwd, sl 1, K1, psso, K4.
7th row K3, *K2 tog, yfwd, K1, yfwd, sl 1, K1, psso, K5, rep from * to last 8 sts, K2 tog, yfwd, K1, yfwd, sl 1, K1, psso, K3.
9th row K2, *K2 tog, yfwd, K3, yfwd, sl 1,

K1, psso, K3, rep from * to last 9 sts, K2 tog, yfwd, K3, yfwd, sl 1, K1, psso, K2.
11th row As 7th.
13th row As 9th.
15th row K4, *yfwd, sl 1, K2 tog, psso, yfwd, K7, rep from * to last 7 sts, yfwd, sl 1, K2 tog, psso, yfwd, K4.
17th row K to end.
19th row K11, *K2 tog, yfwd, K8, rep from * to end.
21st row K10, *K2 tog, yfwd, K8, rep from * to last st, K1.
23rd row K9, *K2 tog, yfwd, K8, rep from *

to last 2 sts, K2.
25th row K8, *K2 tog, yfwd, K1, yfwd, sl 1, K1, psso, K5, rep from * to last 3 sts, K3.
27th row K7, *K2 tog, yfwd, K3, yfwd, sl 1, K1, psso, K3, rep from * to last 4 sts, K4.
29th row As 25th.
31st row As 27th.
33rd row K9, *yfwd, sl 1, K2 tog, psso, K7, rep from * to last 2 sts, K2.
35th row As 17th.
36th row As 2nd.
These 36 rows form the pattern.

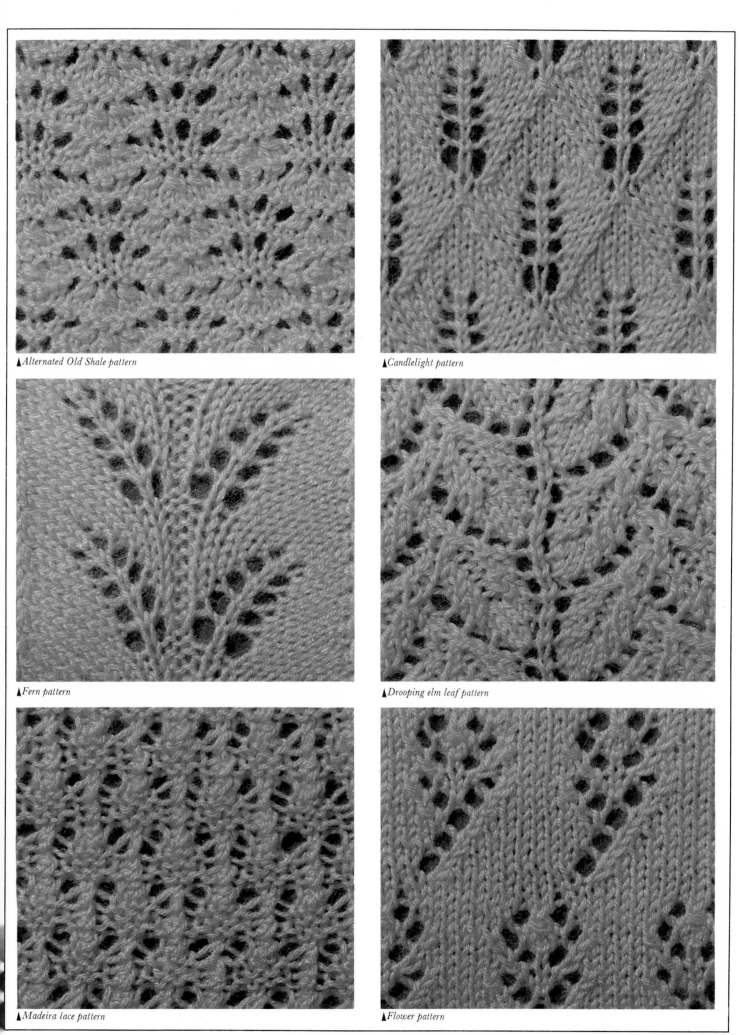

▲Alternated Old Shale pattern

▲Candlelight pattern

▲Fern pattern

▲Drooping elm leaf pattern

▲Madeira lace pattern

▲Flower pattern

53

basic jersey design

Long sleeved crew neck version

Short sleeved V-neck version

Long-sleeved V-neck version
Lacy jersey can be made in any stitch on p. 46 & 47 ▶

Sizes

To fit 34[36:38]in bust
Length to shoulder, 21[21½:22]in
Long sleeve seam, 17[17½:18]in
Short sleeve seam, 4in
The figures in brackets [] refer to the 36 and 38in sizes respectively

Tension

7 sts and 9 rows to 1in over st st worked on No.10 needles

Materials

Long sleeved version 11[12:13] x 1oz balls
Lee Target Motoravia 4 ply
Short sleeved version 9[10:11] x 1oz balls
One pair No.10 needles
One pair No.12 needles
Set of 4 No.12 needles pointed at both ends

Back

Using No.12 needles cast on 127[133:139] sts.
1st row K1, *P1, K1, rep from * to end.
2nd row P1, *K1, P1, rep from * to end.
Rep these 2 rows for 1½in, ending with a 2nd row.
Change to No.10 needles. Beg with a K row cont in st st, or any of the patt given on pages 46 and 47, until work measures 14in from beg, or required length to underarm, ending with a WS row.

Shape armholes

Keeping sequence of patt used correct, cast off at beg of next and every row 5 sts twice and 2 sts 4 times. Dec one st at each end of next and foll 5 alt rows. 97[103:109]sts. Cont without shaping until armholes measure 7[7½:8]in from beg, ending with a WS row.

Shape neck and shoulders

Next row Patt 34[36:38] sts, turn and leave rem sts on holder.
Complete this side first.
Next row Cast off 2 sts, patt to end.
Next row Cast off 7[7:8] sts, patt to end.
Rep last 2 rows twice more. Patt 1 row, then cast off rem 7[9:8] sts.
With RS of work facing, sl first 29[31:33] sts on to holder for centre back neck, rejoin yarn to rem sts, patt to end.
Next row Cast off 7[7:8] sts, patt to end.
Next row Cast off 2 sts, patt to end.
Rep last 2 rows twice more. Cast off rem 7[9:8] sts.

Front (crew neck)

Work as given for back until armhole shaping is completed. Cont without shaping until armholes measure 5[5½:6]in from beg, ending with a WS row.

Shape neck

Next row Patt 40[42:44] sts, turn and leave rem sts on holder.
Complete this side first. Cast off at beg of next and every alt row 3 sts once and 2 sts twice. Dec one st at neck edge on every alt row until 28[30:32] sts rem. Cont without shaping until armhole measures same as back to shoulder, ending at armhole edge.

Shape shoulder

Cast off at beg of next and every alt row 7[7:8] sts 3 times and 7[9:8] sts once.
With RS of work facing, sl first 17[19:21] sts on to holder for centre front neck, rejoin yarn to rem sts and patt to end. Patt 1 row. Complete to match first side, reversing shaping.

Front (v-neck)

Work as given for back to underarms.
Shape armholes and divide for neck
1st row Cast off 5 sts, patt 58[61:64] sts, turn

and leave rem sts on holder.
Complete this side first.
2nd row Patt to end.
3rd row Cast off 2 sts, patt to last 2 sts, K2 tog.
4th row Patt to end.
5th row Cast off 2 sts, patt to end.
6th row P2 tog, patt to end.
Dec one st at armhole edge on next and foll 5 alt rows, *at the same time* cont dec one st at neck edge on every 3rd row until 28[30:32] sts rem. Cont without shaping until armhole measures same as back to shoulder, ending at armhole edge.

Shape shoulder

Work as given for crew neck.
With RS of work facing, sl first st on to holder for centre front, rejoin yarn to rem sts and patt to end.
Next row Cast off 5 sts, patt to end.
Next row K2 tog, patt to end.
Complete to match first side, reversing shaping.

Long sleeves

Using No.12 needles cast on 55[55:61] sts. Work 1½in rib as given for back, ending with a 2nd row. Change to No.10 needles. Beg with a K row cont in st st or patt as given for back, inc one st at each end of 3rd and every foll 8th[6th:8th] row until there are 91[95:99] sts. Cont without shaping until sleeve measures 17[17½:19]in from beg, ending with a WS row.

Shape top

Cast off 5 sts at beg of next 2 rows. Dec one st at each end of next and foll 10[11:12] alt rows. 59[61:63] sts. Cast off at beg of next and every row 2 sts 8[8:10] times, 3 sts 6 times, 4 sts 4 times and 9[11:9] sts once.

Short sleeves

Using No.12 needles cast on 85[85:91] sts. Work 1in rib as given for back, ending with a 2nd row. Change to No.10 needles. Beg with a K row, cont in st st, or patt as given for back, inc one st at each end of 3rd and every foll 8th[6th:8th] row until there are 91[95:99] sts. Cont without shaping until sleeve measures 4in from beg, ending with a WS row.

Shape top

Work as given for long sleeves.

Crew neckband

Join shoulder seams. Using set of 4 No.12 needles and with RS of work facing, K up 9 sts down right back neck, K across back neck sts, K up 9 sts up left back neck ** and 27 sts down left front neck, K across front neck sts, then K up 27 sts up right front neck. 118[122:126] sts. Cont in rounds of K1, P1 rib for 2½in. Cast off in rib. Fold neckband in half to WS and sl st down.

V-neckband

Work as given for crew neck to **, K up 60[64:68] sts down left front neck, K centre front st from holder and mark with coloured thread, then K up 60[64:68] sts up right front neck. 168[178:188] sts. Work in rounds of K1, P1 rib as foll:
Next round Rib to 2 sts before centre front st, K2 tog, P1, sl 1, K1, psso, rib to end.
Rep last round for 1¼in. Cast off in rib, still dec at centre front.

To make up

Press each piece under a damp cloth with a warm iron. Set in sleeves. Join side and sleeve seams. Press seams.

Striped & checked patterns

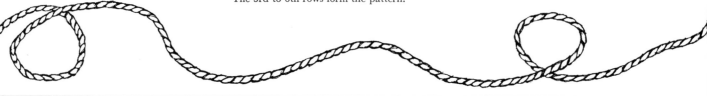

Random stripe pattern

Using A cast on any number of stitches.
1st row With A, K to end.
2nd row With A, P to end.
Continue in st st, join in B and work 1 row, then join in C and work 3 rows C, 1 row A, 3 rows B, 1 row C, 2 rows A, 1 row C, 1 row B, 1 row A, 1 row C, 1 row B.
These 18 rows form the pattern.

Mock houndstooth pattern

Using A cast on a number of stitches divisible by 3 + 2.
1st row With A, K to end.
2nd row With A, P to end.
3rd row With B, K3, *sl 1, K2, rep from * to last 2 sts, sl 1, K1.
4th row With B, P to end.
5th row With A, K1, *sl 1, K2, rep from * to last st, K1.
6th row As 2nd.
The 3rd to 6th rows form the pattern.

Woven stitch in two colours

Using A cast on a number of stitches divisible by 2.
1st row With A, K to end.
2nd row With A, P to end.
3rd row With B, K1, *yfwd, sl 1 P-wise, ybk, K1 rep from * to last st, K1.
4th row With B, P to end.
5th row With A, K2, *yfwd, sl 1 P-wise, ybk, K1, rep from * to end.
6th row As 2nd.
The 3rd-6th rows form the pattern.

Woven stripe pattern

Using A cast on a number of stitches divisible by 2.
1st row With A, K to end.
2nd row With A, P to end.
3rd row With B, K1, *yfwd, sl 1 P-wise, ybk, K1, rep from * to last st, K1.
4th row With B, P to end.
5th row With B, K to end.
6th row As 4th.
7th row With A, K2, *yfwd, sl 1 P-wise, ybk, K1, rep from * to end.
8th row As 2nd.
9th row As 3rd.
10th row As 4th.
11th row As 5th.
12th row As 6th.
13th row As 7th.
14th row As 8th.
These 14 rows form the pattern.

Vertical stripe pattern

Using A cast on a number of stitches divisible by 4 + 3.
1st row With A, K to end.
2nd row With A, P to end.
3rd row With B, K3, *sl 1, K3, rep from * to end.
4th row With B, P3, *sl 1, P3, rep from * to end.
5th row With A, K1, *sl 1, K3, rep from * to last 2 sts, sl 1, K1.
6th row With A, P1, *sl 1, P3, rep from * to last 2 sts, sl 1, P1.
The 3rd-6th rows form the pattern.

Brick pattern

Using A cast on a number of stitches divisible by 4 + 3.
1st row With A, K to end.
2nd row With A, K to end.
3rd row With B, K3, *sl 1, K3, rep from * to end.
4th row With B, P3, *sl 1, P3, rep from * to end.
5th row As 1st.
6th row As 2nd.
7th row With B, K1, *sl 1, K3, rep from * to last 2 sts, sl 1, K1.
8th row With B, P1, *sl 1, P3, rep from * to last 2 sts, sl 1, P1.
These 8 rows form the pattern.

Chevron stripe pattern

Using A cast on a number of stitches divisible by 14 + 3.
1st row With A, K1, K2 tog, *K5, yfwd, K1, yfwd, K5, sl 1, K2 tog, psso, rep from * to last 14 sts, K5, yfwd, K1, yfwd, K5, sl 1, K1, psso, K1.
2nd row With A, K1, P1, *K5, K into back of next st — called K1B —, K1, K1 B, K5, P1, rep from * to last st, K1.
These 2 rows form the pattern.
Repeat these 2 rows using two or more colours as required, changing colour after a 2nd pattern row.

Check pattern

Using A cast on a number of stitches divisible by 4 + 3.
1st row With A, K to end.
2nd row With A, P to end.
3rd row With B, K1, sl 2 P-wise, *K1. sl 3 P-wise, rep from * to last 4 sts, K1, sl 2 P-wise, K1.
4th row With B, P1, sl 1, *P3, sl 1, rep from * to last st, P1.
5th row With A, K3, *sl 1 P-wise, K3, rep from * to end.
6th row With A, P to end.
7th row With B, K2, *sl 3 P-wise, K1, rep from * to last st, K1.
8th row With B, P3, *sl 1, P3, rep from * to end.
9th row With A, K1, sl 1 P-wise, *K3, sl 1 P-wise, rep from * to last st, K1.
10th row As 6th.
The 3rd-10th rows form the pattern.

Two-colour brioche stitch

Using A cast on a number of stitches divisible by 2 + 1.
1st row With A, K to end.
2nd row As 1st.
3rd row With B, K1, *K into the loop below the next st — called K1 below—, K1, rep from * to end.
4th row With B, K to end.
5th row With A, K2, *K1 below, K1, rep from * to last st, K1.
6th row With A, K to end.
The 3rd to 6th rows form the pattern.

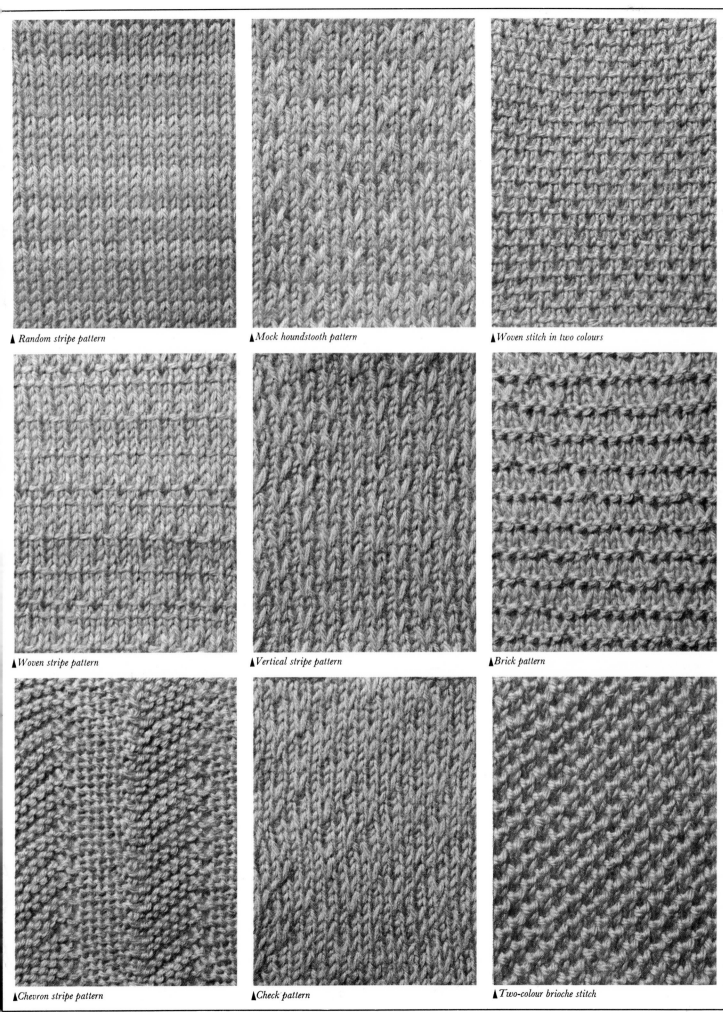

▲ *Random stripe pattern*

▲ *Mock houndstooth pattern*

▲ *Woven stitch in two colours*

▲ *Woven stripe pattern*

▲ *Vertical stripe pattern*

▲ *Brick pattern*

▲ *Chevron stripe pattern*

▲ *Check pattern*

▲ *Two-colour brioche stitch*

Jacquard patterns & motifs

Wavy striped pattern
Using A cast on a number of stitches divisible by 4 + 1.
1st row With A, K to end.
2nd row With A, P to end.
3rd row K1 B, *K3 A, K1 B, rep from * to end.
4th row P2 B, *P1 A, P3 B, rep from * to last 3 sts, P1 A, P2 B.
5th row With B, K to end.
6th row With B, P to end.
7th row K1 C, *K3 B, K1 C, rep from * to end.
8th row P2 C, *P1 B, P3 C, rep from * to last 3 sts, P1 B, P2 C.
9th row With C, K to end.
10th row With C, P to end.
11th row K1 A, *K3 C, K1 A, rep from * to end.
12th row P2 A, *P1 C, P3 A, rep from * to last 3 sts, P1 C, P2 A.
These 12 rows form the pattern.

Houndstooth check
Using A cast on a number of stitches divisible by 4.
1st row K2 A, *K1 B, K3 A, rep from * to last 2 sts, K1 B, K1 A.
2nd row *P1 A, P3 B, rep from * to end.
3rd row *K1 A, K3 B, rep from * to end.
4th row P2 A, *P1 B, P3 A, rep from * to last 2 sts, P1 B, P1 A.
These 4 rows form the pattern.

Key pattern in three colours
Using A cast on a number of stitches divisible by 8 + 1.
1st row With A, K to end.
2nd row With A, P to end.
3rd row K2 A, *K1 B, K3 A, rep from * to last 3 sts, K1 B, K2 A.
4th row P1 A, *P1 B, P1 C, P1 B, P1 A, (P1 B, P1 A) twice, rep from * to end.
5th row K1 B, *K3 A, K1 B, K3 C, K1 B, rep from * to end.
6th row P1 A, *P1 B, P1 C, P1 B, P5 A, rep from * to end.
7th row As 3rd.
8th row *P3 A, P1 B, P1 A, P1 B, P1 C, P1 B, rep from * to last st, P1 A.
9th row K1 B, *K3 C, K1 B, K3 A, K1 B, rep from * to end.
10th row P1 A, *P1 B, P3 A, P1 B, P1 C, P1 B, P1 A, rep from * to end.
The 3rd to 10th rows form the pattern.
Note: If working this pattern as a border, rep the 3rd row at the end, to complete the pattern.

Greek key pattern
Using A cast on a number of stitches divisible by 16.
1st row With A, K to end.
2nd row With A, P to end.
3rd row With B, K to end.
4th row With B, P to end.
5th to 8th rows Rep the 1st and 2nd rows twice.
9th row *K14 B, K2 A, rep from * to end.
10th row *P2 A, P14 B, rep from * to end.
11th row *K2 B, K10 A, K2 B, K2 A, rep from * to end.
12th row *P2 A, P2 B, P10 A, P2 B, rep from * to end.
13th row *K2 B, K2 A, K6 B, K2 A, K2 B, K2 A, rep from * to end.
14th row *P2 A, P2 B, P2 A, P6 B, P2 A, P2 B, rep from * to end.
15th row *(K2 B, K2 A) 4 times, rep from * to end.
16th row *(P2 A, P2 B) 4 times, rep from * to end.
17th row *K2 B, K2 A, K2 B, K2 A, K6 B, K2 A, rep from * to end.
18th row *P2 A, P6 B, P2 A, P2 B, P2 A, P2 B, rep from * to end.
19th row *K2 B, K2 A, K2 B, K10 A, rep from * to end.
20th row *P10 A, P2 B, P2 A, P2 B, rep from * to end.
21st row *K2 B, K2 A, K12 B, rep from * to end.
22nd row *P12 B, P2 A, P2 B, rep from * to end.
23rd to 26th rows Rep the 1st and 2nd rows twice.
27th row As 3rd row.
28th row As 4th row.
These 28 rows complete the pattern for border.
If working as an all-over pattern, rep the 5th to 28th rows.

Hexagon pattern
When working this pattern, use a separate ball of yarn for each motif, and twist the yarns on the wrong side of work where they join on every row.
Using 3 colours, cast on 10 sts in each of the colours, A, B and C, making a number of stitches divisible by 30.
1st row *K10 C, K10 B, K10 A, rep from * to end.
2nd row *P10 A, P10 B, P10 C, rep from * to end.
3rd row As 1st.
4th row As 2nd.
5th row *K1 B, K8 C, K2 A, K8 B, K2 C, K8 A, K1 B, rep from * to end.
6th row *P2 B, P6 A, P4 C, P6 B, P4 A, P6 C, P2 B, rep from * to end.
7th row *K3 B, K4 C, K6 A, K4 B, K6 C, K4 A, K3 B, rep from * to end.
8th row *P4 B, P2 A, P8 C, P2 B, P8 A, P2 C, P4 B, rep from * to end.
9th row *K5 B, K10 A, K10 C, K5 B, rep from * to end.
10th row *P5 B, P10 C, P10 A, P5 B, rep from * to end.
11th to 12th rows Rep the 9th and 10th rows.
13th row As 9th.
14th row As 8th.
15th row As 7th.
16th row As 6th.
17th row As 5th.
18th row As 2nd.
These 18 rows form the pattern.

Diamond pattern
Using A cast on a number of stitches divisible by 12 + 1.
1st row *K2 A, K2 B, K2 A, K1 B, K3 A, K2 B, rep from * to last st, K1 A.
2nd row P1 A, *P2 B, P3 A, P1 B, P2 A, P2 B, P2 A, rep from * to end.
3rd row K1 B, *K2 A, K2 B, K3 A, K1 B, K2 A, K2 B, rep from * to end.
4th row *P2 B, P2 A, P1 B, P3 A, P2 B, P2 A, rep from * to last st, P1 B.
5th row *K2 B, K2 A, K1 B, K3 A, K2 B, K2 A, rep from * to last st, K1 B.
6th row P1 B, *P2 A, P2 B, P3 A, P1 B, P2 A, P2 B, rep from * to end.
7th row K1 A, *K2 B, K3 A, K1 B, K2 A, K2 B, K2 A, rep from * to end.
8th row *P2 A, P2 B, P2 A, P1 B, P3 A, P2 B, rep from * to last st, P1 A.
9th row *K2 A, K1 B, K2 A, K2 B, K3 A, K2 B, rep from * to last st, K1 A.
10th row P1 A, *P2 B, P3 A, P2 B, P1 B, P2 A, rep from * to end.
11th row K1 B, *K3 A, K2 B, K2 A, K1 B, K2 A, K2 B, rep from * to end.
12th row *P2 B, P2 A, P1 B, P2 A, P2 B, P3 A, rep from * to last st, P1 B.
13th row K1 B, *K2 A, K2 B, K2 A, K2 B, K3 A, K1 B, rep from * to end.
14th row P1 B, *P3 A, P2 B, P2 A, P2 B, P2 A, P1 B, rep from * to end.
15th row *K2 A, K2 B, K2 A, K2 B, K2 A, K1 B, K1 A, rep from * to last st, K1 A.
16th row *P2 A, P1 B, P2 A, P2 B, P2 A, P2 B, P1 A, rep from * to last st, P1 A.
17th row *K2 A, K1 B, K2 A, K2 B, K2 A, K2 B, K1 A, rep from * to last st, K1 A.
18th row *P2 A, P2 B, P2 A, P2 B, P2 A, P1 B, P1 A, rep from * to last st, P1 A.
19th row K1 B, *K3 A, K2 B, K2 A, K2 B, K2 A, K1 B, rep from * to end.
20th row P1 B, *P2 A, P2 B, P2 A, P2 B, P3 A, P1 B, rep from * to end.
21st row *K2 B, K2 A, K1 B, K2 A, K2 B, K3 A, rep from * to last st, K1 B.
22nd row P1 B, *P3 A, P2 B, P2 A, P1 B, P2 A, P2 B, rep from * to end.
23rd row K1 A, *K2 B, K3 A, K2 B, K2 A, K1 B, K2 A, rep from * to end.
24th row *P2 A, P1 B, P2 A, P2 B, P3 A, P2 B, rep from * to last st, P1 A.
These 24 rows form the pattern.

Fleur de lys
Using A cast on a number of stitches divisible by 6 + 1.
1st row K3 A, *K1 B, K5 A, rep from * to last 4 sts, K1 B, K3 A.
2nd row P2 A, *P3 B, P3 A, rep from * to last 5 sts, P3 B, P2 A.
3rd row As 1st.
4th row P1 B, *P5 A, P1 B, rep from * to end.
5th row K2 B, *K3 A, K3 B, rep from * to last 5 sts, K3 A, K2 B.
6th row As 4th.
These 6 rows form the pattern.

Ship motif border
Cast on a number of stitches divisible by 20 + 1.
1st row With B, K to end.
2nd row With B, P to end.
3rd row With A, K to end.
4th row With A, P to end.
5th row *K1 B, K2 A, K1 B, K4 A, K6 B, K3 A, K1 B, K2 A, rep from * to last st, K1 B.
6th row P1 A, *P1 A, P1 B, P3 A, P8 B, P4 A, P1 B, P2 A, rep from * to end.
Continue in pattern from chart.

▲Wavy striped pattern

▲Houndstooth check

▲Key pattern in three colours

▲Greek key pattern

▲Hexagon pattern

▲Diamond pattern

▲Chart for ship motif

REP 20 STS

□ —A
× —B
○ —C

▲Fleur de lys

▲Ship motif border

Fair Isle patterns

These patterns are all worked from charts, as given below.

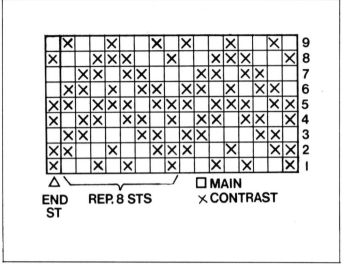

Pattern No.1 Narrow border pattern — 9 rows.
Cast on a number of stitches divisible by 8 plus 1.

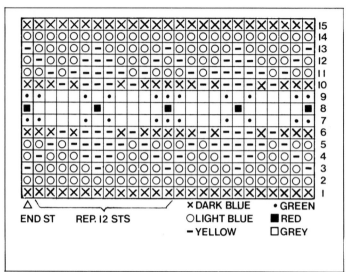

Pattern No.2 Border pattern — 15 rows.
Cast on a number of stitches divisible by 12 plus 1.

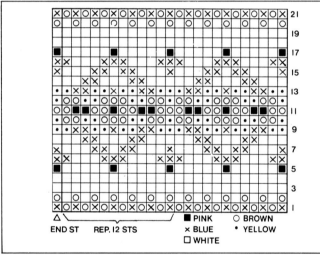

Pattern No.3 Border pattern — 21 rows.
Cast on a number of stitches divisible by 12 plus 1.

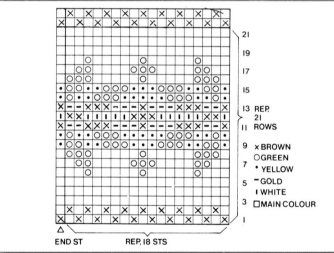

Pattern No.4 Border pattern — 23 rows — first 21 rows can be repeated for an all-over pattern. Cast on a number of stitches divisible by 18 plus 1.

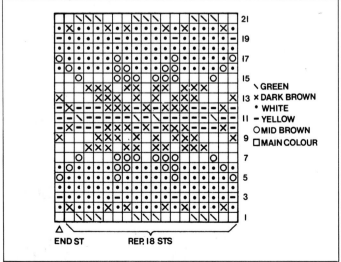

Pattern No.5 Border pattern — 21 rows.
Cast on a number of stitches divisible by 18 plus 1.

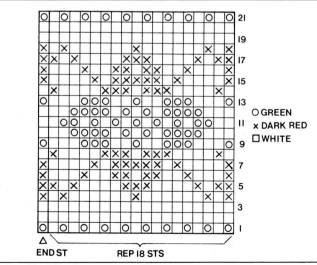

Pattern No.6 Border pattern — 21 rows.
Cast on a number of stitches divisible by 18 plus 1.

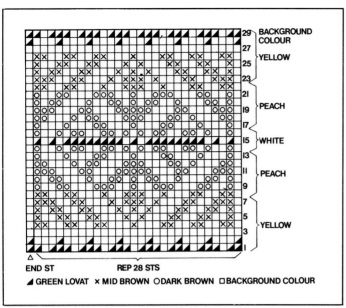

Pattern No.7 Wider border pattern — 29 rows.
Cast on a number of stitches divisible by 28 plus 1.

Key for Pattern No.7:
◣ GREEN LOVAT   × MID BROWN   ○ DARK BROWN   □ BACKGROUND COLOUR

(Pattern No.7 row labels: BACKGROUND COLOUR, YELLOW, PEACH, WHITE, PEACH, YELLOW; END ST, REP 28 STS)

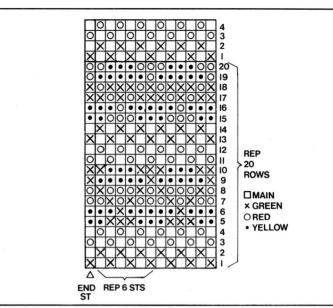

Pattern No.8 All-over pattern — repeat of 20 rows.
Cast on a number of stitches divisible by 6 plus 1.

REP 20 ROWS
□ MAIN
× GREEN
○ RED
• YELLOW

END ST   REP 6 STS

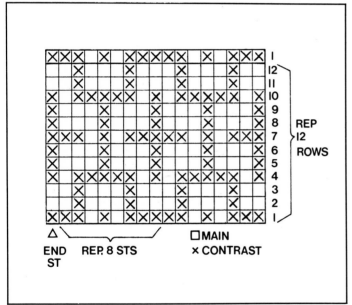

Pattern No.9 All-over pattern — repeat of 12 rows.
Cast on a number of stitches divisible by 8 plus 1.

REP 12 ROWS
END ST   REP. 8 STS   □ MAIN   × CONTRAST

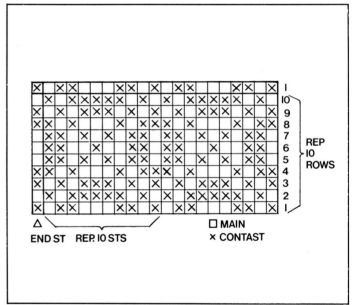

Pattern No.10 All-over pattern — repeat of 10 rows.
Cast on a number of stitches divisible by 10 plus 1.

REP 10 ROWS
END ST   REP. 10 STS   □ MAIN   × CONTAST

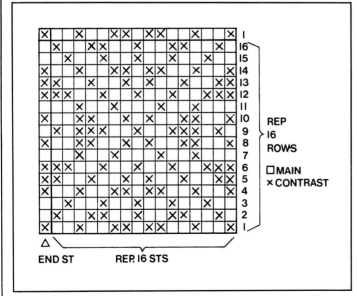

Pattern No.11 All-over pattern — repeat of 16 rows.
Cast on a number of stitches divisible by 16 plus 1.

REP 16 ROWS
□ MAIN
× CONTRAST
END ST   REP. 16 STS

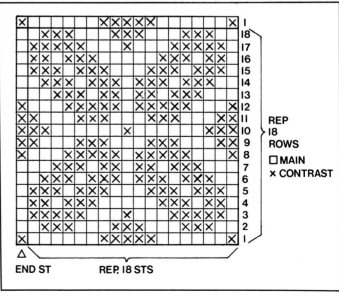

Pattern No.12 All-over pattern — repeat of 18 rows.
Cast on a number of stitches divisible by 18 plus 1.

REP 18 ROWS
□ MAIN
× CONTRAST
END ST   REP. 18 STS

knitting abbreviations

alt	alternate(ly)
approx	approximate(ly)
beg	begin(ning)
cont	continu(e)(ing)
dec	decrease
foll	follow(ing)
g st	garter stitch
in	inch(es)
inc	increase
K	knit
K up	pick up and knit
K-wise	knitwise
No.	number
psso	pass slipped stitch over
patt	pattern
P	purl
P up	pick up and purl
P-wise	purlwise
rem	remain(ing)
rep	repeat
RS	right side
sl	slip
sl st	slip stitch
st(s)	stitch(es)
st st	stocking stitch
tbl	through back of loop
tog	together
WS	wrong side
yd(s)	yard(s)
ybk	yarn back
yfwd	yarn forward
yon	yarn over needle
yrn	yarn round needle

CONVERSION FROM CENTIMETRES TO INCHES (based on 1cm. = .3937in.)

cm.	in.	cm.	in.	cm.	in.
1	$\frac{1}{2}$	36	$14\frac{1}{4}$	71	28
2	$\frac{3}{4}$	37	$14\frac{1}{2}$	72	$28\frac{1}{4}$
3	$1\frac{1}{4}$	38	15	73	$28\frac{3}{4}$
4	$1\frac{1}{2}$	39	$15\frac{1}{4}$	74	$29\frac{1}{4}$
5	2	40	$15\frac{3}{4}$	75	$29\frac{1}{2}$
6	$2\frac{1}{4}$	41	$16\frac{1}{4}$	76	30
7	$2\frac{3}{4}$	42	$16\frac{1}{2}$	77	$30\frac{1}{4}$
8	$3\frac{1}{4}$	43	17	78	$30\frac{3}{4}$
9	$3\frac{1}{2}$	44	$17\frac{1}{4}$	79	31
10	4	45	$17\frac{3}{4}$	80	$31\frac{1}{2}$
11	$4\frac{1}{4}$	46	18	81	32
12	$4\frac{3}{4}$	47	$18\frac{1}{2}$	82	$32\frac{1}{4}$
13	5	48	19	83	$32\frac{3}{4}$
14	$5\frac{1}{2}$	49	$19\frac{1}{4}$	84	33
15	6	50	$19\frac{3}{4}$	85	$33\frac{1}{2}$
16	$6\frac{1}{4}$	51	20	86	$33\frac{3}{4}$
17	$6\frac{3}{4}$	52	$20\frac{1}{2}$	87	$34\frac{1}{4}$
18	7	53	$20\frac{3}{4}$	88	$34\frac{3}{4}$
19	$7\frac{1}{2}$	54	$21\frac{1}{4}$	89	35
20	$7\frac{3}{4}$	55	$21\frac{3}{4}$	90	$35\frac{1}{2}$
21	$8\frac{1}{4}$	56	22	91	$35\frac{3}{4}$
22	$8\frac{3}{4}$	57	$22\frac{1}{2}$	92	$36\frac{1}{4}$
23	9	58	$22\frac{3}{4}$	93	$36\frac{1}{2}$
24	$9\frac{1}{2}$	59	$23\frac{1}{4}$	94	37
25	$9\frac{3}{4}$	60	$23\frac{1}{2}$	95	$37\frac{1}{2}$
26	$10\frac{1}{4}$	61	24	96	$37\frac{3}{4}$
27	$10\frac{3}{4}$	62	$24\frac{1}{2}$	97	$38\frac{1}{4}$
28	11	63	$24\frac{3}{4}$	98	$38\frac{1}{2}$
29	$11\frac{1}{2}$	64	$25\frac{1}{4}$	99	39
30	$11\frac{3}{4}$	65	$25\frac{1}{2}$	100	$39\frac{1}{2}$
31	$12\frac{1}{4}$	66	26	101	$39\frac{3}{4}$
32	$12\frac{1}{2}$	67	$26\frac{1}{2}$	102	$40\frac{1}{4}$
33	13	68	$26\frac{3}{4}$	103	$40\frac{1}{2}$
34	$13\frac{1}{2}$	69	$27\frac{1}{4}$	104	41
35	$13\frac{3}{4}$	70	$27\frac{1}{2}$	105	$41\frac{1}{2}$

From 0 to .125 is rounded down to 0
From .26 to .375 is rounded down to .25
From .51 to .625 is rounded down to .50
From .76 to .875 is rounded down to .75
from .126 to .24 is rounded up to .25
from .376 to .49 is rounded up to .50
from .626 to .74 is rounded up to .75

from .876 to .99 is rounded up to 1.00
(based on 1 cm = .3937in)

SYMBOLS

An asterisk, (*), shown in a pattern row denotes that the stitches shown after this sign must be repeated from that point.

Square brackets, [ ], denote instructions for larger sizes in the pattern. Round brackets, ( ), denote that this section of the pattern is to be worked for all sizes.

Tension—this is the most important factor in successful knitting. Unless you obtain the tension given for each design, you will not obtain satisfactory results.

PART TWO

Patterns
for you to knit
for men, women
and children

In this section you can practice all the skills described in the first half of this book, or adapt the patterns to suit yourself if you are already an expert knitter. The 36 patterns use lots of different stitches, styles and techniques: they include jerseys, jackets, trouser suits, skirts, cardigans, hats, scarves, gloves and mitts. There are Fair Isle and Aran patterns with charts to follow, stripes, checks and spots, Scandinavian style designs and embroidered motifs. There are garments to suit any taste or mood, and they feature many different types of yarn. Each pattern is coded with stars to indicate the standard of knitting required:

*   Easy: for the beginner
** Not so easy: you'll need some experience
***Complicated: for the experienced knitter

However, you can be sure there is nothing here which is not covered in the technique section, so any problems can be instantly solved.

1,2

Casual zipped jacket with a dropped shoulder line—and matching hat. The boy's jersey has a contrast pattern at the lower edge and cuffs

Jacket: knit
Jersey: knit
Sizes: jacket to fit 86.5[91.5:96.5]cm (34[36:38]in) bust
Jersey to fit 66.0 [71.0:76.0]cm (26[28: 30]in) chest
(Pullovers not included)

*

3

*Ribbed jerseys with
optional motif*

Knit
*Sizes to fit 86.5[91.5:
96.5:101.5:106.5:112.0]cm
(34[36:38:40:
42:44]in) chest/bust*

**

1 *Casual zipped jacket and matching pull on hat*

Sizes
To fit 34[36:38]in bust
Length to shoulder, 28[28½:29]in
Sleeve seam, 18[18½:19]in
The figures in brackets [] refer to the 36 and 38in sizes respectively
Tension
5 sts and 7 rows to 1in over st st worked on No.7 needles
Materials
21[22:23] balls Robin Vogue Double Double Knitting
One pair No.7 needles
One pair No.9 needles
26 in open-ended zip

Back
Using No.9 needles cast on 102[108:114] sts.
1st row *K1, P1, rep from * to end.
Rep this row for 1½in to form moss st edge.
Change to No.7 needles. Beg with a K row cont in st st until work measures 4in from beg, ending with a P row.
Shape sides
Next row K5, K2 tog, K to last 7 sts, sl 1, K1, psso, K5.
Cont dec in this way on every 8th row until 88[94:100] sts rem. Cont without shaping until work measures 19in from beg, ending with a P row.
Inc one st at each end of next and every foll 4th row until there are 94[100:106] sts. Mark each end of last row with coloured thread. Cont without shaping until work measures 7½[8:8½]in from markers, ending with a P row.
Shape shoulders
Cast off at beg of next and every row 6 sts 8 times, 5[6:7] sts 4 times and 26[28:30] sts once.

Left front
Using No.9 needles cast on 52[54:58] sts. Work 1½in moss st as given for back, inc one st at end of last row on 36in size only. Change to No.7 needles. Beg with a K row and keeping 4 sts at front edge in moss st, cont in st st until work measures 4in from beg, ending with a WS row.
Shape side
Keep moss st border correct throughout.
Next row K5, K2 tog, K to last 4 sts, moss st to end.
Cont dec in this way on every 8th row until 45[48:51] sts rem. Cont without shaping until work measures 19in from beg, ending with a WS row. Inc one st at beg of next and every foll 4th row twice more. Mark side edge of last row with coloured thread. Cont without shaping until work measures 6½[7:7½]in from marker, ending with a WS row.
Shape neck
Next row K to last 10[11:12] sts, turn and leave rem sts on holder.
Cast off 2 sts at beg of next row and dec one st at beg of foll 2 alt rows, ending with a P row.
Shape shoulder
Cast off at beg of next and every alt row 6 sts 4 times and 5[6:7] sts twice.

Right front
Work as given for left front, reversing shaping.

Sleeves
Using No.7 needles cast on 56 sts, and work from side edge to side edge.
1st row (P1, K1) 13 times, K to end.
2nd row Cast on 52[54:56] sts, P to last 25 sts, rib 25 sts. 108[110:112] sts.
Working first 25 sts in rib and rem sts in st st as now set, work 4 rows. Inc one st at end of next and every 6th row 8 times in all. Cont without shaping until work measures 8[8½:9]in from beg, ending with a WS row. Dec one st at end of next and every 6th row 8 times in all. Work 4 rows, ending with a RS row. Cast off 52[54:56] sts at beg of next row. Work 1 row. Cast off rem 56 sts.

Collar
Join shoulder seams. Using No.9 needles and with RS of work facing, K across 10[11:12] sts of right front neck, K up 73[75:77] sts round neck, K across 10[11:12] sts of left front neck. 93[97:101] sts. Keeping moss st border at both front edges correct, work 3½in K1, P1 rib. Cast off in patt.

Pockets (make 2)
Using No.9 needles cast on 39 sts. Work 6in K1, P1 rib. Cast off in rib.

To make up
Press each piece under a damp cloth with a warm iron. Sew shaped edge of sleeves into armholes between markers. Join side and sleeve seams. Fold ribbing on sleeves to RS. Sew on pockets, noting that cast on edge and cast off edge form sides of pockets. Sew in zip, placing bottom of zip at top edge of moss st border, and noting that zip ends about 1½in from top of collar. Press seams.

Cap
Using No.7 needles cast on 39 sts. Work 21in K1, P1 rib. Cast off in rib. Using No.9 needles and with RS of work facing, K up 109 sts along one long side. Work 1½in K1, P1 rib, ending with a RS row. Change to No.7 needles. Beg with a K row, cont in st st for 1½in, ending with a P row.
Shape top
Next row *K16, K2 tog, rep from * to last st, K1.
Next row P to end.
Next row *K15, K2 tog, rep from * to last st, K1.
Cont dec in this way on every alt row until 7 sts rem, ending with a K row. Break off yarn, thread through rem sts, draw up and fasten off.

To make up
Press st st part under a damp cloth with a warm iron. Join seam. Turn up brim as required.

2 *Boy's jersey with contrast pattern at lower edge and cuffs*

Sizes
To fit 26[28:30]in chest
Length to shoulder, 16½[18:19½]in
Sleeve seam, 13[14:15]in
The figures in brackets [] refer to the 28 and 30in sizes respectively
Tension
6 sts and 8 rows to 1in over st st worked on No.9 needles
Materials
9[10:11] balls Jaeger Donegal in main shade, A
1 ball of contrast colour, B
One pair No.9 needles
One pair No.11 needles
Set of 4 No.11 needles pointed at both ends

Back
Using No.11 needles and A, cast on 82[90:94] sts.
1st row *K1, P1, rep from * to end.
Rep this row 5 times more for moss st hem.
Change to No.9 needles. Beg with a K row cont in st st. Join in B. Commence patt.
1st row K2 A, *2 B, 2 A, rep from * to end.
2nd row P as 1st row.
3rd row K2 B, *2 A, 2 B, rep from * to end.
4th row P as 3rd row.
Rep these 4 rows twice more, inc 1[0:1] st at each end of last row. Break off B. 84[90:96] sts. Using A only cont in st st until work measures 11[12:13]in from beg, ending with a P row.
Shape armholes
Cast off at beg of next and every row 4 sts twice and 2 sts twice. Dec one st at each end of next and foll 3[4:5] alt rows. 64[68:72] sts. Cont without shaping until armholes measure 5½[6:6½]in from beg, ending with a P row.
Shape shoulders
Cast off at beg of next and every row 6 sts 4 times and 5[6:7] sts twice.
Leave rem 30[32:34] sts on holder for centre back neck.

Front
Work as given for back until front measures same as back to underarm.
Shape armhole and divide for neck
Next row Cast off 4 sts, K38[41:44] sts, turn and leave rem sts on holder.
Complete this side first. Cast off at armhole edge at beg of foll alt row 2 sts once, then dec one st on every alt row 4[5:6] times, *at the same time* dec one st at neck edge on next and every 3rd row until 17[18:19] sts rem. Cont without shaping until armhole measures same as back to shoulder, ending with a P row.
Shape shoulder
Cast off at beg of next and every alt row 6 sts twice and 5[6:7] sts once.
With RS of work facing, rejoin yarn to rem sts and K to end. Complete to match first side, reversing shaping.

Sleeves
Using No.11 needles and A, cast on 34[38:42] sts. Work 6 rows moss st as given for back. Change to No.9 needles. Join in B. Beg with a K row, work 12 rows patt as given for back. Break off B. Using A only cont in st st, inc one st at each end of next and every foll 6th row until there are 62[66:70] sts. Cont without shaping until sleeve measures 13[14:15]in from beg, ending with a P row.
Shape top
Cast off at beg of next and every row 4 sts twice and 2 sts twice. Dec one st at each end of next and every alt row until 32[34:36] sts rem, ending with a P row. Cast off at beg of next and every row 2 sts 6[6:8] times, 3 sts 4 times, then 8[10:8] sts once.

Neckband
Join shoulder seams. Using set of 4 No.11 needles, A and with RS of work facing, K across 30[32:34] back neck sts, K2 tog in centre, K up 40[43:46] sts down left front neck, pick up a loop between sts at centre front and K tbl and K up 40[43:46] sts up right front neck. 110[118:126] sts. Work 6 rounds moss st, noting that centre front st should be a P st on every round, and dec one st at each side of centre front st on every round. Cast off in moss st, still dec one st at each side of centre front.

To make up
Press each piece under a damp cloth with a warm iron. Set in sleeves. Join side and sleeve seams. Press seams.

3 *Ribbed jerseys with optional embroidered motifs at the front*

Sizes
To fit 34[36:38:40:42:44]in chest/bust
Length to shoulder, 24[25:26:27:28:29]in
Sleeve seam, 17[17½:18:18½:18½:19]in
The figures in brackets [] refer to the 36, 38, 40,

No. 3

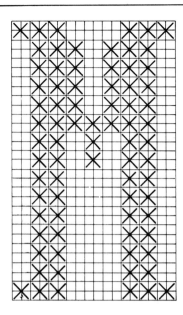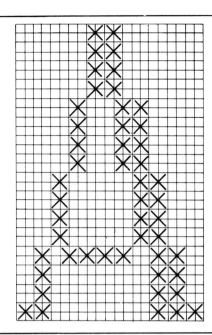

Embroidered motifs for any letter can be plotted on graph as the M and A above.

42 and 44in sizes respectively

Tension
4 sts and 5 rows to 1in over st st worked on No.5 needles

Materials
12[13:14:15:16:17] balls Wendy Swiftknit Double Double Knitting in main shade, A
1 ball of contrast colour, B
One pair No.5 needles
One pair No.7 needles

Back
Using No.7 needles and A, cast on 73[77:81:85: 89:93] sts.
1st row (RS) K1, *P1, K1, rep from * to end.
2nd row P1, *K1, P1, rep from * to end.
Rep these 2 rows for 1½in, ending with a 2nd row. Change to No.5 needles. Cont in rib until work measures 16½[17:17½:18:18½:19]in from beg, ending with a WS row.
Shape armholes
Cast off at beg of next and every row 5 sts twice and 2[2:3:3:4:4] sts twice. Dec one st at each end of next and foll 2[3:3:4:4:5] alt rows. 53[55:57: 59:61:63] sts. Cont without shaping until armholes measure 7½[8:8½:9:9½:10]in from beg, ending with a WS row.
Shape shoulders
Cast off at beg of next and every row 5[5:6:6:6:6] sts 4 times and 6[6:5:5:6:6] sts twice.
Leave rem 21[23:23:25:25:27] sts on holder for back neck.

Front
Using No.7 needles and A, cast on 73[77:81:85: 89:93] sts. Work 1½in rib as given for back, ending with a 2nd row. Change to No.5 needles. Commence patt.
1st row Rib 26[28:30:32:34:36] sts, K21 sts, rib to end.
2nd row Rib 26[28:30:32:34:36] sts, P21 sts, rib to end.
Rep last 2 rows until work measures same as back to underarm, ending with a WS row.
Shape armholes
Work as given for back. Cont without shaping until armholes measure 4½[5:5½:6:6½:7]in from beg, ending with a WS row.
Shape neck
Next row Patt 20[20:21:21:22:22] sts, turn and leave rem sts on holder.
Complete this side first.

Dec one st at neck edge on every alt row until 16[16:17:17:18:18] sts rem. Cont without shaping until armhole measures same as back to shoulder, ending with a WS row.
Shape shoulder
Cast off at beg of next and every alt row 5[5:6:6: 6:6] sts twice and 6[6:5:5:6:6] sts once.
With RS of work facing, sl first 13[15:15:17:17:19] sts on to holder for front neck, rejoin yarn to rem sts and patt to end. Complete to match first side, reversing shaping.

Sleeves
Using No.7 needles and B, cast on 39[41:43:45: 47:49] sts. Work 2 rows rib as given for back. Break off B. Join in A.
Next row Using A, K to end.
Cont in rib using A only until work measures 3[3:3½:3½:4:4]in from beg, ending with a WS row. Change to No.5 needles. Cont in rib, inc one st at each end of next and every foll 10th row until there are 51[53:55:57:59:61] sts. Cont without shaping until sleeve measures 17[17½:18:18½: 18½:19]in from beg, ending with a WS row.
Shape top
Cast off 5 sts at beg of next 2 rows. Dec one st at each end of next and every alt row until 17 sts rem, ending with a WS row. Cast off at beg of next and every row 2 sts 4 times and 9 sts once.

Neckband
Join right shoulder seam. Using No.7 needles, A and with RS of work facing, K up 18 sts down left front neck, K across front neck sts, K up 17 sts up right front neck, then K across back neck sts. 69[73:73:77:77:81] sts. Work 5[5:5½:5½:6:6]in rib, ending with a 2nd row. Break off A. Join in B.
Next row Using B, K to end.
Next row Using B, rib to end.
Cast off in rib.

To make up
Join left shoulder and neckband seam. Set in sleeves. Join side and sleeve seams. Press seams lightly under a dry cloth with a cool iron. Embroider initials on front if required, noting that initials are worked in cross-st, and every st covers 2 sts of knitting and 2 rows.

 Matching striped cap, mitts and scarf, snug for a cold day

Sizes
Cap to fit an average head
Mitts to fit an average hand
Scarf 8in by 60in
Tension
7 sts and 10 rows to 2in over st st worked on No.5 needles
Materials
Icelandic Lopi Sheep Wool
Cap and mitts 1 hank each of 4 contrast colours, A, B, C and D
Scarf 1 hank each of 4 contrast colours, A, B, C and D
One pair No.5 needles
One pair No.6 needles
Note
Cap and mitts: when working in rib, always K first row at each change of colour

Cap
Using No.6 needles and B, cast on 75 sts.
1st row K1, *P1, K1, rep from * to end.
2nd row P1, *K1, P1, rep from * to end.
Rep these 2 rows twice more. Change to No.5 needles. Join in A, C and D. Cont in rib as now set, working 8 rows C, 4 rows B, 10 rows D, then 2 rows A. Break off B, C and D.
Cont using A only.
Shape top
Next row K1, *P1, sl 1, K2 tog, psso, rep from * to last 2 sts, P1, K1. 39 sts.
Work 3 rows rib without shaping.
Next row K1, *K2 tog, rep from * to end. 21 sts. P1 row without shaping.
Next row K1, *K2 tog, rep from * to end. 11 sts. Break off yarn, thread through rem sts, draw up and fasten off.

To make up
Join seam.

Mitts right hand
Using No.5 needles and A, cast on 35 sts.
Work 10 rows rib as given for cap.
Next row Rib 6 sts, sl 1, K2 tog, psso, rib 17 sts, sl 1, K2 tog, psso, rib to end. 31 sts.

4

*Matching striped cap,
mitts and scarf*

Knit
*Sizes: cap to fit an
average head, mitts to
fit an average hand.
Scarf: 21cm (8in) by 152cm (60in)*

*

5

*Twinset with a
striped jersey and a
short sleeved cardigan
with a striped collar*

Knit
*Sizes to fit 81.5[86.5:91.5]cm
(32[34:36]in) bust*

*

6 7

Twinset in a two-
colour checked
pattern with plain
bands at the edge

Jersey and cardigan
with cap sleeves
worked in three-
colour stripes

Knit
Sizes to fit 86.5/91.5cm
(34/36in) bust

Knit
Size to fit 81.5cm
(32in) bust

**

**

Work 7 rows rib without shaping.
Next row Rib 6 sts, sl 1, K2 tog, psso, rib 13 sts, sl 1, K2 tog, psso, rib to end. 27 sts.
Work 1 row rib without shaping. Change to No.6 needles. Join in B. Using B, work 6 rows rib, inc one st at end of last row. 28 sts. Change to No.5 needles. Beg with a K row cont in st st working 2 rows B. Join in C. Work 8 rows C.
Divide for thumb
Next row Using C, K14 sts, sl next 6 sts onto holder for thumb, cast on 6 sts, K8 sts.
Cont in st st, work 1 row C and 4 rows B. Join in D. Work 12 rows D. Break off B, C and D. Cont using A only.

Shape top
Next row K1, K2 tog, K9, sl 1, K1, psso, K2 tog. K9, sl 1, K1, psso, K1. 24 sts.
Next row P to end.
Next row K1, K2 tog, K7, sl 1, K1, psso, K2 tog, K7, sl 1, K1, psso, K1. 20 sts.
Cont dec in this way on every alt row twice more. 12 sts.
Next row P6 sts, turn.
Fold work in half. Cast off P-wise, taking one st from each needle tog.
Thumb
Using No.5 needles, C and with RS of work facing. cast on 4 sts, K up 6 sts from holder. Beg with a P row, work 11 rows st st.
Next row *K2 tog, rep from * to end.
Break off yarn, thread through rem sts, draw up and fasten off.

Mitts left hand
Work as given for right mitt, reversing shaping and position of thumb.

To make up
Press work under a damp cloth with a warm iron. Join seams. Press seams.

Scarf
Using No.5 needles and B, cast on 28 sts. Beg with a K row, cont in st st throughout, working (8 rows B, 8 rows A, 12 rows D, 4 rows B, 10 rows C) 7 times, then 8 rows B. Cast off.

To make up
Press work under a damp cloth with a warm iron.
Fringe Using A, cut yarn into 12in lengths. Using 2 strands, knot into every alt st along each end. Trim fringe.

 Striped twinset with short sleeved cardigan

Sizes
To fit 32[34:36]in bust
Jersey length to shoulder, 21[21½:22]in
Sleeve seam, 17[17½:18]in
Jacket length to shoulder, 25[25½:26]in
Sleeve seam, 10in including cuff
The figures in brackets [] refer to the 34 and 36in sizes respectively
Tension
7 sts and 9 rows to 1in over st st worked on No.10 needles with 4 ply; 6 sts and 8 rows to 1in over st st worked on No.9 needles with Double Knitting
Materials
Jersey 8[8:9] balls Sunbeam Hyland Superwash 4 ply in main shade, A
6[7:8] balls of contrast colour, B
One pair No.10 needles
One pair No.11 needles
Set of 4 No.12 needles pointed at both ends
Jacket 21[22:23] balls Sunbeam Hyland Double

Knitting in contrast colour, B
4[4:4] balls of main shade, A
One pair No.9 needles
One pair No.11 needles
One No.11 circular Twin Pin
7 buttons

Jersey back
Using No.12 needles and A, cast on 106[114:122] sts.
1st row K2, *P2, K2, rep from * to end.
2nd row P2, *K2, P2, rep from * to end.
Rep these 2 rows for 6in, ending with a 2nd row.
Join in B. Change to No.10 needles. Beg with a K row, cont in st st working 2 rows B, 2 rows A, 4 rows B, 4 rows A throughout, *at the same time* inc one st at each end of every 10th row until there are 116[124:132] sts. Cont without shaping until work measures 14in from beg, ending with a P row.
Shape armholes
Cast off at beg of next and every row 4 sts twice, 3 sts twice, 2 sts 4 times and one st 10[12:14] times. 84[90:96] sts. Cont without shaping until armholes measure 7[7½:8]in from beg, ending with a P row.
Shape neck and shoulder
Next row (RS) K25[27:29] sts, turn and leave rem sts on holder.
Complete this side first.
Next row Cast off 2 sts, P to end.
Next row Cast off 4[5:5] sts, K to end.
Rep last 2 rows twice more, then first of them again. Cast off rem 5[4:6] sts.
With RS of work facing, sl first 34[36:38] sts on to holder for centre back neck, rejoin yarn to rem sts and K to end. Complete to match first side, reversing shaping.

Front
Work as given for back until armhole shaping is completed. Cont without shaping until armholes measure 4½[5:5½]in from beg, ending with a P row.
Shape neck
Next row K36[38:40] sts, turn and leave rem sts on holder.
Complete this side first. Cast off at beg of next and every alt row 3 sts twice, 2 sts 4 times, then one st 5 times, ending with a P row.
Shape shoulder
Cast off at beg of next and every alt row 4[5:5] sts 3 times and 5[4:6] sts once.
With RS of work facing, sl first 12[14:16] sts on to holder for centre front neck, rejoin yarn to rem sts and K to end. Complete to match first side, reversing shaping.

Sleeves
Using No.12 needles and B, cast on 50[54:58] sts.
Work 3in rib as given for back, ending with a 2nd row. Change to No.10 needles. Beg with a K row cont in st st, working in striped patt as given for back, inc one st at each end of 1st and every foll 8th row until there are 82[86:90] sts. Cont without shaping until sleeve measures 17[17½:18]in from beg, ending with a P row.
Shape top
Cast off at beg of next and every row 4 sts twice, one st 34[36:38] times, 2 sts 6[6:8] times, 3 sts 4 times, 4 sts twice and 8[10:8] sts once.

Neckband
Join shoulder seams. Using set of 4 No.12 needles, A and with RS of work facing, K up 12 sts down right back neck, K across back neck sts, K up 12 sts up left back neck and 37 sts up left front neck, K across front neck sts, K up 37 sts up right front neck. 144[148:152] sts. Work 1¼in in rounds of K2, P2 rib. Cast off in rib.

To make up
Press each piece under a damp cloth with a warm iron. Set in sleeves. Join side and sleeve seams.

Press seams.

Jacket back
Using No.11 needles and A, cast on 106[110:118] sts. Work 10 rows rib as given for Jersey back, inc 0[1:0] st at each end of last row. 106[112:118] sts. Break off A. Change to No.9 needles. Join in B. Beg with a K row cont in st st until work measures 16½in from beg, ending with a K row.
Next row (WS) K to end to reverse st st.
Beg with a P row cont in reverse st st until work measures 17½in from beg, ending with a K row.
Shape armholes
Cont in reverse st st throughout, cast off at beg of next and every row 4 sts twice, 2 sts 4 times, then one st 10[12:14] times. 80[84:88] sts. Cont without shaping until armholes measure 7½[8:8½]in from beg, ending with a K row.
Shape neck and shoulder
Next row P26[27:28] sts, turn and leave rem sts on holder.
Complete this side first. Cast off at neck edge at beg of next and every alt row 3 sts twice and 2 sts twice, *at the same time* cast off at armhole edge on every alt row 4 sts 3 times and 4[5:6] sts once.
With RS of work facing, rejoin yarn to rem sts, cast off first 28[30:32] sts, P to end.
K one row.
Complete to match first side, reversing shaping.

Left front
Using No.9 needles and B, cast on 34 sts for pocket. Beg with a K row work 5in st st, ending with a K row. Leave sts on holder.
Using No.11 needles and A, cast on 50[54:58] sts. Work 10 rows rib as given for back, inc one st at end of last row on 32in size only and dec one st at end of last row on 36in size only. 51[54:57] sts. Break off A. Change to No.9 needles. Join in B. Beg with a K row cont in st st until work measures 6in from beg, ending with a P row.
Pocket top
Next row (K2, P2) 9 times, K to end.
Next row P15[18:21] sts, *K2, P2, rep from * to end.
Rep these 2 rows 4 times more.
Next row K2, cast off next 34 sts in rib, K to end.
Next row P15[18:21] sts, P across sts of pocket lining, P2.
Cont in st st until work measures 16½in from beg, then change to reverse st st as given for back.
Cont without shaping until work measures same as back to underarm, ending with a K row.
Shape armhole
Cast off at beg of next and every alt row 4 sts once, 2 sts twice, and one st 5[6:7] times. 38[40:42] sts.
Cont without shaping until armhole measures 3½[4:4½]in from beg, ending with a P row.
Shape neck
Cast off at beg of next and every alt row 4[5:6] sts once, 3 sts twice, 2 sts twice, one st 4 times, then one st at beg of every 4th row 4 times.
Cont without shaping until armhole measures 7½[8:8½]in from beg, ending with a K row.
Shape shoulder
Cast off at beg of next and every alt row 4 sts 3 times and 4[5:6] sts once.

Right front
Work as given for left front, reversing shaping.

Sleeves
Using No.9 needles and B, cast on 74[77:80] sts. Beg with a K row work 6in st st, ending with a K row. Change to reverse st st as given for back.
Cont in reversed st st until sleeve measures 10in from beg, ending with a K row.
Shape top
Cast off at beg of next and every row 4 sts twice, 2 sts 4 times, one st 20[22:24] times, 2 sts 8 times,

3 sts 4 times and 10[11:12] sts once.

Edging
Join shoulder seams. Using No.11 circular Twin Pin, A and with RS of work facing, K up 134[138:142] sts up right front edge, 134[138:142] sts round neck, then 134[138:142] sts down left front edge.
Next row (P2, K2) 33[34:35] times, K up 1, P2, K up 1, K2, (P2, K2) 33[34:35] times, K up 1, P2, K up 1, *K2, P2, rep from * to end.
Cont in rib as now set for 2 more rows, inc at corners on every row.
Next row (buttonhole row) Rib 10[12:14] sts, (cast off 2 sts, rib 18 sts) 6 times, cast off 2 sts, rib to end, still inc at corners.
Next row Rib to end, still inc at corners and casting on 2 sts above those cast off in previous row.
Work 3 more rows, still inc at corners. Cast off in rib.

Collar
Using No.11 needles and A, cast on 138[142:148] sts. Work in rib as given for back, *at the same time* working (2 rows A, 2 rows B, 4 rows A, 4 rows B) 3 times, K the first row at each change of colour. Cast off in rib. Using No.11 needles, B and with RS of work facing, K up 30 sts along side of collar. Rib 2 rows. Cast off in rib. Work other side in same way.

To make up
Press each piece under a damp cloth with a warm iron. Set in sleeves. Join side and sleeve seams. Sew collar to inside neck, at beg of ribbed edging. Sew down pocket linings. Press seams. Sew on buttons. Fold cuff edge of sleeve over double to RS.

6 Checked twinset with plain bands at the edges

Sizes
To fit 34/36in bust
Jersey length to shoulder, 20½in
Jacket length to shoulder, 21in
Sleeve seam, 17½in
Tension
6 sts and 8 rows to 1in over st st worked on No.9 needles
Materials
Jersey 8 balls Sunbeam Hyland Double Knitting in main shade, A
7 balls of contrast colour, B
Jacket 11 balls in main shade, A
9 balls of contrast colour, B
One pair No.9 needles; One pair No.11 needles
One No.11 circular Twin Pin

Jersey back
Using No.11 needles and A, cast on 110 sts. Work 1½in g st. Change to No.9 needles. Commence patt. Join in B.
1st row K4 A, *6 B, 6 A, rep from * to last 10 sts, 6 B, 4 A.
2nd row P as 1st row.
Rep last 2 rows twice more and first of them once more.
8th row P4 B, *6 A, 6 B, rep from * to last 10 sts, 6 A, 4 B.
9th row K as 8th row.
Rep last 2 rows twice more and first of them once more. These 14 rows form patt and are rep throughout. Cont in patt until work measures 13½in from beg, *at the same time* inc one st at each end of next and every foll 20th row until there are 116 sts, ending with a P row.

Shape armholes
Cast off at beg of next and every row 4 sts 4 times. 3 sts twice, 2 sts 6 times, then one st 8 times. 74 sts. Cont without shaping until armholes measure 7in from beg, ending with a P row.
Shape neck and shoulder
Next row Patt 23, turn and leave rem sts on holder.
Complete this side first. Cast off at beg of next and every alt row 3 sts 3 times, *at the same time* cast off at armhole edge on every alt row 5 sts twice and 4 sts once.
With RS of work facing, sl first 28 sts on to holder for centre back neck, rejoin yarn to hem sts, patt to end. Complete to match first side, reversing shaping.

Front
Work as given for back until armholes measure 5½in from beg, ending with a P row.
Shape neck
Next row Patt 29 sts, turn and leave rem sts on holder.
Complete this side first. Cast off at beg of next and every alt row 4 sts once, 3 sts once and 2 sts 3 times, ending with a P row.
Shape shoulder
Next row Cast off 5 sts, patt to last 2 sts, K2 tog.
Next row Patt to end.
Rep last 2 rows once more. Cast off rem 4 sts. With RS of work facing, sl first 16 sts on to holder for centre front neck, rejoin yarn to rem sts and patt to end. Complete to match first side, reversing shaping.

Neckband
Join right shoulder seam. Using No.11 needles, A and with RS of work facing, K up 26 sts down left front neck, K across front neck sts, K up 26 sts up right front neck and 12 sts down right back neck, K across back neck sts, then K up 12 sts up left back neck. 120 sts. Work 1in g st, ending with a RS row. Cast off.

Armbands
Join left shoulder seam. Using No.11 needles, A and with RS of work facing, K up 126 sts round armhole. Work 1in g st, ending with a RS row. Cast off.

To make up
Press each piece under a damp cloth with a warm iron. Join side seams. Press seams.

Jacket back
Using No.11 needles and A, cast on 121 sts. Work 1½in g st. Change to No.9 needles. Commence patt.
1st row K2 A, * 3 B, 3 A, rep from * to last 5 sts, 3 B, 2 A.
2nd row P as 1st row.
Rep last 2 rows once more.
5th row K2 B, * 3 A, 3 B, rep from * to last 5 sts, 3 A, 2 B.
6th row P as 5th row.
Rep last 2 rows once more. These 8 rows form patt and are rep throughout. Cont in patt until work measures 13½in from beg, ending with a P row.
Shape armholes
Cast off at beg of next and every row 4 sts twice. 3 sts 4 times, 2 sts 6 times, then one st 8 times. 81 sts. Cont without shaping until armholes measure 7½in from beg, ending with a P row.
Shape neck and shoulder
Next row Patt 24 sts, turn and leave rem sts on holder.
Complete this side first. Cast off at beg of next and every alt row 2 sts 3 times, *at the same time* cast off at armhole edge on every alt row 6 sts 3 times. With RS of work facing, rejoin yarn to rem sts, cast off first 33 sts, patt to end. Complete to match first side, reversing shaping.

Left front
Using No.11 needles and A, cast on 57 sts. Work 1½in g st. Change to No.9 needles. Commence patt.
1st row K2 A, *3 B, 3 A, rep from * to last st, 1 A.
2nd row P4 A, *3 B, 3 A, rep from * to last 5 sts, 3 B, 2 A.
Rep last 2 rows once more.
5th row K2 B, *3 A, 3 B, rep from * to last st, 1 B.
6th row P4 B, *3 A, 3 B, rep from * to last 5 sts, 3 A, 2 B.
Rep last 2 rows once more. These 8 rows form patt and are rep throughout. Cont in patt until work measures same as back to underarm, ending with a P row.
Shape armhole
Cast off at beg of next and every alt row 4 sts once, 3 sts twice, 2 sts 3 times, then one st 4 times. 37 sts. Cont without shaping until armhole measures 3½in from beg, ending with a RS row.
Shape neck
Cast off at beg of next and every alt row 6 sts once, 3 sts once, 2 sts 3 times, then one st 4 times. 18 sts. Cont without shaping until armhole measures same as back to shoulder, ending with a P row.
Shape shoulder
Cast off at beg of next and every alt row 6 sts 3 times.

Right front
Work as given for left front, reversing patt rows and all shaping.

Sleeves
Using No.11 needles and A, cast on 55 sts. Work 1½in g st. Change to No.9 needles. Cont in patt as given for back, inc one st at each end of every 8th row until there are 83 sts. Cont without shaping until sleeve measures 17½in from beg, ending with a WS row.
Shape top
Cast off at beg of next and every row 4 sts twice, 3 sts 4 times, 2 sts 6 times, one st 16 times, 2 sts 6 times, 3 sts 4 times, then 11 sts once.

Mock pocket top (make 2)
Using No.11 needles and A, cast on 33 sts. Work 1½in g st, ending with a RS row. Cast off.

Edging
Join shoulder seams. Using No.11 circular Twin Pin, A and with RS of work facing, K up 110 sts up right front edge, 140 sts round neck, then 110 sts down left front edge. 360 sts. Work 1in g st, inc one st at each side of corners on every alt row, ending with a RS row. Cast off.

To make up
Press each piece under a damp cloth with a warm iron. Set in sleeves. Join side and sleeve seams. Press seams. Sew on mock pocket tops, 4½in from lower edge.

7 Jersey and cardigan with cap sleeves in three colours

Sizes
To fit 32in bust
Jersey length to shoulder, 20in
Sleeve seam, 17in
Jacket length to shoulder, 21in
Tension
7 sts and 10 rows to 1in over patt worked on No.10 needles with 4 ply; 7 sts and 8 rows to 1in over rib patt worked on No.9 needles with Double Knitting
Materials
Jersey 8 balls each of Sunbeam Courtelle Nylon 4 ply in 3 contrast colours, A, B and C

8

*Unusual long striped
jersey with long sleeves and
a polo collar, worked in
seven colours. It can easily
be adapted to fewer colours.*

*Knit
Sizes to fit 81.5[86.5:91.5]
cm (32[34:36]in) bust*

*

9

*Stunning pull-on cap
and matching double
sided scarf.*

*Knit
Size: scarf 8½ inches
wide by 60 inches long.
Cap to fit an average head*

***

One pair No.10 needles; One pair No.12 needles
Jacket 16 balls of Sunbeam Courtelle Nylon
Double Knitting in main shade, A
3 balls each of contrast colours, B and C
One pair No.9 needles
6 buttons

Jersey back
Using No.12 needles and A, cast on 117 sts. Work
6 rows g st. Change to No.10 needles. Commence
patt. Join in C.
1st row (RS) Using C, K to end.
2nd row Using C, K to end.
3rd row Using C, P to end.
4th row Using C, K to end. Join in B.
5th–8th rows Using B as 1st–4th rows.
9th–12th rows Using A as 1st–4th rows.
These 12 rows form patt and are rep throughout.
Cont in patt until work measures 13in from beg,
ending with a WS row.
Shape armholes
Cast off at beg of next and every row 3 sts twice,
2 sts 8 times, one st 4 times, then dec one st at
each end of every 4th row 3 times. 85 sts. Cont
without shaping until armholes measure 7in from
beg, ending with a WS row.
Shape neck and shoulder
Cast off 4 sts at beg of next 4 rows.
Next row Cast off 3 sts, patt 15 sts, turn and leave
rem sts on holder.
Complete this side first. Cast off at neck edge on
next and every alt row 2 sts 3 times, *at the same time*
cast off at armhole edge on every alt row 3 sts
3 times.
With RS of work facing, rejoin yarn to rem sts,
cast off first 33 sts, patt to end. Complete to match
first side, reversing shaping.

Front
Work as given for back until armholes measure
5in from beg, ending with a WS row.
Shape neck
Next row Patt 37 sts, turn and leave rem sts on
holder.
Complete this side first. Cast off at neck edge on
next and every alt row 3 sts twice, 2 sts 3 times,
then one st 3 times, ending with a WS row.
Shape shoulder
Next row Cast off 4 sts, patt to last 2 sts, K2 tog.
Next row Patt to end.
Rep last 2 rows once more. Cast off at beg of next
and every alt row 3 sts 4 times.
With RS of work facing, rejoin yarn to rem sts,
cast off first 11 sts, patt to end. Complete to match
first side, reversing shaping.

Sleeves
Using No.12 needles and A, cast on 49 sts.
1st row K1, *P1, K1, rep from * to end.
2nd row P1, *K1, P1, rep from * to end.
Rep these 2 rows for 3in, ending with a 2nd row.
Change to No.10 needles. Cont in patt as given for
back, inc one st at each end of next and every
foll 8th row until there are 81 sts. Cont without
shaping until sleeve measures 17in from beg,
ending with a WS row.
Shape top
Cast off at beg of next and every row 3 sts twice,
2 sts 6 times, one st 10 times, then dec one st at
each end of every 3rd row 8 times. Cast off at
beg of next and every row one st 8 times, 2 sts
6 times, 3 sts twice then 11 sts once.

Collar
Using No.10 needles and length of contrast yarn,
cast on 75 sts. Break off contrast yarn. Join in C.
Cont in striped patt as given for back until work
measures 16in from beg, ending with a 3rd patt
row of stripe in A. Take out contrast colour at
cast on edge. Using A, graft beg and end of collar
tog.

To make up
Join shoulder seams. Set in sleeves. Join side and
sleeve seam. Sew on collar with WS of collar
outside, then fold collar over to RS. Press seams.

Jacket back
Using No.9 needles and A, cast on 129 sts. Work
8 rows rib as given for jersey. Join in C.
Next row Using C, K to end.
Next row Using C, rib to end.
Rep last row 6 times more. Break off C. Join in B.
Using B, rep last 8 rows. Break off B. Using A,
rep last 8 rows. Using A, cont in rib until work
measures 12in from beg, ending with a WS row.
Shape sleeves
Inc one st at each end of next and foll alt row.
Rib one row. Cast on at beg of next and every
row 2 sts twice, 3 sts 6 times, then 4 sts twice.
163 sts. Cont without shaping until work measures
17½in from beg, then work 8 rows B, 8 rows C, as
given at beg of jacket back. Cont in A only until
work measures 20½in, ending with a WS row.
Shape neck
Next row Rib 64 sts, turn and leave rem sts on
holder.
Complete this side first. Cast off at beg of next
and every alt row 4 sts twice, then 3 sts once,
ending with a WS row. Cast off rem 53 sts.
With RS of work facing, rejoin yarn to rem sts,
cast off first 35 sts, rib to end. Complete to match
first side, reversing shaping.

Left front
Using No.9 needles and A, cast on 69 sts. Work
as given for back to beg of sleeves, ending with
a WS row.
Shape sleeve
Inc one st at beg of next and foll alt row, ending
with a WS row. Cast on at beg of next and every
alt row 2 sts once, 3 sts 3 times, then 4 sts once.
86 sts. Cont without shaping until work measures
17½in from beg, ending with a WS row. Join in B.
Next row Using B, K to end.
Next row Using B, rib to end.
Rep last row 3 times more, ending at front edge.
Shape neck
Keeping striped patt correct to match back, cast
off at beg of next and every alt row 10 sts once,
4 sts twice, 3 sts twice, 2 sts 3 times, then one st
3 times. 53 sts. Cont without shaping until work
measures same as back to shoulder, ending with
a WS row. Cast off.
Mark positions for 6 buttons, first to come at beg
of C stripe at beg, and last to come in centre of
B stripe at neck with 4 more evenly spaced
between.

Right front
Work as given for left front, reversing shaping,
making buttonholes as markers are reached as foll:
Next row (RS) Rib 3 sts, cast off 3 sts, rib to end.
Next row Rib to end, casting on 3 sts above those
cast off on previous row.

Neckband
Join shoulder seams. Using No.9 needles, A and
with RS of work facing, K up 103 sts round neck.
Work ¾in rib. Cast off in rib.

To make up
Join side and sleeve seams. Sew on buttons.

8 Unusual, long striped jersey with polo collar

Sizes
To fit 32[34:36]in bust
Length to shoulder, 33[33½:34]in
Sleeve seam, 18½in

The figures in brackets [] refer to the 34 and 36in
sizes respectively
Tension
7 sts and 9 rows to 1in over st st worked on No.10
needles
Materials
Sunbeam Hyland 4 ply Superwash
3[3:4] balls in main shade, A
2[3:3] balls of contrast colours, B and C
2[2:2] balls of contrast colours, D, E, F and G
One pair No.10 needles
One pair No.12 needles
Set of 4 No.12 needles pointed at both ends

Back
Using No.12 needles and A, cast on 123[131:139]
sts.
1st row K1, *P1, K1, rep from * to end.
2nd row P1, *K1, P1, rep from * to end.
Rep these 2 rows 5 times more. Join in B. Using B,
rib 12 more rows. Break off B. Change to No.10
needles. Beg with a K row cont in st st for 12 rows
more. Join in contrast colours as required,
working 12 rows each in C, D, E, F, G, C, A, B, A,
B, A, *at the same time* dec one st at each end of every
20th row until 111[119:127] sts rem. Cont in st st
working 12 rows each in C, D, E, F, G, then
6 rows C, *at the same time* inc one st at each end
of 1st and every foll 16th row until there are
119[127:135] sts. 26in.
Shape armholes
Cont in C, cast off at beg of next and every row
6 sts twice, then 2[3:4] sts 4 times, ending with
a P row.
Cont in striped patt, dec one st at each end of next
and every alt row until 91[95:99] sts rem. Cont
without shaping until armholes measure 7[7½:8]in
from beg, ending with a P row.
Shape neck and shoulder
Next row Cast off 6 sts, K25[26:27] sts, turn and
leave rem sts on holder.
Complete this side first.
Next row Cast off 4 sts, P to end.
Next row Cast off 6 sts, K to end.
Rep last 2 rows once more. P 1 row. Cast off rem
5[6:7] sts.
With RS of work facing, sl first 29[31:33] sts on to
holder for centre back neck, rejoin yarn to rem sts
and K to end.
Complete to match first side,
reversing shaping.

Front
Work as given for back until armholes measure
5[5½:6]in from beg, ending with a P row.
Shape neck
Next row K35[36:37] sts, turn and leave rem sts
on holder.
Complete this side first.
Cast off at beg of next and every alt row 2 sts
4 times. Dec one st at neck edge on foll 4 alt rows,
ending with a P row.
Shape shoulder
Cast off at beg of next and every alt row 6 sts
3 times and 5[6:7] sts once.
With RS of work facing, sl first 21[23:25] sts on to
holder for centre front neck, rejoin yarn to rem sts
and K to end.
Complete to match first side,
reversing shaping.

Sleeves
Using No.12 needles and A, cast on 61[63:65] sts.
Work in rib as given for back. Change to No.10
needles. Beg with a K row, cont in st st, inc one
st at each end of every 12th[12th:10th] row until
there are 83[87:91] sts, *at the same time* cont in
striped patt working 12 rows each of A, B, A,
C, D, E, F, G, C, A, B, A. 234 rows from beg.
Shape top
Using B, cast off 6 sts at beg of next 2 rows. Cont
in striped patt, working 10 more rows B, 12 A,

12 C, 8[10:12] D, *at the same time* dec one st at each end of next and every alt row •13[14:15] times, ending with a P row. Cast off at beg of next and every row 2 sts 12 times, 3 sts 4 times and 9[11:13] sts once.

Collar
Join shoulder seams. Using set of 4 No.12 needles, C and with RS of work facing, K up 10 sts down right back neck, K across back neck sts, K up 10 sts up left back neck and 24 sts down left front neck, K across front neck sts, then K up 24 sts up right front neck. 118[122:126] sts. Cont in rounds of K1, P1 rib working 11 rounds C, then 12 rounds each of D, E, F, G, C, A, B and 11 rounds in A. Cast off in A.
108 rounds. 12in.

To make up
Press each piece under a damp cloth with a warm iron. Set in sleeves. Join side and sleeve seams. Press seams.

9 Pull-on cap and matching scarf

Sizes
Scarf 8½in wide and 60in long
Cap to fit an average head
Tension
5½ sts and 7 rows to 1in over st st worked on No.8 needles
Materials
15 balls Wendy Double Knitting Nylonised in main shade, A
3 balls of contrast colour, B
3 balls of contrast colour, C
1 ball of contrast colour, D
One No.8 circular Twin Pin
Set of 4 No.8 needles pointed at both ends
One No.10 circular Twin Pin

Scarf
Using No.8 circular Twin Pin and A, cast on 96 sts. Work 4 rounds st st. **. Join in D, work 2 rounds D. Join in C, work 2 rounds C. Commence patt.
9th round *K2 A, 5 C, 1 A, rep from * to end.
10th round As 9th.
11th round *K3 A, 3 C, 2 A, rep from * to end.
12th round As 11th.
13th round *K4 A, 1 C, 3 A, rep from * to end.
14th round As 13th.
15th round *K1 C, 7 A, rep from * to end.
16th round *K2 C, 5 A, 1 C, rep from * to end.
17th round *K1 A, 2 C, 3 A, 2 C, rep from * to end.
18th round *K1 B, 1 A, 2 C, 1 A, 2 C, 1 A, rep from * to end.
19th round *K1 A, 1 B, 1 A, 3 C, 1 A, 1 B, rep from * to end.
20th–29th rounds Work from 18th round back to 9th round.
Work 2 rounds C, 2 rounds D and 4 rounds A.
38th round *K1 B, 7 A, rep from * to end.
39th round *K2 B, 5 A, 1 B, rep from * to end.
40th round As 38th. **.
Work 4 rounds A.
45th round *K5 A, 1 B, 2 A, rep from * to end.
46th round *K4 A, 3 B, 1 A, rep from * to end.
47th round As 45th.
Rep last 14 rounds until work measures 54in from beg, ending with a 4th round in A. Rep from ** to **. Cast off.

To make up
Press work under a damp cloth with a warm iron. Using A or colours required, make fringe along each end of scarf.

Cap
Using No.10 circular Twin Pin and A, cast on 120 sts. Work in rounds of K1, P1 rib for 2½in. Change to set of 4 No.8 needles and work from ** to ** as given for scarf.
Shape top
1st round Using A, K to end.
2nd round Using A, *K2 tog, K6, rep from * to end. 105 sts.
3rd round As 1st.
4th round Using A, *K2 tog, K5, rep from * to end. 90 sts.
5th round *K4 A, 1 B, 1 A, rep from * to end.
6th round *K3 A, 3 B, rep from * to end.
7th round As 5th.
8th round As 1st.
9th round Using A, *K2 tog, K4, rep from * to end. 75 sts.
Using A only, cont dec in this way on every 4th round 3 times more. 30 sts. Work 1 round without shaping.
23rd round *K2 tog, rep from * to end.
Break off yarn, thread through rem sts, draw up and fasten off.

To make up
Press as given for scarf. Fold ribbing in half to WS and sl st down.

10 Four variations on a toddler's dress

Sizes
To fit 20[22:24]in chest
Length to shoulder, 15¼[16¾:18¼]in, adjustable
Long sleeve seam, 8[9¼:10½]in, adjustable
Short sleeve seam, 2[2½:3]in
Side edge of pants, 6[7:8]in, excluding frill
The figures in brackets [] refer to the 22 and 24in sizes respectively
Tension
7½ sts and 10 rows to 1in over st st worked on No.11 needles
Materials
Robin Tricel/Nylon Perle 4 ply
Dress A 4[4:5] balls in main shade, A
2[2:3] balls of contrast colour, B
Pants A 2[2:2] balls of contrast colour, B
Oddments of main shade, A
Dress B 5[5:6] balls in main shade, A
1[1:1] ball each of contrast colours, B and C
Pants B 2[2:2] balls in main shade, A
Oddments of contrast colours, B and C
Dress C 5[5:6] balls in main shade, A
2[2:3] balls each of contrast colours, B and C
Pants C 2[2:2] balls in main shade, A
Oddments of contrast colours, B and C
Dress D 5[5:6] balls in main shade, A
1[1:1] ball each of contrast colours, B and C
Pants D 2[2:2] balls in main shade, A
Oddments of contrast colours, B and C
One pair No.11 needles
10[10:12]in zip fastener
1¼yd narrow ribbon, optional
Waist length of elastic
Narrow elastic for legs

Dress A back
Using No.11 needles and A, cast on 145[158: 171] sts. K 5 rows g st. Commence skirt patt.
1st row (RS) *K2, inc 1 by picking up and K loop lying between needles, K4, sl 1 P-wise, K2 tog, psso, K4, inc 1, rep from * to last 2 sts, K2.
2nd row P to end.
These 2 rows form chevron patt. Cont in patt until work measures 5[5½:6]in from beg, measured at side edge and ending with a WS row.
Shape skirt
Next row (dec row) *K2, inc 1, K1, sl 1 P-wise,

K1, psso, K1, sl 1 P-wise, K2 tog, psso, K1, K2 tog, K1, inc 1, rep from * to last 2 sts, K2. 123[134: 145] sts.
Next row P to end.
Next row *K2, inc 1, K3, sl 1 P-wise, K2 tog, psso, K3, inc 1, rep from * to last 2 sts, K2.
Rep last 2 rows until work measures 6[6½:7]in from beg, ending with a WS row.
Next row (dec row) *K2, inc 1, K1, sl 1 P-wise, K1, psso, sl 1 P-wise, K2 tog, psso, K2 tog, K1, inc 1, rep from * to last 2 sts, K2. 101[110:119] sts.
Next row P to end.
****Next row** *K2, inc 1, K2, sl 1 P-wise, K2 tog, psso, K2, inc 1, rep from * to last 2 sts, K2.**
Rep last 2 rows until work measures 6½[7:7½]in from beg, or required length to waist less 1½in, ending with a WS row.***
Divide for back opening
Next row Patt 49[53:58] sts, K2 tog, turn and leave rem sts on holder. 50[54:59] sts.
Complete this side first. Keeping patt and number of sts correct, cont in patt until work measures 8[8½:9]in from beg, or required length to waist, ending with a WS row.**** Break off A. Join in B and complete using B only.
Shape waist
Next row *K4, sl 1 P-wise, K2 tog, psso, K2, rep from * 4[5:5] times more, K5[K0:K5] sts. 40[42:47] sts.
Ribbon slotting
Next row K to end.
Next row (eyelet hole row) *K1, yfwd, K2 tog, rep from * to last 1[0:2] sts, K1[0:2].
Next row K to end.
Beg with a K row, cont in st st until work measures 3¼[3¾:4¼]in from eyelet hole row, ending with a P row.
Shape armhole
Cast off 4[4:6] sts at beg of next row. P 1 row.
Dec one st at beg of next and foll 4[5:6] alt rows. 31[32:34] sts. Cont without shaping until armhole measures 4[4½:5]in from beg, ending with a P row.
Shape shoulder
Cast off at beg of next and every alt row 6 sts twice and 6[6:8] sts once. Leave rem 13[14:14] sts on holder for centre back neck.
With RS of work facing, rejoin A to rem sts, K0[K2 tog: K0], patt to end. 50[54:59] sts.
Complete to match first side, reversing shaping.

Dress A front
Work as given for back to ***. Cont across all sts, omitting back opening, and work as given for back to ****. Break off A. Join in B and complete using B only.
Shape waist
Next row (dec row) *K4, sl 1 P-wise, K2 tog, K2, rep from * to last 2 sts, K2. 79[86:93] sts.
Ribbon slotting
Next row K to end.
Next row (eyelet hole row) *K1, yfwd, K2 tog, rep from * to last 1[2:0] sts, K1[2:0].
Next row K to end.
Beg with a K row cont in st st until work measures same as back to underarm, ending with a P row.
Shape armholes
Cast off 4[4:6] sts at beg of next 2 rows. Dec one st at each end of next and foll 4[5:6] alt rows. 61[66:67] sts. Cont without shaping until armholes measure 2¾[3:3¼]in from beg, ending with a P row.
Shape neck
Next row K24[26:26] sts, turn and leave rem sts on holder.
Complete this side first. Dec one st at neck edge on next and every alt row until 18[18:20] sts rem. Cont without shaping until armhole measures same as back to shoulder, ending at armhole edge.
Shape shoulder
Cast off at beg of next and every alt row 6 sts

10

*Variations on a theme—from
left to right, dresses C, A, D, B*

Knit
*Sizes to fit 51.0[56.0:61.0]cm
(20[22:24]in) chest*

***

twice and 6[6:8] sts once.

With RS of work facing, sl first 13[14:15] sts onto holder and leave for centre neck, rejoin yarn to rem sts and K to end. Complete to match first side, reversing shaping.

Frilled sleeve

Join shoulder seams. Using No.11 needles, B and with RS of work facing, K up 69[73:77] sts round armhole. K 4 rows g st.**

Next row Cast off 12[14:16] sts, K into front then into back of each of next 45 sts including last st left after casting off, cast off 12[14:16] sts. 90 sts. Break off B. Join in A.

Next row *K2, inc 1, K3, sl 1 P-wise, K2 tog, psso, K3, inc 1, rep from * to last 2 sts, K2.

Next row K2, P to last 2 sts, K2.

Rep last 2 rows 7 times more. K 5 rows g st. Cast off.

Neckband

Using No.11 needles, B and with RS of work facing, K across sts on left back neck holder, K up 18[20:22] sts down left front neck, K across sts on front neck holder, K up 18[20:22] sts up right front neck and K across sts on right back neck holder. 75[82:87] sts. K 4 rows g st. Cast off.

To make up

Press each piece under a damp cloth with a cool iron. Join side seams. Sew in zip to back opening to come to top of neckband. Cut ribbon in half, or using A make 2 twisted cords 20[24:28]in long. Thread ribbon or cord through eyelet holes at waist to tie at centre front, securely sewing each cord on either side of centre back opening. Press seams.

Dress B back

Work as given for Dress A back to ****, casting on in A and working skirt in stripes of 6 rows B, 6 rows C and 6 rows A throughout. Complete using A only.

Dress B front

Work as given for Dress A front, working skirt and completing as given for Dress B back.

Short sleeves

Using No.11 needles and A, cast on 74[74:74] sts. K 5 rows g st. Join in B. Beg with chevron patt row marked ** to **, as given for dress back, work 6 rows patt ending with a WS row. Break off B. Join in C and work 6 more rows patt. Break off C. Cont using A only.

Next row (dec row) K2 tog[K4:K10], *K2 tog, K2, rep from * to last 4[2:8] sts, (K2 tog) twice [K2:K8]. 54[57:60] sts.

Beg with a P row cont in st st until sleeve measures 2[2½:3]in from beg, ending with a P row.

Shape top

Cast off 4[4:6] sts at beg of next 2 rows. Dec one st at each end of next and every alt row until 16 sts rem, ending with a P row. Cast off 2 sts 6 times. Cast off rem 4 sts.

Neckband

Join shoulder seams. Using No.11 needles, A and with RS of work facing, work as given for Dress A.

To make up

Press as given for Dress A. Set in sleeves. Join side and sleeve seams. Complete as for Dress A.

Dress C back

Work as given for Dress A back to ****, casting on in A and working skirt in A throughout. Complete as given for Dress A, working bodice in stripes of 4 rows B, 4 rows C and 4 rows A throughout.

Dress C front

Work as given for Dress A front, working skirt and completing as given for Dress C back.

Long sleeves

Using No.11 needles and A, cast on 42[45:48] sts. K 5 rows g st. Join in B. Beg with a K row cont in st st, working stripes of 4 rows B, 4 rows C and 4 rows A throughout, *at the same time* inc one st at each end of 15th and every foll 8th row until there are 54[57:60] sts. Cont without shaping until sleeve measures 8[9½:10½]in from beg, or required length to underarm, ending with a P row and same stripe as back and front armholes.

Shape top

Keeping striped patt correct, work as given for short sleeves.

Neckband

Work as given for Dress B.

To make up

Work as given for Dress B.

Dress D back

Work as given for Dress A back to ****, casting on in A and working skirt in stripes of 4 rows A, 2 rows B, 4 rows C and 2 rows B throughout. Complete using A only.

Dress D front

Work as given for Dress A front, working skirt and completing as given for Dress D back.

Neckband

Work as given for Dress A.

Armbands

Work as given for frilled sleeve to **. Cast off.

To make up

Work as given for Dress A.

Pants left side (all versions)

Using No.11 needles and correct sequence of colours to match skirt of dress required, cast on 119[128:137] sts. K 5 rows g st. Commence patt.

1st row *K2, inc 1, K2, sl 1 P-wise, K2 tog, psso, K2, inc 1, rep from * to last 2 sts, K2.

2nd row P to end.

Keeping patt correct as now set, work 10 more rows. Break off contrast colours and complete to match bodice of dress required.

Next row (dec row) *K4, sl 1 P-wise, K2 tog, psso, K2, rep from * to last 2 sts, K2. 93[100:107] sts.

Next row K to end.

Next row (eyelet hole row) *K1, yfwd, K2 tog, rep from * to last 0[1:2] sts, K0[1:2].

Next row K to end.

Beg with a K row work 2 rows st st.

Shape crutch

Cont in st st, cast off for back edge 3 sts at beg of next and foll alt row, then dec one st at same edge on every foll 4th row 4 times in all, *at the same time* cast off 2 sts at front edge on foll alt row and dec one st at same edge on every alt row 8 times in all. 73[80:87] sts. Cont without shaping until work measures 6[7:8]in from eyelet hole row, ending with a P row.

Shape back

Next row K to last 24 sts, turn.

Next row Sl 1, P to end.

Next row K to last 32 sts, turn.

Next row Sl 1, P to end.

Cont working 8 sts less in this way on next and every alt row 4[5:6] times more.

Next row K to end.

Next row (hemline) K all sts tbl.

Beg with a K row work 8 rows st st. Cast off.

Pants right side

Work as given for left side, reversing all shaping.

To make up

Press as given for dress. Join centre front and centre back seams. Join leg seams. Fold waistband to WS at hemline and sl st down. Press seams. Thread elastic through waistband. Thread elastic through eyelet holes of legs.

11 *Patterned mittens*

Size

To fit average hand

Tension

7½ sts and 10 rows to 1in over st st worked on No.11 needles

Materials

2 balls Patons Purple Heather 4 ply
One pair No.11 needles
One pair No.12 needles

Right mitten

Using No.12 needles cast on 51 sts.

1st row *K1, P1, rep from * to last st, K1.

2nd row K1, *K1, P1, rep from * to end.

Rep these 2 rows until work measures 2in, ending with a 1st row.

Next row K1, *inc in next st, rib 6, rep from * 6 times more, P1. 58 sts.

Change to No.11 needles. Commence patt.

1st row K4, (P2 tog) twice, yon, (K1, yfwd) twice, K1, yrn, (P2 tog) 4 times, yon, (K1, yfwd) twice, K1, yrn, (P2 tog) twice, K32.

2nd row K1, P to last st, K1.

3rd row K to end.

4th row As 2nd.

These 4 rows form patt. Cont in patt until work measures 3¼in from beg, ending with a WS row.

Shape thumb

Next row Patt 30 sts, K up 1, K2, K up 1, K26. Work 1 row.

Next row Patt 30 sts, K up 1, K4, K up 1, K26. Work 1 row.

Cont inc in this way on every alt RS row, keeping the inc sts in st st and working in patt for main part of mitten, until there are 20 sts in thumb shaping. 76 sts in all.

Next row K1, P25, sl next 20 sts on to contrast thread and leave for thumb, turn and cast on 2 sts to replace original 2 sts for thumb, turn and P to end. 58 sts.

Cont in patt until 64 rows have been worked, 16 complete patts.

Shape top

Next row K2, K2 tog, K5, K1, yfwd, K1, yrn, (P2 tog) 4 times, yon, K1, yfwd, K6, sl 1, K1, psso, K2, K2 tog, K22, sl 1, K1, psso, K2.

Next row K1, P to last st, K1.

Next row K2, K2 tog, K20, sl 1, K1, psso, K2, K2 tog, K20, sl 1, K1, psso, K2.

Next row K1, P to last st, K1.

Cont in this way working patt over 12 sts only, with st st at either side, dec on every RS row until 30 sts rem.

Next row (K2 tog) 15 times. 15 sts.

Work 1 row.

Next row (K3 tog) 5 times. 5 sts.

Break off yarn, thread through rem sts, draw up and fasten off.

Thumb

Return to sts left on contrast thread and place on needle, rejoin yarn and cast on one st. Using No.12 needles and beg with a K row, work in st st, dec one st at beg of 4th row and end of 9th row. 19 sts. Cont in st st until thumb measures 2in ending with a WS row.

Shape top

Next row K1, (K2 tog) 9 times. 10 sts.

Work 1 row.

Next row (K2 tog) 5 times. 5 sts.

Break off yarn, thread through rem sts, draw up

and fasten off.

Left mitten
Work as given for right mitten, reversing position of thumb and patt rows by working from end to beg, as foll:
1st row K32, (P2 tog) twice, yon, (K1, yfwd) twice, K1, yrn, (P2 tog) 4 times, yon, (K1, yfwd) twice, K1, yrn, (P2 tog) twice, K4.

To make up
Press under a damp cloth with a warm iron. Join side seam. Press seams.

12 Aran mittens

Size
To fit average hand
Tension
7½ sts and 10 rows to 1in over st st worked on No.11 needles
Materials
2 balls Patons Purple Heather 4 ply
One pair No.11 needles
One pair No.12 needles
Cable needle

Right mitten
Using No.12 needles cast on 51 sts.
1st row *K1, P1, rep from * to last st, K1.
2nd row K1, *K1, P1, rep from * to end.
Rep these 2 rows until work measures 2in, ending with a 1st row.
Next row K2, *inc in next st, rib 4, rep from * to last 4 sts, inc in next st, rib 3. 61 sts.
Change to No.11 needles. Commence patt.
1st row (K1, P1) twice, sl next 2 sts on to cable needle and hold at front of work, K2, K2 from cable needle, K2 – called Tw2F –, (P1, K1) twice, K 2nd st on left hand needle in front of first st, K first st and sl both sts off needle tog – called Cr2R –, K 2nd st on left hand needle tbl, K first st and sl both sts off needle tog – called Cr2L –, (K1, P1) twice, Tw2F, P1, (P1, K1) 16 times.
2nd row (K1, P1) 16 times, K1, P6, K1, P1, K1, P6, K1, P1, K1, P6, K2, P1, K1.
3rd row (K1, P1) twice, K2, sl next 2 sts on to cable needle and hold at back of work, K2, K2 from cable needle – called Tw2B –, P2, K1, Cr2R, K2, Cr2L, K1, P2, Tw2B, P1, (P1, K1) 16 times.
4th row (K1, P1) 16 times, K1, P6, K2, P8, K2, P6, K2, P1, K1.
5th row (K1, P1) twice, Tw2F, P1, K1, Cr2R, K4, Cr2L, K1, P1, Tw2F, P1, (P1, K1) 16 times.
6th row (K1, P1) 16 times, K1, P6, K1, P10, K1, P6, K2, P1, K1.
7th row (K1, P1) twice, Tw2B, P1, Cr2R, K6, Cr2L, P1, Tw2B, P1, (P1, K1) 16 times.
8th row As 6th.
9th row (K1, P1) twice, Tw2F, P1, K1, Cr2L, K6, Cr2R, P1, Tw2F, P1, (P1, K1) 16 times.
10th row As 4th.
11th row (K1, P1) twice, Tw2B, P2, Cr2L, K4, Cr2R, P2, Tw2B, P1, (P1, K1) 16 times.
12th row As 4th.
13th row (K1, P1) twice, Tw2F, P1, K1, Cr2L, K2, Cr2R, P1, K1, P1, Tw2F, P1, (P1, K1) 16 times.
14th row As 2nd.
15th row (K1, P1) twice, Tw2B, P2, K1, P1, Cr2L, Cr2R, P1, K1, P2, Tw2B, P1, (P1, K1) 16 times.
16th row (K1, P1) 16 times, K1, P6, K2, P1, K1, P4, K1, P1, K2, P6, K2, P1, K1.
These 16 rows form patt and are rep throughout, keeping Aran patt for back of mittens and moss st for palm.
Shape thumb
Next row Aran patt 35 sts as 1st row, K up 1,

K1, K up 1, moss st 25 sts.
Next row Moss st 25 sts, P3, Aran patt 35 sts as 2nd row.
Next row Aran patt 35 sts as 3rd row, K up 1, K3, K up 1, moss st 25 sts.
Cont in this way, inc 2 sts for thumb shaping on every alt RS row, working in patt and keeping thumb sts in st st. Cont until there are 21 sts in thumb shaping.
Next row Patt 25 sts, sl next 21 sts on to thread for thumb, inc in next st to replace st used at beg of thumb shaping, patt to end. 61 sts.
Cont in patt until 3 complete patts and 15 rows of 4th patt have been worked.
Shape top
Next row (WS) P1, *K1, P1, rep from * to end.
Next row (RS) P2 tog, (K1, P1) 13 times, K1, P3 tog, K1, (P1, K1) 13 times, P2 tog.
Next row K1, *P1, K1, rep from * to end.
Next row K2 tog, P1, (K1, P1) 12 times, K3 tog, P1, (K1, P1) 12 times, K2 tog.
Cont in rib, dec 4 sts on every RS row until 9 rows of rib have been worked and 45 sts rem.
Work 1 more row rib.
Next row K1, (K2 tog) 22 times.
P 1 more row.
Next row K1, (K2 tog) 11 times. 12 sts.
P 1 more row.
Break off yarn, thread through rem sts, draw up and fasten off.

Work thumb
Return to sts on thread and with RS of work facing K across 21 sts, inc in last st. 22 sts.
Beg with a P row, work in st st dec one st at beg of 5th row and one st at end of 10th row. 20 sts.
Cont in st st until thumb measures 2in from join with main part of mitten, ending with a WS row.
Shape top
Next row (K2 tog) 10 times. 10 sts.
P 1 more row.
Break off yarn, thread through rem sts, draw up and fasten off.

Left mitten
Work as given for right mitten, reversing position of thumb and patt rows.

To make up
Press lightly under a damp cloth with a warm iron, avoiding ribbing. Join side and thumb seams. Press seams.

13 Gloves with medallion motif

Size
To fit average hand
Tension
7½ sts and 10 rows to 1in over st st worked on No.11 needles
Materials
3 balls Patons Purple Heather 4 ply
Set of 4 No.11 needles pointed at both ends

Right Glove
Using No.11 needles cast on 48 sts and arrange them as foll: 24 sts on 1st needle, 12 sts on 2nd needle and 12 sts on 3rd needle.
Cuff
P 4 rounds.
Next round K all sts to form first fold line.
P 12 rounds.
Next round K all sts to form 2nd fold line.
K 22 rounds.
Commence patt.
1st round K11, yfwd, K1, yfwd, K to end.
2nd and every alt round until 12th K to end.
3rd round K10, yfwd, K2 tog, K1, sl 1, K1, psso, yfwd, K to end.

5th round K9, yfwd, K2 tog, K3, sl 1, K1, psso, yfwd, K to end.
7th round K8, yfwd, K2 tog, K2, yfwd, K1, yfwd, K2, sl 1, K1, psso, yfwd, K2, sl 1, K1, psso, yfwd, K to end.
9th round K7, yfwd, K2 tog, K2, yfdw, K2 tog, K1, sl 1, K1, psso, yfwd, K2, sl 1, K1, psso, yfwd, K to end.
11th round K6, K2 tog, yfwd, K2, K2 tog, yfwd, K3, yfwd, sl 1, K1, psso, K2, yfwd, sl 1, K1, psso, K to end.
Divide sts for thumb
12th round K24 (Note on left glove this should be K38), K next 10 sts and sl on to contrast thread for thumb, cast on 10 sts to replace them, K to end of round.
13th round As 11th.
14th and every alt round K to end.
15th round K7, K2 tog, yfwd, K2, K2 tog, yfwd, K1, yfwd, sl 1, K1, psso, K2, yfwd, sl 1, K1, psso, K to end.
17th round K8, K2 tog, yfwd, K1, K2 tog, K1, sl 1, K1, psso, K1, yfwd, sl 1, K1, psso, K to end.
19th round K9, K2 tog, yfwd, K3, yfwd, sl 1, K1, psso, K to end.
21st round K10, K2 tog, yfwd, K1, yfwd, sl 1, K1, psso, K to end.
23rd round K10, K2 tog, K1, sl 1, K1, psso, K to end.
24th round K to end.
This completes the medallion patt.
K 12 more rounds.
Divide sts for fingers
Sl next 5 sts on to 4th needle and leave, then sl next 38 sts on to thread, leaving last 5 sts on needle.
Little finger
With back of glove facing, K5 sts, cast on 3 sts, K5 sts from last needle. 13 sts.
Work in K rounds until finger measures 2in.
Shape top
K2 tog at beg of every foll round until 3 sts rem.
Break off yarn, thread through rem sts, draw up and fasten off.
Third finger
With back of glove facing, pick up and K6 sts from holding thread, cast on 3 sts, K last 6 sts from holding thread, pick up and K3 sts along cast on sts at base of little finger. 18 sts.
Work in K rounds until finger measures 2¾in, then shape top as for little finger.
Middle finger
Work as given for third finger but cont K rounds until finger measures 3in.
First finger
With back of glove facing, pick up and K rem 14 sts from thread, pick up 4 sts from cast on edge at base of middle finger. 18 sts.
Work as given for third finger.
Thumb
With palm of glove facing, pick up and K10 sts left on thread for thumb, pick up and K one st between lower and upper thumb opening, pick up and K9 sts along cast on edge, pick up and K one st between edges of thumb opening. 21 sts.
Arrange evenly on 3 needles and K 2 rounds.
Next round K, dec 1 st at each side of thumb opening over each of the picked up sts. 19 sts.
Cont to K in rounds until thumb measures 2in, then shape top as given for little finger.

Left Glove
Work as given for right glove altering thumb position by working note given in 12th round of medallion patt. Work fingers in reverse order.

To make up
Fasten off finger ends securely. Press glove lightly under slightly damp cloth with a warm iron. Turn in first fold of cuff and st st loosely to RS. Turn up rem part of cuff to RS. Give final light press to hold in place.

11-13

*Pretty patterned mittens,
warm tough Aran mitts and
gloves with a
diamond motif.*

*Knit
Sizes to fit
an average hand*

**

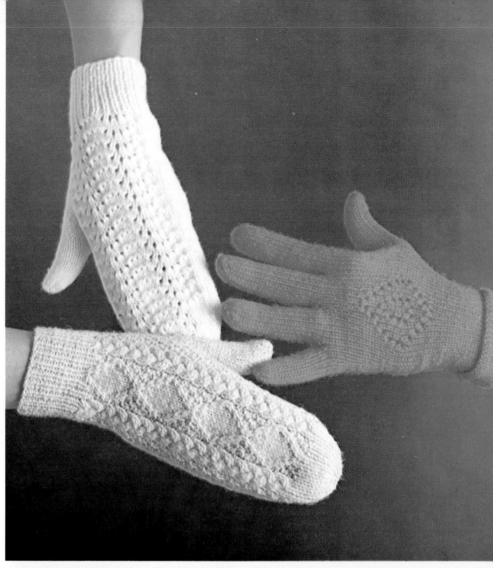

14,15

*Fashionable and authentic
Fair Isle pill-box and
matching mittens (right)
or beret and
matching scarf (left).*

*Knit
Sizes: pill-box and
beret to fit an
average head;
mittens to fit an
average hand; scarf 18cm
(7in) by 162cm (64in)*

***

16

Traditional Aran
jersey to knit with
set-in sleeves and
a polo collar.

*Knit
Sizes to fit 86.5[91.5:
96.5:101.5]cm
(34[36:38:40]in) bust*

***

17

Gay chequerboard
jersey worked in
garter stitch—the
design is worked in strips
which are sewn together
afterwards.

*Knit
Size to fit 86.5|91.5cm
(34|36in) bust*

**

NOS. 14 & 15

Chart for pill-box (Key as given for mitts)

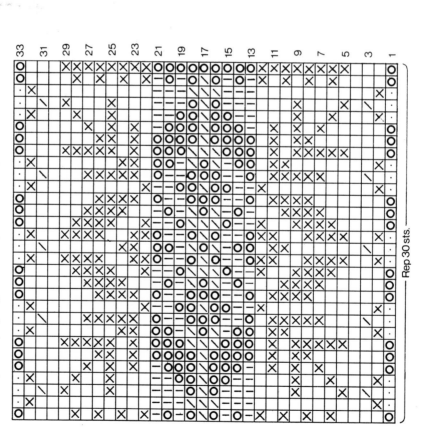

Chart for beret and scarf

24 rows

Rep 18 sts.

A
B
C
D
E
□ X o — |

Chart for mitts

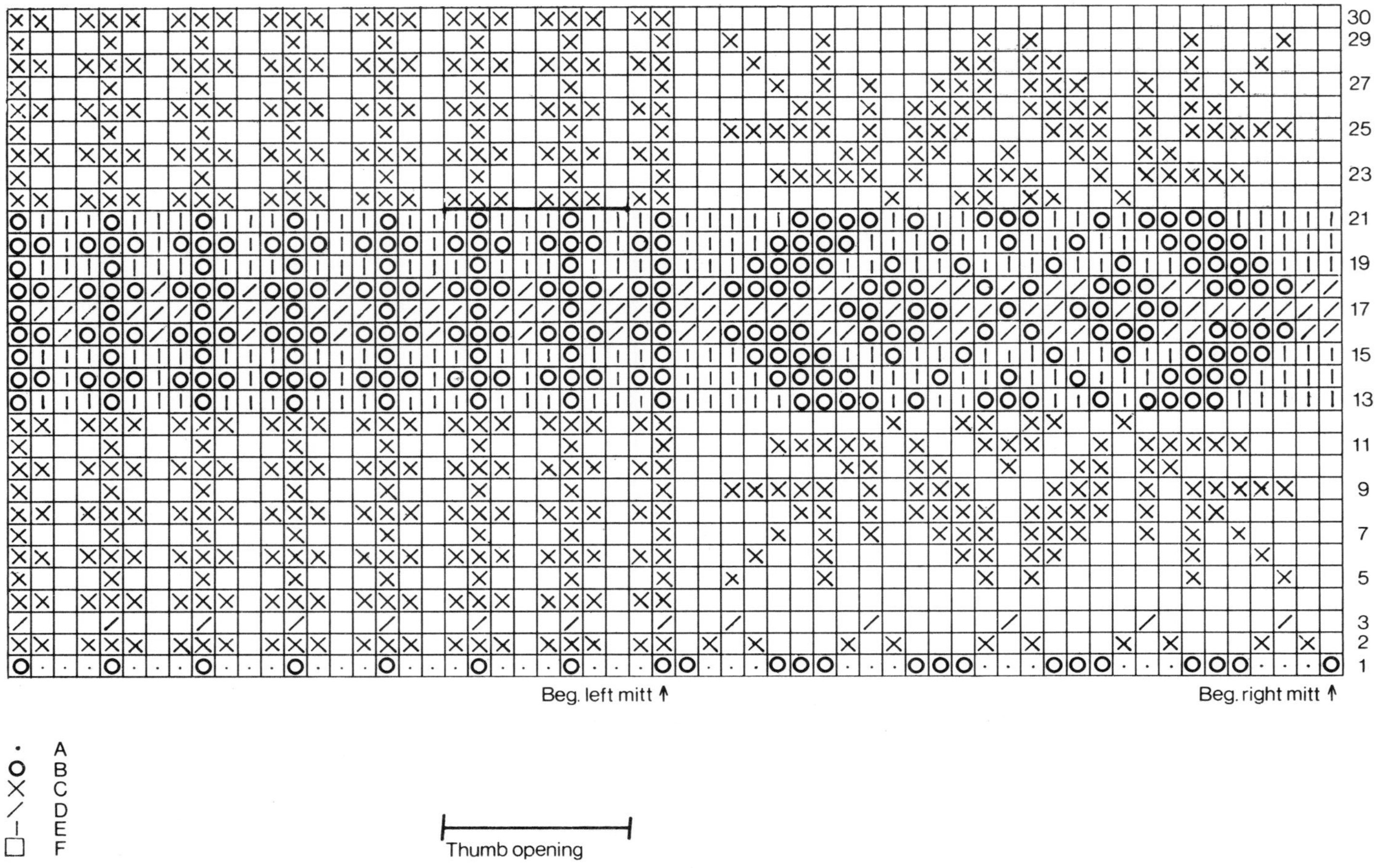

Thumb opening

Beg. right mitt ←

Beg. left mitt ←

30 29 27 25 23 21 19 17 15 13 11 9 7 5 3 2 1

A
B
C
D
E
F

• O × \ — □

14 Fair Isle pill-box and matching mittens

Size
Pill-box to fit average head
Mittens to fit average hand
Tension
8 sts and 10 rows to 1in over st st worked on No.12 needles
Materials
H. & O. Shetland Fleece distributed by Templetons
Pill-box 2 balls of main shade, A
1 ball each of 5 contrast colours, B, C, D, E and F
Mittens 1 ball of main shade, A
1 ball each of 5 contrast colours, B, C, D, E and F
Set of 4 No.12 needles pointed at both ends
Foam rubber for lining pill-box
Note When working Fair Isle patt, strand colours across back of work

Pill-box
Using set of 4 No.12 needles and A, cast on 180 sts. Work in rounds of K1, P1 rib for 4in. K 2 rounds. Cont in rounds of st st, working Fair Isle patt from chart for 33 rounds, then K 1 round using A.
Next round Using A, *P5, P2 tog, P6, P2 tog, rep from * to end. 156 sts.
Using A, P 1 round, K 1 round, then K13 sts of next round.
Shape top
1st round *(K1 B, 3A) twice, (K1 B, 4A) twice, (K1 B, 3A) twice, rep from * to end.
2nd round *(K1 F, 1C) 4 times, 4F, 3C, 4F, (1C, 1F) 3 times, 1C, rep from * to end.
3rd round *K2 F, 1C, 3F, 1C, 4F, 2C, 1F, 2C, 4F, 1C, 3F, 1C, 1F, rep from * to end.
4th round *(K1 F, 1C) 3 times, 4F, 2C, K3 tog F, 2C, 4F, (1C, 1F) twice, 1C, rep from * to end.
5th round *K1 C, 3F, 1C, 4F, 2C, 3F, 2C, 4F, 1C, 3F, rep from * to end.
6th round *(K1 F, 1C) twice, 4F, 2C, 1F, K3 tog F, 1F, 2C, 4F, 1C, 1F, 1C, rep from * to end.
7th round *K2 F, 1C, 4F, 2C, 5F, 2C, 4F, 1C, 1F, rep from * to end.
8th round *K1 F, 1C, 4F, 2C, 2F, K3 tog F, 2F, 2C, 4F, 1C, rep from * to end.
9th round *K1 C, 4F, 2C, 7F, 2C, 4F, rep from * to end.
10th round *K4 E, 2B, 3E, K3 tog E, 3E, 2B, 3E, rep from * to end.
11th round *K3 E, 2B, 9E, 2B, 2E, rep from * to end.
12th round *K2 E, 2B, 4E, K3 tog E, 4E, 2B, 1E, rep from * to end.
13th round *K1 D, 2B, 11D, 2B, rep from * to end.
14th round *K1 D, 2B, 4D, K3 tog D, 4D, 2B, rep from * to end.
15th round *K1 D, 2B, 9D, 2B, rep from * to end.
16th round *K1 E, 2B, 3E, K3 tog E, 3E, 2B, rep from * to end.
17th round *K1 E, 2B, 7E, 2B, rep from * to end.
18th round *K1 E, 2B, 2E, K3 tog E, 2E, 2B, rep from * to end.
19th round *K1 F, 2C, 5F, 2C, rep from * to end.
20th round *K1 F, 2C, 1F, K3 tog F, 1F, 2C, rep from * to end.
21st round *K1 F, 2C, 3F, 2C, rep from * to end.
22nd round *K1 F, 2C, K3 tog F, 2C, rep from * to end.
23rd round *K1 F, 2C, rep from * to end.
24th round *K1 F, 1C, K3 tog C, 1C, rep from * to end.
25th round *K1 F, K3 tog C, rep from * to end.

Break off yarn, thread through rem sts, draw up and fasten off.

Pill-box trim
Using set of 4 No.12 needles and one strand each of A and C, cast on 8 sts. Work in rounds of st st for 1in.
Next round *K2 tog, rep from * to end.
Break off yarn, thread through rem sts, draw up and fasten off.

To make up
Press under a damp cloth with a warm iron. Sew trim to top pf pill-box. Cut a strip of foam rubber 4in deep and 22in long, then cut a circle 12in diameter. Sew circle inside top of pill-box. Sew long strip into side of pill-box and turn ribbing over the foam rubber to inside and sl st down.

Right mitten
Using set of 4 No.12 needles and A, cast on 58 sts. Work in rounds of K1, P1 rib for 3in. K 2 rounds. Cont in rounds of st st, working Fair Isle patt from chart for 21 rounds.
Divide for thumb
Next round Patt 31 sts, sl next 8 sts on to holder, cast on 8 sts, patt to end.
Cont in patt from chart until 30 rounds have been completed, then rep 5th-30th rounds, omitting thumb opening, then work the 3rd, 2nd and 1st rounds.
Shape top
Using A throughout.
Next round *K1, sl 1, K1, psso, K23, K2 tog, K1, rep from * once more.
Next round *K1, sl 1, K1, psso, K21, K2 tog, K1, rep from * once more.
Cont to dec in this way on every round until 18 sts rem. Graft, or cast off 2 sets of sts tog, making sure that dec come at each side.
Work thumb
Using set of 4 No. 12 needles and A, K across 8 sts on holder, K up 8 sts from cast on sts. Cont in rounds of st st for 2¼in.
Shape top
Next round *K2 tog, rep from * to end.
Rep last round once more.
Break off yarn, thread through rem sts, draw up and fasten off.

Left mitten
Work as given for right mitten, reversing patt so that commencement of round comes at outside of hand and working thumb opening, as foll:
Next round Patt 19, sl next 8 sts on to holder, cast on 8 sts, patt to end.

To make up
Press under a damp cloth with a warm iron.

15 Fair Isle beret and matching scarf

Size
Beret to fit average head
Scarf 7in wide by 64in long
Tension
As given for pill-box and mittens
Materials
H. & O. Shetland Fleece distributed by Templetons
Beret 2 balls of main shade, A
1 ball each of 4 contrast colours, B, C, D and E
Scarf 10 balls of main shade, A
1 ball each of 4 contrast colours, B, C, D and E
Set of 4 No. 12 needles pointed at both ends
Set of 4 No. 13 needles pointed at both ends
Note When working Fair Isle patt, strand colours across back of work

Beret
Using set of 4 No. 13 needles and B, cast on 132 sts. Work in rounds of K1, P1 rib for 1½in. Change to set of 4 No. 12 needles.
Next round *K1, K twice into next st, rep from * to end. 198 sts.
Next round *K1 B, 1A, rep from * to end.
Using A, K 1 round, then cont in Fair Isle patt from chart, working the 24 rounds once, then the first 16 rounds again.
Next round Using A, *K2, K2 tog, K3, K2 tog, rep from * to end. 154 sts.
Work centre
1st round *K1 B, 1A, rep from * to end.
2nd round Using B, K to end.
3rd round *K1 A, 10B, rep from * to end.
4th round *K1 B, 1A, 8B, 3A, 8B, 1A, rep from * to end.
5th round *K1 A, 1B, 1A, 6B, 1A, K3 tog A, 1A, 6B, 1A, 1B, rep from * to end.
6th round *(K1 B, 1A) twice, 4B, 1A, K3 tog B, 1A, 4B, 1A, 1B, 1A, rep from * to end.
7th round *K1 A, 1B, 1A, 4B, 5A, 4B, 1A, 1B, rep from * to end.
8th round *K1 C, 1A, 4C, 2A, K3 tog C, 2A, 4C, 1A, rep from * to end.
9th round *K1 A, 4C, 7A, 4C, rep from * to end.
10th round *K4 C, 3A, K3 tog C, 3A, 3C, rep from * to end.
11th round *K3 C, 9A, 2C, rep from * to end.
12th round *K2 E, 4A, K3 tog E, 4A, 1E, rep from * to end.
13th round *K1 E, 11A, rep from * to end.
14th round *K1 E, 4A, K3 tog E, 4A, rep from * to end.
15th round *K1 D, 9A, rep from * to end.
16th round *K1 D, 3A, K3 tog D, 3A, rep from * to end.
17th round *K1 D, 7A, rep from * to end.
18th round *K1 D, 2A, K3 tog D, 2A, rep from * to end.
19th round *K1 D, 5A, rep from * to end.
20th round *K1 B, 1A, K3 tog B, 1A, rep from * to end.
21st round *K1 B, K3 tog A, rep from * to end.
22nd round Using A, *K2 tog, rep from * to end.
Using one strand each of A and B, work 6 rounds st st on these 7 sts.
Next round K3 tog, K1, K3 tog.
Break off yarn, thread through rem sts, draw up and fasten off.

To make up
Press under a damp cloth with a warm iron. Fold ribbing in half to WS and sl st down.

Scarf
Using set of 4 No. 12 needles and A, cast on 108 sts. K 2 rounds st st.
Next round K4, (yfwd, K2 tog, K7) 11 times, yfwd, K2 tog, K3. ****
Cont in rounds of st st for 1in. Work Fair Isle patt from chart, working the 24 rounds, then first 15 rounds again. Using A only cont in st st until work measures 58in from beg. Rep Fair Isle patt rounds as given at beg. Using A only, cont in rounds of st st for 1in. Rep from ** to **. K 2 rounds st st. Cast off.

To make up
Press as given for beret. Cut strands of A and B into 9in lengths, then taking 18 strands tog at a time, make a tassel in each pair of holes along each end.

16 *Aran jersey with a polo collar*

Sizes
To fit 34 [36:38:40]in bust
Length to shoulder, 22½ [23:23½:24]in
Sleeve seam, 17 [17½:17½:18]in
The figures in brackets [] refer to the 36, 38 and 40in sizes respectively

Tension
5 sts and 7 rows to 1in over double moss st worked on No.8 needles

Materials
15[17:19:21] balls Patons Capstan
One pair No.8 needles
One pair No.10 needles
Set of 4 No.8 needles pointed at both ends
Set of 4 No.10 needles pointed at both ends
Cable needle

Back
Using No.10 needles cast on 113[119:125:131] sts.
1st row K1, *P1, K1, rep from * to end.
2nd row P1, *K1, P1, rep from * to end.
Rep these 2 rows 3 times more. Change to No.8 needles. Commence patt.

1st row K1[0:1:0], (P1, K1) 11[13:14:16] times, K2, (P5, K2) twice, P1, K6, P1, K3, (sl next st on to cable needle and hold at back of work, K1 tbl then P1 from cable needle – called Cr2RP –) 3 times, K1, (sl next st on to cable needle and hold at front of work, P1 then K1 tbl from cable needle – called Cr2LP –) 3 times, K3, P1, K6, P1, (K2, P5) twice, K2, (K1, P1) 11[13:14:16] times, K1[0:1:0].
2nd row P1[0:1:0], (K1, P1) 11[13:14:16] times, (K5, P2) twice, K1, P6, K1, P3, (P1 tbl, K1) 3 times, P1, (K1, P1 tbl) 3 times, P3, K1, P6, K1, (P2, K5) twice, P2, (P1, K1) 11[13:14:16] times, P1[0:1:0].
3rd row P1[0:1:0], (K1, P1) 11[13:14:16] times, K2, P4, sl next st on to cable needle and hold at back of work, K1 then P1 from cable needle – called Tw2R –, sl next st on to cable needle and hold at front of work, P1 then K1 from cable needle – called Tw2L –, P4, K2, P1, K2, K into front, back and front of next st then into front and back of next st, making 5 sts from 2, turn, P5, turn, K5, turn, P5, sl 2nd, 3rd and 4th sts over 1st st, turn and K2 – called B2 –, K2, P1, K2, (Cr2RP) 3 times, P1, K1, K1, (Cr2LP) 3 times, K2, P1, K2, B2, K2, P1, K2, P4, Tw2R, Tw2L, P4, K2, (P1, K1) 11[13:14:16] times, P1[0:1:0].
4th row K1[0:1:0], (P1, K1) 11[13:14:16] times, P2, K4, P1, K2, P1, K4, P2, K1, P6, K1, P2, (P1 tbl, K1) 3 times, P1, K1, P1, (K1, P1 tbl) 3 times, P2, K1, P6, K1, P2, K4, P1, K2, P1, K4, P2, (K1, P1) 11[13:14:16] times, K1[0:1:0].
5th row The 23[26:29:32] sts at each end are worked in double moss st as given for the 1st-4th rows and will now be referred to as, patt 23[26:29:32] sts, K2, P3, Tw2R, P2, Tw2L, P3, K2, P1, K6, P1, K1, (Cr2RP) 3 times, (K1, P1) twice, K1, (Cr2LP) 3 times, K1, P1, K6, P1, K2, P3, Tw2R, P2, Tw2L, P3, K2, patt 23[26:29:32] sts.
6th row Patt 23[26:29:32] sts, P2, K3, P1, K4, P1, K3, P2, K1, P6, K1, P1, (P1 tbl, K1) 3 times, (P1, K1) twice, P1, (K1, P1 tbl) 3 times, P1, K1, P6, K1, P2, K3, P1, K4, P1, K3, P2, patt 23[26:29:32] sts.
7th row Patt 23[26:29:32] sts, K2, P2, Tw2R, P4, Tw2L, P2, K2, P1, K6, P1, (Cr2RP) 3 times, (K1, P1) 3 times, K1, (Cr2LP) 3 times, P1, K6, P1, K2, P2, Tw2R, P4, Tw2L, P2, K2, patt 23[26:29:32] sts.
8th row Patt 23[26:29:32] sts, P2, K2, P1, K6,

P1, K2, P2, K1, P6, K1, (P1 tbl, K1) 3 times, (P1, K1) 3 times, P1, (K1, P1 tbl) 3 times, K1, P6, K1, P2, K2, P1, K6, P1, K2, P2, patt 23[26:29:32] sts.
9th row Patt 23[26:29:32] sts, K2, (P5, K2) twice, P1, K6, P1, sl next st on to cable needle and hold at front of work, K1 then K1 tbl from cable needle – called Cr2LK –, (Cr2LP) twice, (P1, K1) 3 times, P1, (Cr2RP) twice, sl next st on to cable needle and hold at back of work, K1 tbl then K1 from cable needle – called Cr2RK –, P1, K6, P1, (K2, P5) twice, K2, patt 23[26:29:32] sts.
10th row Patt 23[26:29:32] sts, P2, (K5, P2) twice, K1, P6, K1, P1, (P1 tbl, K1) 3 times, (P1, K1) twice, P1, (K1, P1 tbl) 3 times, P1, K1, P6, K1, (P2, K5) twice, P2, patt 23[26:29:32] sts.
11th row Patt 23[26:29:32] sts, K2, P4, Tw2R, Tw2L, P4, K2, P1, K2, B2, K2, P1, K1, Cr2LK, (Cr2LP) twice, (P1, K1) twice, P1, (Cr2RP) twice, Cr2RK, K1, P1, K2, B2, K2, P1, K2, P4, Tw2R, Tw2L, P4, K2, patt 23[26:29:32] sts.
12th row As 4th.
13th row Patt 23[26:29:32] sts, K2, P3, Tw2R, P2, Tw2L, P3, K2, P1, K6, P1, K2, Cr2LK, (Cr2LP) twice, P1, K1, P1, (Cr2RP) twice, Cr2RK, K2, P1, K6, P1, K2, P3, Tw2R, P2, Tw2L, P3, K2, patt 23[26:29:32] sts.
14th row Patt 23[26:29:32] sts, P2, K3, P1, K4, P1, K3, P2, K1, P6, K1, P3, (P1 tbl, K1) 3 times, P1, (K1, P1 tbl) 3 times, P3, K1, P6, K1, P2, K3, P1, K4, P1, K3, P2, patt 23[26:29:32] sts.
15th row Patt 23[26:29:32] sts, K2, P2, Tw2R, P4, Tw2L, P2, K2, P1, K6, P1, K3, Cr2LK, (Cr2LP) twice, P1, (Cr2RP) twice, Cr2RK, K3, P1, K6, P1, K2, P2, Tw2R, P4, Tw2L, P2, K2, patt 23[26:29:32] sts.
16th row Patt 23[26:29:32] sts, P2, K2, P1, K6, P1, K2, P2, K1, P6, K1, P4, (P1 tbl, K1) 5 times, P1 tbl, P4, K1, P6, K1, P2, K2, P1, K6, P1, K2, P2, patt 23[26:29:32] sts.
These 16 rows form patt. Cont in patt until work measures 15in from beg, ending with a WS row.

Shape armholes
Cast off 7 sts at beg of next 2 rows. Dec one st at each end of next and foll 3[4:5:6] alt rows. 91[95:99:103] sts. Cont without shaping until armholes measure 7½ [8:8½:9]in from beg, ending with a WS row.

Shape shoulders
Cast off at beg of next and every row 9[10:10:11] sts 4 times and 9[9:10:10] sts twice. Leave rem 37[37:39:39] sts on holder for centre back neck.

Front
Work as given for back until armholes measure 5 [5½:6:6½]in from beg, ending with a WS row.

Shape neck
Next row Patt 36[38:39:41] sts, turn and leave rem sts on holder.
Cast off 2 sts at beg of next and foll alt row. Dec one st at neck edge on foll 5 alt rows. 27[29:30:32] sts. Cont without shaping until armhole measures same as back to shoulder, ending with a WS row.

Shape shoulder
Cast off at beg of next and every alt row 9[10:10:11] sts twice and 9[9:10:10] sts once.
With RS of work facing, sl first 19[19:21:21] sts on holder and leave for centre neck, rejoin yarn to rem sts and patt to end. Complete to match first side, reversing shaping.

Sleeves
Using No.10 needles cast on 43[45:47:49] sts. Work 2in rib as given for back, ending with a 2nd row. Change to No.8 needles. Commence patt.

1st row K0[1:0:1], (P1, K1) 2[2:3:3] times, P1, K6, P1, K3, (Cr2RP) 3 times, K1, (Cr2LP) 3 times, K3, P1, K6, P1, (K1, P1) 2[2:3:3] times, K0[1:0:1].
2nd row P0[1:0:1], (K1, P1) 2[2:3:3] times, K1, P6, K1, P3, (P1 tbl, K1) 3 times, P1, (K1, P1 tbl) 3 times, P3, K1, P6, K1, (P1, K1) 2[2:3:3] times, P0[1:0:1].
3rd row P0[1:0:1], (K1, P1) 2[2:3:3] times, P1, K2, B2, K2, P1, K2, (Cr2RP) 3 times, K1, P1, K1, (Cr2LP) 3 times, K2, P1, K2, B2, K2, P1, (P1, K1) 2[2:3:3] times, P0[1:0:1].
4th row K0[1:0:1], (P1, K1) 2[2:3:3] times, K1, P6, K1, P2, (P1 tbl, K1) 3 times, P1, K1, P1, (K1, P1 tbl) 3 times, P2, K1, P6, K1, (K1, P1) 2[2:3:3] times, K0[1:0:1].
Cont in patt as now set, working centre 19 sts as given for centre 19 sts of back, and working B2 on every 8th row, inc one st at each end of next and every 6th row until there are 73[75:77:79] sts and working extra sts into double moss st. Cont without shaping until sleeve measures 17 [17½:17½:18]in from beg. Mark each end of last row with coloured thread and work a further 1½in, ending with a WS row and noting that sleeve from marked point is set into armhole shaping and is not included in sleeve seam.

Shape top
Cast off 4 sts at beg of next 16 rows. Cast off rem 9[11:13:15] sts.

Collar
Join shoulder seams. Using set of 4 No.10 needles and with RS of work facing, K up 18 sts down left front neck, K across front neck sts on holder, K up 18 sts up right front neck and K across back neck sts on holder. 92[92:96:96] sts. Cont in rounds of K1, P1 rib for 2in. Change to set of 4 No.8 needles. Cont in rib for a further 4in. Cast off loosely in rib.

To make up
Press each piece under a damp cloth with a warm iron. Set in sleeves, sewing last 1½in from marked point to cast off sts at underarm. Join side and sleeve seams. Press seams.

17 *Chequerboard jersey in garter stitch*

Size
To fit 34/36in bust
Length to back neck, 22in
Sleeve seam, 17in

Tension
5 sts and 9⅛ rows to 1in over g st worked on No.6 needles

Materials
Pingouin Super
7 balls of main shade, A
3 balls of contrast colour, B
2 balls each of contrast colours, C and D
One pair No.6 needles
One pair No.7 needles

Note
This design is worked in strips which are sewn tog afterwards

Back
1st strip
Using No.6 needles and A, cast on 13 sts and beg at right side seam. Work 24 rows g st. Cont in g st, work 24 rows B, 24 rows C, 24 rows D, 24 rows A and 24 rows B.

Shape armhole
Using C, cast off at beg of next and every alt row 3 sts twice, 2 sts once and one st 3 times,

18

Belted jackets for the
whole family, with
bands of traditional
patterns on body and
sleeves for the expert
knitter, or the jacket
can be knitted in one
colour

Knit
Sizes: adults to fit 81.5
[91.5:101.5:112.0]cm
(32[36:40:44]in) chest/bust
Child's to fit 66.0
[71.0:76.0]cm (26[28:
30]in) chest

***

19

Warm jersey with an
optional embroidered
flower in two colours
on the front.

Knit and embroidery
Sizes to fit 86.5
[91.5:96.5]cm (34[36:
38]in) bust

**

ending with a RS row. Leave rem 2 sts on holder.
2nd strip
Using No.6 needles and B, cast on 13 sts. Cont
in g st, working 24 rows each in B, C, D, A, B,
C, then 11 rows D.
Join strips for shoulder
Next row K to end, K2 sts of 1st strip from
holder. 15 sts.
Keeping colour sequence correct, cont in g st
until 202 rows have been worked from beg.
Shape shoulder
Cast off at beg of next and every alt row 3 sts
5 times.
3rd strip
Using No.6 needles and C, cast on 13 sts. Cont
in g st, working 24 rows each in C, D, A and
B, until 212 rows have been worked from beg.
Next row Cast off 2 sts, K to end. 11 sts. K 1
row. Cast off rem sts.
4th strip
Using No.6 needles and D, cast on 13 sts for
centre back. Cont in g st, working 24 rows each
in D, A, B, and C, until 214 rows have been
worked from beg. Cast off.
5th strip
Work as given for 3rd strip, reversing shaping
at top.
6th strip
Work as given for 2nd strip, reversing shaping
but do not complete until 7th strip has been
worked.
7th strip
Work as given for 1st strip, reversing shaping
and working the 2 rem sts from this strip with
the 6th strip for armhole.

Front
1st strip
Using No.6 needles and D, cast on 13 sts and
beg at left side seam. Work as given for 1st
strip of back.
2nd strip
Using No.6 needles and C, cast on 13 sts. Work
as given for 2nd strip of back.
3rd strip
Using No.6 needles and B, cast on 13 sts. Work
as given for 3rd strip of back until 193 rows
have been worked from beg.
Shape neck
Cast off 3 sts at beg of next row and 2 sts at
beg of next row. Cast off one st at beg of foll 4
alt rows. 4 sts. Cont in g st, keeping colour
sequence correct until 214 rows have been
worked from beg. Cast off.
4th strip
Using No.6 needles and A, cast on 13 sts for
centre front. Cont in g st, keeping colour
sequence correct, until 190 rows have been
worked from beg.
Shape neck
Next row K3 sts, turn and K3.
Next row Cast off 10 sts, K to end.
Next row K3 sts, turn and K3. Cast off.
5th strip
Work as given for 3rd strip of front, reversing
shaping.
6th strip
Work as given for 2nd strip of front, reversing
shaping and completing as given for 6th strip
of back.
7th strip
Work as given for 1st strip of front, reversing
shaping and completing as given for 7th strip
of back.

Sleeves
Using No.6 needles and A, cast on 36 sts. Cont
in g st, working in A throughout, inc one st at
each end of every 12th row until there are 60
sts. Cont without shaping until sleeve measures
17in from beg.
Shape top

Cast off 3 sts at beg of next 2 rows. K2 tog at
each end of next and every alt row until 8 sts
rem. Cast off.

Collar
Using No.7 needles and A, cast on 84 sts. Cont
in g st, using A throughout until work measures
2½in from beg. Change to No.6 needles and cont
in g st for a further 2½in. Cast off.

To make up
Do not press. Join all strips tog, matching the
squares. Join shoulder seams. Set in sleeves.
Join side and sleeve seams. Join side seam of
collar. Sew on cast on edge of collar to neck
edge. Fold collar in half to outside. Press all
seams very lightly under a damp cloth with a
cool iron.

18 Belted jackets for the whole family

Sizes
Adults' jacket to fit 32[36:40:44]in bust/chest
Length to shoulder, 28[29:30:31]in, adjustable
Sleeve seam, 17½[18:18½:19]in, adjustable
Children's jacket to fit 26[28:30]in chest
Length to shoulder, 18[20:22]in, adjustable
Sleeve seam, 13[14:15]in, adjustable
The figures in brackets [] refer to the 36, 40 and
44in adults' sizes and the 28 and 30in children's
sizes respectively
Tension
7 sts and 10 rows to 2in overst st worked on No.5
needles
Materials
Icelandic Lopi Sheep Wool
Adults' jacket 7[8:9:10] hanks in main shade, A
1 hank each of contrast colours, B and C
Children's jacket 4[4:5] hanks in main shade, A
1 hank each of contrast colours, B and C
One pair No.5 needles
One pair No.7 needles

Adults' jacket back
Using No.7 needles and A, cast on 62[70:78:86] sts.
1st row K2, *P2, K2, rep from * to end.
2nd row P2, *K2, P2, rep from * to end.
Rep these 2 rows 2[2:3:3] times more. Change to
No.5 needles. Beg with a K row work 2 rows st st.
Join in B and C. Cont in st st working 9 rows patt
from chart I, noting the exact st on which rows
end and beg, as patt multiples are not intended
to fit exactly. Break off B and C. **. Using A, cont
in st st until work measures 17in from beg, ending
with a P row, or required length to underarm
less 4in. Join in B and C. Cont in st st working
19 rows patt from chart II, noting the exact st on
which rows end and beg. Break off B and C. Using
A, P 1 row.
Shape armholes
Cont using A throughout, cast off at beg of next
and every row 3 sts twice and 2 sts twice. Dec
one st at each end of next and foll 2[3:4:5] alt
rows. 46[52:58:64] sts. Cont without shaping until
armholes measure 7[8:9:10]in from beg, ending
with a P row.
Shape shoulders
Cast off at beg of next and every row 4[5:5:6] sts
4 times, 4[4:6:6] sts twice and 22[24:26:28] sts
once.

Adults' jacket left front
Using No.5 needles and A, cast on 18[18:22:22] sts
for pocket lining. Beg with a K row work 4[4:5:5]in
st st, ending with a P row. Leave sts on holder.
Using No.7 needles and A, cast on 34[38:42:46] sts.
Work as given for back to **. Using A, cont in st st

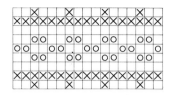

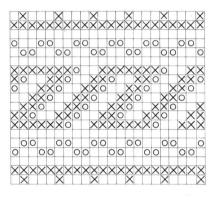

CHART I

CHART II

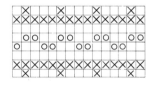

CHART III

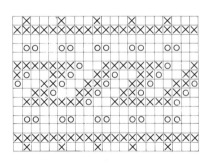

CHART IV

- ☐ Main colour
- ☒ 1st contrast
- ⊙ 2nd contrast

until work measures 7in from beg, ending with a P row.

Pocket top

Next row K8[10:10:12] sts, (P2, K2) 5[5:6:6] times, K to end.

Next row P8[10:10:12] sts, (K2, P2) 5[5:6:6] times, P to end.

Rep last 2 rows once more, then first of them again.

Next row P8[10:10:12] sts, cast off next 18[18:22:22] sts in rib, P to end.

Next row K8[10:10:12] sts, K across pocket lining sts, K to end.

Using A, cont in st st until work measures 4in less than back to underarm, ending with a P row. Join in B and C. Work first 4 rows patt from chart II.

Shape front

Cont in patt until 19 rows of chart II have been completed, dec one st at end of next and every foll 4th row. Break off B and C. Using A, P 1 row.

Shape armhole

Cont to dec one st at front edge on every foll 4th row, *at the same time* cast off at armhole edge 3 sts once and 2 sts once, then dec one st 3[4:5:6] times. Cont to dec one st at front edge on every foll 4th row until 12[14:16:18] sts rem. Cont without shaping until armhole measures same as back to shoulder, ending at armhole edge.

Shape shoulder

Cast off at beg of next and every alt row 4[5:5:6] sts twice and 4[4:6:6] sts once.

Adults' jacket right front

Work as given for left front, reversing all shaping.

Sleeves

Using No.7 needles and A, cast on 34[34:38:38] sts. Work 3in rib as given for back, ending with a 2nd row and inc one st at each end of last row on 36 and 44in sizes only. 34[36:38:40] sts. Change to No.5 needles. Beg with a K row cont in st st, inc one st at each end of 3rd and every foll 8th row until there are 46[48:50:52] sts. Cont without shaping until sleeve measures 13½[14:14½:15]in from beg, ending with a P row, or required length to underarm less 4in. Join in B and C. Cont in st st working 19 rows patt from chart II. Break off B and C. Using A, P 1 row.

Shape top

Cont using A throughout, cast off at beg of next and every row 3 sts twice and 2 sts twice. Dec one st at each end of next and foll 4[5:6:7] alt rows, ending with a P row. 26 sts. Cast off at beg of next and every row 2 sts 6 times, 3 sts twice and 8 sts once.

Front band and collar

Using No.7 needles and A, cast on 14 sts. Beg with a K row work 18in st st, or until band measures same length as front to beg of shaping. Cont in st st, inc one st at each end of next and every foll 4th row until there are 40[42:44:46] sts. Cont without shaping until collar reaches to centre back neck. Cast off. Make 2nd piece in same way.

Belt

Using No.7 needles and A, cast on 14 sts. Beg with a K row work 48[50:52:54]in st st, or required length. Cast off.

To make up

Press each piece under a damp cloth with a warm iron. Join shoulder seams. Set in sleeves. Join side and sleeve seams. Sew down pocket linings. Join collar at centre back. Sew on front band and collar, with collar seam at centre back neck. Fold in half to WS and sl st down. Fold belt in half lengthwise and join seam. Join short ends. Press seams.

Children's jacket back

Using No.7 needles and A, cast on 50[54:58] sts.

1st row K2, *P2, K2, rep from * to end.
2nd row P2, *K2, P2, rep from * to end.

Rep these 2 rows twice more. Change to No.5 needles. Beg with a K row work 2 rows st st. Join in B and C. Cont in st st working 8 rows patt from chart III, noting the exact st on which rows end and beg as patt multiples are not intended to fit exactly. Break off B and C. **. Using A, cont in st st until work measures 10[11½:13]in from beg, ending with a P row, or required length to underarm less 3in. Join in B and C. Cont in st st working 15 rows patt from chart IV, noting the exact st on which rows end and beg. Break off B and C. Using A, P 1 row.

Shape armholes

Cont using A throughout, cast off 3 sts at beg of next 2 rows. Dec one st at each end of next and foll 2[3:4] alt rows. 38[40:42] sts. Cont without shaping until armholes measure 5[5½:6]in from beg, ending with a P row.

Shape shoulders

Cast off at beg of next and every row 5[5:6] sts twice, 4[5:5] sts twice and 20 sts once.

Children's jacket left front

Using No.5 needles and A, cast on 14 sts for pocket lining. Beg with a K row work 3½in st st, ending with a K row. Leave sts on holder.

Using No.7 needles and A, cast on 26[28:30] sts.

1st row *K2, P2, rep from * to last 2[4:2] sts, K2, P0[2:0].

2nd row K0[2:0], P2, *K2, P2, rep from * to end.

Rep these 2 rows twice more. Change to No.5 needles and cont as given for back to **. Using A, cont in st st until work measures 5in from beg, ending with a P row.

Pocket top

Next row K8 sts, (P2, K2) 4 times, K to end.
Next row P4[6:8] sts, (K2, P2) 4 times, P to end.

Rep last 2 rows once more.

Next row K8 sts, cast off 14 sts in rib, K to end.

Next row P4[6:8] sts, P across pocket lining sts, P to end.

Work as given for back until front measures same as back to underarm, ending with a P row.

Shape armhole and front edge

Next row Cast off 3 sts, K to last 2 sts, K2 tog. Dec one st at armhole edge on foll 3[4:5] alt rows, *at the same time* dec one st at front edge on every alt row until 9[10:11] sts rem. Cont without shaping until armhole measures same as back to shoulder, ending at armhole edge.

19 *Warm jersey with flower embroidery*

Sizes

To fit 34 [36:38]in bust
Length to shoulder, 22 [22½:23]in
Sleeve seam, 17½in
The figures in brackets [] refer to the 36 and 38in sizes respectively

Tension

6 sts and 8 rows to 1in over st st worked on No.9 needles

Materials

20[21:22] balls Lister Lavenda Double Knitting in main shade, A
1 ball each of contrast colours, B and C or 2 skeins of embroidery wool in B and C
One pair No.9 needles
One pair No.11 needles
Set of 4 No.11 needles pointed at both ends

Back

Using No.11 needles and A, cast on 106[114:118] sts.

1st row K2, *P2, K2, rep from * to end.

2nd row P2, *K2, P2, rep from * to end.

Rep these 2 rows for 2in, ending with a 2nd row and inc one st at each end of last row on 34 and 38in sizes only. 108[114:120] sts. Change to No. 9 needles. Beg with a K row cont in st st until work measures 15in from beg, ending with a P row.

Shape armholes

Cast off at beg of next and every row 4 sts twice and 2 sts twice. Dec one st at each end of next and foll 5[6:7] alt rows. 84[88:92] sts. Cont without shaping until armholes measure 7 [7½: 8]in from beg, ending with a P row.

Shape shoulders and neck

Next row K33[34:35] sts, turn and leave rem sts on holder.

Next row Cast off 3 sts, P to end.

Next row Cast off 6 sts, K to end.

Rep last 2 rows twice more. P 1 row. Cast off rem 6[7:8] sts.

With RS of work facing, sl first 18[20:22] sts on holder and leave for centre back neck, rejoin yarn to rem sts and K to end. Complete to match first side, reversing shaping.

Front

Work as given for back until armhole shaping is completed. Cont without shaping until armholes measure 5 [5½:6]in from beg, ending with a P row.

Shape neck

Next row K36[37:38]sts, turn and leave rem sts on holder.

Cast off at beg of next and every alt row 3 sts once and 2 sts twice. Dec one st at neck edge on next and foll 4 alt rows. Cont without shaping until armhole measures same as back to shoulder, ending with a P row.

Shape shoulder

Cast off at beg of next and every alt row 6 sts 3 times and 6[7:8] sts once.

With RS of work facing, sl first 12[14:16] sts on to holder and leave for centre neck, rejoin yarn to rem sts and K to end. Complete to match first side, reversing shaping.

Sleeves

Using No.11 needles and A, cast on 42[46:50] sts. Work 2in rib as given for back, ending with a 2nd row and inc 8 sts evenly across last row. 50[54:58] sts. Change to No.9 needles. Beg with a K row cont in st st, inc one st at each end of every 8th row until there are 78[82:86] sts. Cont without shaping until sleeve measures 17½in from beg, ending with a P row.

Shape top

Cast off 4 sts at beg of next 2 rows. Dec one st at each end of next and foll 9[10:11] alt rows, ending with a P row. Cast off at beg of next and every row 2 sts 10 times, 3 sts 4 times and 4 sts twice. Cast off rem 10[12:14] sts.

Neckband

Join shoulder seams. Using set of 4 No. 11 needles, A and with RS of work facing, K up 12 sts down right back neck, K across back neck sts, K up 12 sts up left back neck and 21 sts down left front neck, K across front neck sts, then K up 21 sts up right front neck. 96[100:104] sts. Work in rounds of K2, P2 rib for 3½in. Cast off loosely in rib.

To make up

Press each piece under a damp cloth with a warm iron. Set in sleeves. Join side and sleeve seams. Embroider flower motif on front, working from chart in Swiss darning. Press seams.

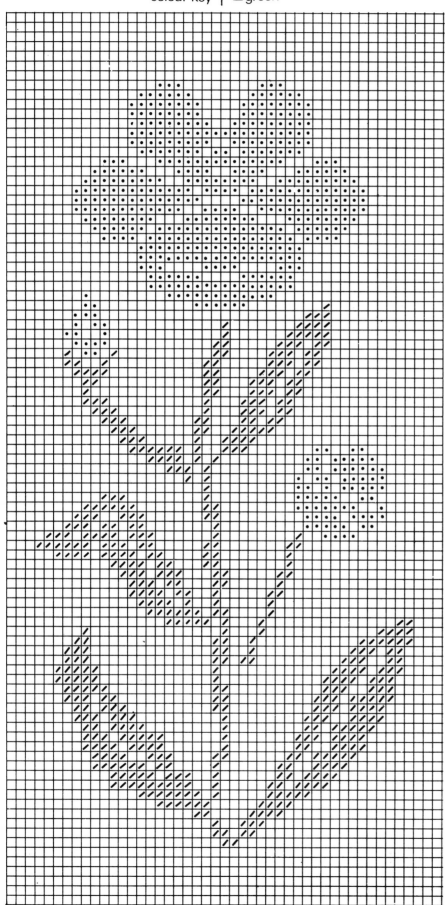

NO. 19

colour key

⊡ red
☑ green

Mini jersey with cap sleeves

Sizes
To fit 32 [34:36]in bust
Length to shoulder, 18 [18½:19]in
The figures in brackets [] refer to the 34 and 36in sizes respectively

Tension
7 sts and 11 rows to 1in over g st worked on No.10 needles

Materials
4[5:5] balls Mademoiselle Pingouin in main shade, A
1 ball each in contrast colours, B and C
One pair No.10 needles

Back
Using No.10 needles and A, cast on 98[102:106] sts.
1st row K2, *P2, K2, rep from * to end.
2nd row P2, *K2, P2, rep from * to end.
Rep these 2 rows 3 times more. Cont in g st, inc one st at each end of every 8th[8th:6th] row until there are 118[126:134] sts. Cont without shaping until work measures 10in from beg, ending with a WS row.

Shape armholes
Cast off 12[13:14] sts at beg of next 2 rows. 94[100:106] sts. Cont without shaping until armholes measure 8 [8½:9]in from beg, ending with a WS row.

Shape shoulders
Cast off at beg of next and every row 6[7:7] sts 4 times and 6[6:8] sts twice. Cast off rem 58 [60:62] sts.

Front
Work as given for back until armholes measure 1½in from beg, ending with a WS row.
Next row K26[28:30] B, K42[44:46] C, K26 [28:30] B.
Next row K26[28:30] B, P42[44:46] C, K26 [28:30] B.
Rep these 2 rows 7 times more.
Next row K10[11:12] B, K74[78:82]C, K10[11: 12] B.
Next row K10[11:12] B, P74[78:82] C, K10[11: 12] B.
Rep last 2 rows until armholes measure 5 [5½: 6]in from beg, ending with a WS row.

Shape neck
Next row Patt 36[38:40] sts, turn and leave rem sts on holder.
Cast off at neck edge on next and every alt row 4 sts once, 3 sts once, 2 sts twice and one st 7 times. 18[20:22] sts. Cont without shaping until armhole measures same as back to shoulder, ending with a WS row.

Shape shoulder
Cast off at beg of next and every alt row 6[7:7] sts twice and 6[6:8] sts once.
With RS of work facing, rejoin yarn to rem sts and cast off first 22[24:26] sts, patt to end.
Complete to match first side, reversing shaping.

Sleeves
Using No.10 needles and B, cast on 112[116: 120] sts. Work 20 rows g st. Break off B. Join in A and cont in g st until work measures 3½in from beg.

Shape top
Cast off 2 sts at beg of next 46[48:50] rows.
Cast off rem 20 sts.

Neckband
Using No.10 needles and B, cast on 5 sts. Work in g st until band measures 20 [20½:21]in from beg. Cast off.

20

Mini-jersey with an unusual cap sleeve worked in garter and stocking stitch in three colours.

Knit
Sizes to fit 81.5[86.5:91.5]cm (34[36:38]in) bust

***

To make up

Join shoulder seams. Sew neckband round neck. Join side seams. Set sleeves into armholes, sewing the curved part into the armhole but not the cast off sts at underarms. The first 4 rows of A and the border in B on the sleeves are then sewn to back and front, continuing in a straight line down from armhole. Press seams very lightly under a dry cloth with a cool iron.

21 Collage jersey with a V-neck in eight colours

Sizes

To fit 34[36]in bust
Length to shoulder, 19½[20]in
Sleeve seam, 19in
The figures in brackets [] refer to the 36in size only.

Tension

6½ sts and 9 rows to 1in over st st worked on No.10 needles

Materials

Jaeger Celtic-Spun
1[1] ball each of 8 contrast colours, A, B, C, D, E, F, G and H
One pair No.10 needles
One pair No.11 needles

Note

Use separate ball of yarn for each colour, twisting yarns at back of work when changing colour

Back

Using No.11 needles and A, cast on 76[80] sts.
Work 6in K2, P2 rib, working 1 or 2 rows in each colour at random and carrying yarn up sides of work. Change to No.10 needles.
Next row P2 sts, inc 1 by picking up loop lying between sts and P tbl, *P4 sts, inc 1, rep from * to last 2 sts, P2. 95[100] sts.
Commence patt, inc one st at each end of every 6th row until there are 115[120] sts.
1st row K25[27] A, 23 B, 23 C, 24[27] D.
2nd row P24[27] D, 23 C, 23 B, 25[27] A.
3rd row K25[27] A, 23 B, 23 C, 24[27] D.
4th row P28[31] D, 29 C, 21 B, 17[19] A.
5th row K17[19] A, 21 B, 29 C, 28[31] D.
6th row Inc one st at each end, P29[32] D, 29 C, 21 B, 18[20] A. 97[102] sts.
7th row K22[24] A, 20 B, 35 C, 20[23] D.
8th row P20[23] D, 35 C, 20 B, 22[24] A.
9th row K23[25] A, 20 B, 35 C, 19[22] D.
10th row P24[27] D, 30 C, 30 B, 13[15] A.
11th row K13[15] A, 24 B, 11 E, 26 C, 23[26] D.
12th row Inc one st at each end, P24[27] D, 29 C, 8 E, 24 B, 14[16] A. 99[104] sts.
13th row K17[19] A, 21 B, 8 E, 29 C, 24[27] D.
14th row P24[27] D, 29 C, 12 E, 17 B, 17[19] A.
15th row K17[19] A, 17 B, 20 E, 31 C, 14[17] D.
16th row P14[17] D, 31 C, 20 E, 34[36] B.
17th row K34[36] B, 20 E, 31 C, 14[17] D.
18th row Inc one st at each end, P19[22] D, 27 C, 25 E, 30[32] B. 101[106] sts.
19th row K30[32] B, 32 E, 20 C, 19[22] D.
20th row P19[22] D, 20 C, 32 E, 30[32] B.
21st row K30[32] B, 32 E, 20 C, 19[22] D.
22nd row P21[24] D, 23 C, 38 E, 19[21] B.
23rd row K19[21] B, 38 E, 44[47] C.
24th row Inc one st at each end, P45[48] C, 58[60] E. 103[108] sts.
25th row K43[45] E, 24 F, 36[39] C.
26th row P36[39] C, 24 F, 43[45] E.
27th row K25[27] E, 25 G, 22 F, 31[34] C.
28th row P31[34] C, 33 F, 14 G, 25[27] E.
29th row K25[27] E, 14 G, 33 F, 31[34] C.
30th row Inc one st at each end, P39[42] C, 31 F, 16 G, 19[21] E. 105[110] sts.
31st row K19[21] E, 16 G, 31 F, 39[42] C.

32nd row P40[43] C, 31 F, 16 G, 18[20] E.
33rd row K19[21] E, 20 G, 38 F, 28[31] C.
34th row P28[31] C, 38 F, 22 G, 17[19] E.
35th row K17[19] E, 15 G, 14 H, 32 F, 27[30] C.
36th row Inc one st at each end, P28[31] C, 32 F, 14 H, 33[35] G. 107[112] sts.
37th row K33[35] G, 21 H, 32 F, 21[24] C.
38th row P21[24] C, 32 F, 21 H, 33[35] G.
39th row K36[38] G, 25 H, 26 F, 20[23] C.
40th row P20[23] C, 26 F, 25 H, 36[38] G.
41st row K37[39] G, 24 H, 29 F, 17[20] C.
42nd row Inc one st at each end, P11[14] C, 15 B, 23 F, 46 H, 14[16] G. 109[111] sts.
43rd row K30[32] G, 30 H, 23 F, 15 B, 11[14] C.
44th row P14[17] C, 21 B, 17 F, 27 H, 30[32] G.
45th row K31[33] G, 33 H, 17 F, 14 B, 14[17] C.
46th row P15[18] C, 13 B, 17 F, 44 H, 20[22] G.
47th row K20[22] G, 43 H, 19 F, 21 B, 6[9] C.
48th row Inc one st at each end, P11[14] C, 29 B, 7 F, 44 H, 20[22] G. 111[116] sts.
49th row K27[29] G, 40 H, 9 F, 24 B, 11[14] C.
50th row P12[15] C, 24 B, 32 F, 16 H, 27[29] G.
51st row K28[30] G, 16 H, 34 F, 25 B, 8[11] C.
52nd row P24[27] C, 17 B, 27 F, 34 H, 9[11] G.
53rd row K9[11] G, 38 H, 24 F, 16 B, 24[27] C.
54th row Inc one st at each end, P26[29] C, 23 B, 16 F, 39 H, 9[11] G. 113[118] sts.
55th row K19[21] G, 30 H, 16 F, 43 B, 5[8] C.
56th row P8[11] C, 40 B, 33 F, 14 H, 18[20] G.
57th row K19[21] G, 13 H, 37 F, 7 E, 29 B, 8[11] C.
58th row P9[12] C, 28 B, 20 E, 33 F, 19 H, 4[6] G.
59th row K5[7] G, 39 H, 12 F, 21 E, 3 B, 31 A, 2[5] C.
60th row Inc one st at each end, P3[6] C, 31 A, 3 B, 22 E, 12 F, 39 H, 5[7] G. 115[120] sts.
61st row K37[39] G, 7 H, 20 F, 15 E, 16 B, 18 A, 2[5] C.
62nd row P9[12] C, 11 A, 16 B, 30 E, 8 F, 4 H, 37[39] G.
63rd row K39[41] G, 3 H, 7 F, 38 E, 9 B, 19[22] A.
64th row P19[22] A, 25 B, 26 E, 3 F, 3 H, 39[41] G.

Shape armholes

65th row Cast off 4 sts, K36[38] G, 3 H, 2 F, 27 E, 25 B, 18[21] A.
66th row Cast off 4 sts, P26[29] A, 13 B, 33 E, 35[37] G.
67th row Cast off 3 sts, K46[48] G, 29 E, 4 B, 25[28] A.
68th row Cast off 3 sts, P22[25] A, 10 B, 23 E, 32 G, 14 [16] D.
69th row Cast off 2 sts, K15[17] D, 32 G, 21 E, 10 B, 21 [24] A.
70th row Cast off 2 sts, P26[29] A, 3 B, 22 E, 26 G, 20[22] D.
71st row Dec one st at beg, K16[18] D, 29 G, 23 E, 6 B, 22[25] A.
72nd row Dec one st at beg, P21[24] A, 6 B, 33 E, 19 G, 16[18] D. 95[100] sts.
73rd row K17[19] D, 38 G, 17 E, 3 B, 20[23] A.
74th row P21[24] A, 2 B, 17 E, 49 G, 6[8] D.
75th row K27[29] D, 29 G, 17 E, 1 B, 21[24] A.
76th row P22[25] A, 34 E, 13 G, 26[28] D.
77th row K26[28] D, 13 G, 48 E, 8[11] A.
78th row P8[11] A, 52 E, 16 G, 19[21] D.
79th row K19[21] D, 44 G, 27 E, 5[8] A.
80th row P19[22] A, 14 E, 44 G, 18[20] D.
81st row K5[7] E, 26 D, 34 G, 11 E, 19[22] A.
82nd row P20[23] A, 10 E, 34 G, 26 D, 5[7] E.
83rd row K8[10] E, 24 D, 34 G, 17 E, 12[15] A.
84th row P13[16] A, 31 E, 19 G, 27 D, 5[7] E.
85th row K19[21] E, 20 D, 15 G, 34 E, 7[10] A.
86th row P8[11] A, 33 E, 16 G, 19 D, 19[21] E.
87th row K20[22] E, 18 D, 17 G, 32 E, 8[11] A.
88th row P18[21] A, 30 E, 24 G, 16 D, 7[9] E.
89th row K8[10] E, 15 D, 25 G, 30 E, 17[20] A.
90th row P17[20] A, 30 E, 6 C, 20 G, 14 D, 8[10] E.
91st row K15[17] E, 17 D, 11 G, 14 C, 22 F, 16[19] A.

92nd row P24[27] A, 14 E, 14 C, 16 G, 12 D, 15[17] E.
93rd row K18[20] E, 9 D, 28 G, 12 C, 10 E, 18[21] A.
94th row P18[21] A, 12 E, 10 C, 29 G, 22 D, 4[6] E.
95th row K5[7] E, 34 D, 17 G, 9 C, 13 E, 17[20] A.
96th row P26[29] A, 8 E, 14 C, 9 G, 33 D, 5[7] E.
97th row K12[14] E, 26 D, 10 G, 14 C, 8 E, 25[28] A.
98th row P25[28] A, 8 E, 14 C, 29 G, 7 D, 12[14] E.
99th row K13[15] E, 21 D, 17 G, 16 C, 24 E, 4[7] A.
100th row P4[7] A, 24 E, 16 C, 31 G, 17 D, 3[5] E.
101st row K3[5] E, 40 D, 9 G, 33 C, 7 E, 3[6] A.
102nd row P3[6] A, 12 E, 35 C, 9 G, 34 D, 2[4] E.
103rd row K7[9] E, 29 D, 9 G, 35 C, 12 E, 3[6] A.

Shape neck

104th row P10 A, 3[5] E, cast off 69[70] sts, P7 D, 6[8] E.
Complete this side first.
105th row K6 E, 7[9] D.
106th row P11[13] D, 2 E.
107th row K3 E, 10[12] D.
108th row P10[12] D, 3 E.
109th row K10 E, 3[5] D.
110th row P11[13] D, 2 E.
111th row K2 E, 11[13] D.
112th row P13[15] D.
113th row K13[15] D.
114th row P10[12] E, 3 D.
115th row K3 D, 10[12] E.
116th row P12[14] E, 1 D.
117th row K10 D, 3[5] E.
118th row P4[6] E, 9 D.
119th row K9 D, 4[6] E.
120th row P9[11] E, 4 D.
121st row K5 D, 8[10] E.
122nd row P8[10] E, 5 D.

36in size only

123rd row K6 D, 9 E.
124th row P15 E.
125th row K15 E.
126th row P15 E.

Both sizes

Cast off.
With RS of work facing, rejoin yarn to rem sts.
105th row K6[8] E, 7 A.
106th row P7 A, 6[8] E.
107th row K11[13] E, 2 A.
108th row P10 A, 3[5] E.
109th row K4[6] E, 9 A.
110th row P9 A, 4[6] E.
111th row K8[10] E, 5 A.
112th row P5 A, 8[10] E.
113th row K9[11] E, 4 A.
114th row P8 A, 5[7] E.
115th row K7[9] E, 6 A.
116th row P11 A, 2[4] E.
117th row K3[5] E, 10 A.
118th row P12 A, 1[3] E.
119th row K9[11] E, 4 A.
120th row P4 A, 9[11] E.
121st row K10[12] E, 3 A.
122nd row P10 A, 3[5] E.

36in size only

123rd row K9 E, 6 A.
124th row P6 A, 9 E.
125th row K10 E, 5 A.
126th row P15 A.

Both sizes

Cast off.

Front

Work as given for back until 40th patt row has been completed.

Divide for neck

41st row K37[39] G, 16 H, turn and leave rem sts on holder.
Complete this side first, still inc at side edge as before on next and every foll 6th row, *at the same time* dec one st at neck edge on every K row,

21

*Super example of
collage knitting for a
V-neck jersey. It is
worked in eight
colours with detailed
row-by-row
instructions*

*Knit
Sizes to fit 86.5
[91.5] cm (34[36] in)
bust*
***

as foll:

42nd row P27[29] H, 27 G, inc one st at end. 54[56] sts.
43rd row K16 G, 11 D, 25[27] H, K2 tog.
44th row P26[28] H, 11 D, 16 G.
45th row K22 G, 20 D, 9[11] H, K2 tog.
46th row P10[12] H, 20 D, 22 G.
47th row K23 G, 20 D, 7[9] H, K2 tog.
48th row P16[18] H, 24 D, 12 G, inc one st at end.
49th row K13 G, 24 D, 13[15] H, K2 tog.
50th row P14[16] H, 24 D, 13 G.
51st row K17 G, 25 D, 7[9] H, K2 tog.
52nd row P8[10] H, 25 D, 17 G.
53rd row K18 G, 25 D, 5[7] H, K2 tog.
54th row P7[9] H, 25 D, 18 G, inc one st at end.
55th row K18 G, 25 D, 5[7] H, K2 tog.
56th row P16[18] H, 25 D, 8 G.
57th row K8 G, 25 D, 14[16] H, K2 tog.
58th row P15[17] H, 25 D, 8 G.
59th row K11 G, 26 D, 9[11] H, K2 tog.
60th row P10[12] H, 26 D, 12 G, inc one st at end.
61st row K12 G, 26 D, 8[10] H, K2 tog.
62nd row P19[21] H, 23 D, 5 G.
63rd row K5 G, 23 D, 17[19] H, K2 tog.
64th row P25[27] H, 21 D, 46[48] sts.

Shape armhole
65th row Cast off 4 sts, K18 D, 22[24] H, K2 tog.
66th row P22[24] H, 19 D.
67th row Cast off 3 sts, K11 D, 8 F, 17[19] H, K2 tog.
68th row P17[19] H, 8 F, 12 D.
69th row Cast off 2 sts, K14 D, 10 F, 9[11] H, K2 tog.
70th row P9[11] H, 10 F, 15 D.
71st row Dec one st, K15 D, 10 F, 6[8] H, K2 tog.
72nd row P6[8] H, 10 F, 16 D.
73rd row K16 D, 10 F, 4[6] H, K2 tog.
74th row P13[15] H, 12 F, 6 D.
75th row K6 D, 12 F, 11[13] H, K2 tog.
76th row P12[14] H, 12 F, 6 D.
77th row K12 D, 8 F, 8[10] H, K2 tog.
78th row P9[11] H, 8 F, 12 D.
79th row K12 D, 10 F, 5[7] H, K2 tog.
80th row P6[8] H, 10 F, 12 D.
81st row K12 D, 10 F, 4[6] H, K2 tog.
82nd row P5[7] H, 10 F, 12 D.
83rd row K15 D, 9 F, 1[3] H, K2 tog.
84th row P2[4] H, 21 F, 3 D.
85th row K3 D, 21 [23] F, K2 tog.
86th row P7[9] G, 18 F.
87th row K18 F, 5[7] G, K2 tog.
88th row P13[15] G, 11 F.
89th row K15 F, 7[9] G, K2 tog.
90th row P14[16] G, 9 F.
91st row K9 F, 12[14] G, K2 tog.
92nd row P14[16] G, 8 F.
93rd row K14 F, 6[8] G, K2 tog.
94th row P7[9] G, 14 F.
95th row K14 F, 5[7] G, K2 tog.
96th row P15[17] G, 5 F.
97th row K5 F, 13[15] G, K2 tog.
98th row P15[17] G, 4 F.
99th row K7 F, 10[12] G, K2 tog.
100th row P11[13] G, 7 F.
101st row K10 F, 6[8] G, K2 tog.
102nd row P13[15] G, 4 F.
103rd row K4 F, 11 [13] G, K2 tog.
104th row P16[18] G.
105th row K14[16] G, K2 tog.
106th row P7[9] G, 8 E.
107th row K8 E, 5[7] G, K2 tog.
108th row P6[8] G, 8 E.
109th row K11 E, 1[3] G, K2 tog.
110th row P2[4] G, 11 E.
111th row K11[13] E, K2 tog. Cont without shaping.
112th row P5[7] G, 7 E.
113th row K7 E, 5[7] G.
114th row P7[9] G, 5 E.
115th row K5 E, 7[9] G.
116th row P8[10] G, 4 E.
117th row K8 E, 4[6] G.
118th row P10[12] G, 2 E.
119th row K2 E, 10[12] G.

120th row P12[14] G.
121st row K12[14] G.
122nd row P12[14] G.
36in size only
123rd row K14 G.
124th row P14 G.
Rep last 2 rows once more.
Both sizes
Cast off.
With RS of work facing, rejoin yarn to rem sts.
41st row K2 tog [sl 1, K2 tog, psso] H, K15 H, 24 F, 13[15] C.
42nd row Inc one st at beg, P14[16] C, 24 F, 16 H. 54[56] sts.
43rd row K2 tog H, K20 H, 19 F, 13[15] C.
44th row P24[26] C, 14 F, 15 H.
45th row K2 tog H, K14 H, 14 F, 23[25] C.
46th row P23[25] C, 14 F, 15 H.
47th row K2 tog H, K21 H, 20 F, 9[11] C.
48th row Inc one st at beg, P10[12] C, 20 F, 22 H.
49th row K2 tog H, K21 H, 20 F, 9[11] C.
50th row P9[11] C, 20 F, 22 H.
51st row K2 tog H, K21 H, 20 F, 8[10] C.
52nd row P8[10] C, 20 F, 22 H.
53rd row K2 tog H, K20 H, 21 F, 7[9] C.
54th row Inc one st at beg, P20[22] C, 16 F, 14 H.
55th row K2 tog H, K12 H, 16 F, 20[22] C.
56th row P21[23] C, 16 F, 12 H.
57th row K2 tog H, K22 H, 20 F, 5[7] C.
58th row P15[17] C, 10 F, 23 H.
59th row K2 tog H, K22 H, 24[26] F.
60th row Inc one st at beg, P19[21] F, 12 B, 17 H.
61st row K2 tog H, K15 H, 12 B, 19[21] F.
62nd row P19[21] F, 20 B, 8 H.
63rd row K2 tog H, K6 H, 21 B, 18[19] F.
64th row P24[26] F, 15 B, 7 H.
65th row K2 tog H, K14 H, 19 B, 11[13] F.

Shape armhole
66th row Cast off 4 sts, P8[10] A, 18 B, 15 H.
67th row K2 tog H, K8 H, 10 E, 13 B, 8[10] A.
68th row Cast off 3 sts, P12[14] A, 6 B, 10 E, 9 H.
69th row K2 tog H, K7 H, 10 E, 6 B, 12[14] A.
70th row Cast off 2 sts, P13[15] A, 8 B, 13 E.
71st row K2 tog E, K11 E, 8 B, 13[15] A.
72nd row Dec one st, P12[14] A, 7 B, 12 E.
73rd row K2 tog E, K14 E, 10 B, 6[8] A.
74th row P6[8] A, 18 B, 7 E.
75th row K2 tog E, K5 E, 18 B, 6[8] A.
76th row P7[9] A, 17 B, 6 E.
77th row K2 tog E, K9 E, 13 B, 6[8] A.
78th row P6[8] A, 13 B, 10 E.
79th row K2 tog E, K14 E, 11 B, 2[4] A.
80th row P2[4] A, 11 B, 15 G.
81st row K2 tog E, K13 E, 11 G, 2[4] A.
82nd row P2[4] A, 11 G, 14 E.
83rd row K2 tog E, K15 E, 8 G, 2[4] A.
84th row P7[9] A, 12 G, 7 E.
85th row K2 tog E, K5 E, 12 G, 7[9] A.
86th row P7[9] A, 12 G, 6 E.
87th row K2 tog E, K11 E, 5 G, 7[9] A.
88th row P7[9] A, 5 G, 12 E.
89th row K2 tog E, K10 E, 5 G, 7[9] A.
90th row P10[12] A, 13 G.
91st row K2 tog G, K11 G, 10[12] A.
92nd row P10[12] A, 12 G.
93rd row K2 tog G, K16 G, 4[6] A.
94th row P4[6] A, 17 G.
95th row K2 tog G, K16 G, 3[5] A.
96th row P4[6] A, 16 G.
97th row K2 tog G, K14 G, 4[6] A.
98th row P15[17] A, 4 G.
99th row K2 tog G, K9 G, 8[10] A.
100th row P8[10] A, 10 G.
101st row K2 tog G, K9 G, 7[9] A.
102nd row P7[9] A, 10 G.
103rd row K2 tog G, K9 G, 6[8] A.
104th row P11[13] A, 5 G.
105th row K2 tog G, K5 G, 11[13] A.
106th row P12[14] A, 3 G.
107th row K2 tog G, 13[15] G.
108th row P14[16] G.
109th row K2 tog G, K12[14] G.

110th row P6[8] D, 7 G.
111th row K2 tog G, K5 G, 6[8] D. 12[14] sts. Cont without shaping.
112th row P7[9] D, 5 G.
113th row K5 G, 7[9] D.
114th row P8[10] D, 4 G.
115th row K9 G, 3[5] D.
116th row P4[6] D, 8 G.
117th row K8 G, 4[6] D.
118th row P8[10] D, 4 G.
119th row K4 G, 8[10] D.
120th row P12[14] D.
121st row K12[14] D.
122nd row P12[14] D.
36in size only
Rep 121st and 122nd rows twice more.
Both sizes
Cast off.

Sleeves
Using No.11 needles and A, cast on 44 sts. Work 6in K2, P2 rib as given for back. Change to No.10 needles. Commence patt.
1st row K11 C, 11 G, 11 D, 11 B.
2nd row P11 B, 11 D, 11 G, 11 C.
Cont in patt, inc one st at each end of next and foll 10th and 20th rows, then every foll 8th row until there are 70[74] sts, as foll:
3rd row Inc one st at each end, K17 C, 11 G, 6 D, 12 B.
4th row P12 B, 6 D, 11 G, 17 C.
5th row K21 C, 9 G, 4 D, 12 B.
6th row P15 B, 5 D, 5 G, 21 C.
7th row K21 C, 5 G, 14 D, 6 B.
8th row P6 B, 15 D, 11 G, 14 C.
9th row K14 C, 11 G, 16 D, 5 B.
10th row Inc one st at each end, P11 B, 12 D, 11 G, 14 C.
11th row K14 C, 11 G, 12 D, 11 B.
12th row P17 B, 9 D, 14 G, 8 C.
13th row K8 C, 14 G, 9 D, 17 B.
14th row P18 B, 11 D, 12 G, 7 C.
15th row K7 C, 12 G, 14 D, 15 B.
16th row P22 B, 10 D, 11 G, 5 C.
17th row K5 C, 20 G, 5 D, 18 B.
18th row P18 B, 5 D, 21 G, 4 C.
19th row K4 C, 22 G, 5 D, 17 B.
20th row Inc one st at each end, P18 B, 18 D, 9 G, 5 C.
21st row K11 C, 11 G, 15 D, 13 B.
22nd row P13 B, 15 D, 11 G, 11 C.
23rd row K12 C, 11 G, 15 D, 12 B.
24th row P19 B, 15 D, 9 G, 7 C.
25th row K7 C, 9 G, 15 D, 19 B.
26th row P8 A, 17 B, 12 D, 7 G, 6 C.
27th row K6 C, 7 G, 12 D, 17 B, 8 A.
28th row Inc one st at each end, P17 A, 14 B, 10 D, 5 G, 6 C.
29th row K6 C, 12 G, 3 D, 14 B, 17 A.
30th row P18 A, 14 B, 10 D, 10 G.
31st row K10 G, 17 D, 15 B, 10 A.
32nd row P10 A, 15 B, 17 D, 10 G.
33rd row K11 G, 17 D, 15 B, 9 A.
34th row P20 A, 14 B, 14 D, 4 G.
35th row K4 G, 15 D, 14 B, 19 A.
36th row Inc one st at each end, P20 A, 14 B, 16 D, 4 G.
37th row K14 G, 11 D, 15 B, 14 A.
38th row P14 A, 15 B, 11 D, 14 G.
39th row K7 G, 7 F, 12 D, 15 B, 13 A.
40th row P24 A, 4 B, 12 D, 7 F, 7 G.
41st row K8 G, 11 F, 8 D, 11 B, 16 A.
42nd row P16 A, 11 B, 8 D, 11 F, 8 G.
43rd row K9 G, 14 F, 5 D, 11 B, 15 A.
44th row Inc one st at each end, P11 E, 10 A, 11 B, 14 F, 10 G.
45th row K11 G, 14 F, 10 B, 10 A, 11 E.
46th row P15 E, 11 A, 6 B, 20 F, 4 G.
47th row K4 G, 21 F, 5 B, 11 A, 15 E.
48th row P16 E, 11 A, 4 B, 22 F, 3 G.
49th row K14 G, 12 F, 3 B, 11 A, 16 E.
50th row P23 E, 7 A, 7 B, 5 F, 14 G.

51st row K14 G, 12 F, 7 A, 23 E.
52nd row Inc one st at each end, P25 E, 7 A, 12 F, 14 G.
53rd row K14 G, 12 F, 12 A, 20 E.
54th row P20 E, 12 A, 15 F, 11 G.
55th row K11 G, 19 F, 14 A, 14 E.
56th row P14 E, 14 A, 19 F, 11 G.
57th row K18 G, 17 F, 10 A, 13 E.
58th row P7 H, 16 F, 17 F, 18 G.
59th row K25 G, 10 F, 16 E, 7 H.
60th row Inc one st at each end, P8 H, 16 E, 10 F, 26 G.
61st row K27 G, 10 F, 16 E, 7 H.
62nd row P12 H, 16 E, 12 F, 20 G.
63rd row K20 G, 12 F, 16 E, 12 H.
64th row P17 H, 12 E, 12 F, 19 G.
65th row K23 G, 8 F, 12 E, 17 H.
66th row P18 H, 15 E, 11 F, 16 G.
67th row K16 G, 11 F, 22 E, 11 H.
68th row Inc one st at each end, P12 H, 23 E, 11 F, 16 G.
69th row K21 G, 13 F, 17 E, 11 H.
70th row P11 H, 17 E, 13 F, 21 G.
71st row K22 G, 13 F, 16 E, 11 H.
72nd row P22 H, 10 E, 22 F, 8 G.
73rd row K8 G, 22 F, 10 E, 22 H.
74th row P29 H, 10 E, 23 F.
75th row K23 F, 10 E, 29 H.
76th row Inc one st at each end, P31 H, 10 E, 23 F.
77th row K15 D, 8 F, 10 E, 31 H.
78th row P31 H, 10 E, 8 F, 15 D.
79th row K23 D, 7 F, 11 E, 23 H.
80th row P15 C, 8 H, 11 E, 7 F, 23 D.
81st row K23 D, 8 F, 11 E, 7 H. 15 C.
82nd row P15 C, 7 H, 15 E, 9 F, 18 D.
83rd row K27 D, 15 E, 7 H, 15 C.
84th row Inc one st at each end, P19 C, 9 H, 10 E, 28 D.
85th row K29 D, 9 E, 9 H, 19 C.
86th row P20 C, 9 H, 24 E, 13 D.
87th row K13 D, 24 E, 16 H, 13 C.
88th row P13 C, 19 H, 22 E, 12 D.
89th row K24 D, 19 E, 11 H, 12 C.
90th row P12 C, 11 H, 19 E, 24 D.
91st row K25 D, 20 E, 10 H, 11 C.
92nd row Inc one st at each end, P22 C, 14 H, 14 E, 18 D.
93rd row K18 D, 14 E, 14 H, 22 C.
94th row P23 C, 14 H, 14 E, 17 D.
95th row K24 D, 14 E, 14 H, 16 C.
96th row P16 C, 14 H, 14 E, 24 D.
97th row K9 B, 16 D, 14 E, 14 H, 15 C.
98th row P23 C, 16 H, 10 E, 10 D, 9 B.
99th row K14 B, 5 D, 10 E, 16 H, 23 C.
100th row Inc one st at each end, P25 C, 16 H, 10 E, 4 D, 15 B. 70[70] sts.
Cont without shaping on 34in size only and inc one st at each end of foll 8th rows twice more on 36in size only.
101st row K16 B, 11 D, 8 E, 15 H, 10 C, 10 G.
102nd row P10 G, 18 C, 15 H, 11 D, 16 B.
103rd row K17 B, 11 D, 14 H, 18 C, 10 G.
104th row P17 G, 16 C, 9 H, 11 D, 17 B.
105th row K20 B, 9 D, 8 H, 16 C, 17 G.
106th row P18 G, 20 C, 8 H, 4 D, 20 B.
107th row K20 B, 4 D, 16 H, 12 C, 18 G.
108th row Inc one st at each end on 36 in size only, P25[26[G, 21 C, 13 D, 11[12] B.
109th row K11[12] B, 13 D, 21 C, 25[26] G.
110th row P29[30] G, 20 C, 11 D, 10[11] B.
111th row K17[18] B, 14 D, 26 C, 13[14] G.
112th row P13[14] G, 26 C, 14 D, 17[18] B.
113th row K24[25] B, 14 D, 20 C, 12[13] G.
114th row P19[20] G, 13 C, 14 D, 24[25] B.
115th row K29[30] B, 10 D, 12 C, 19[20] G.
116th row Inc one st at each end on 36in size only, P26[28] G, 12 C, 19 D, 13[15] B. 70[74] sts.
Cont without shaping.
117th row K13[15] B, 19 D, 12 C, 26[28] G.
118th row P30[32] G, 12 C, 16 D, 12[14] B.
119th row K21[23] B, 7 D, 20 C, 22[24] G.

120th row P22[24] G, 20 C, 7 D, 21[23] B.
121st row K26[28] B, 8 D, 15 C, 21[23] G.
122nd row P32[34] G, 4 C, 8 D, 26[28] B.
123rd row K26[28] B, 8 D, 4 C, 32[34] G.
124th row P36[38] G, 15 D, 19[21] B.
Shape top
125th row Cast off 3 sts, K16[18] B, 15 D, 36[38] G.
126th row Cast off 3 sts, P37[39] G, 11 D, 16[18] B.
127th row Cast off 2 sts, K23[25] B, 12 D, 27[29] G.
128th row Cast off 2 sts, P24[26] G, 12 D, 24[26] B.
129th row Dec one st, K23[25] B, 12 D, 24[26] G.
130th row Dec one st, P22[24] G, 12 D, 24[26] B. 58[62] sts.
131st row Dec one st, K28[30] B, 14 D, 15[17] G.
132nd row Dec one st, P23[25] G, 4 D, 29[31] B.
133rd row Dec one st, K30[32] B, 25[27] G.
134th row Dec one st, P22[24] G, 32[34] B.
135th row Dec one st, K36[38] B, 17[19] G.
136th row Dec one st, P16[18] G, 36[38] B.
137th row Dec one st, K35[37] B, 16[18] G.
138th row Dec one st, P29[31] G, 21[23] B.
139th row Dec one st, K20[22] B, 29[31] G.
140th row Dec one st, P35[37] G, 13[15] B.
141st row Dec one st, K30[32] B, 17[19] G.
142nd row Dec one st, P16[18] G, 30[32] B.
143rd row Dec one st, K30[32] B, 15[17] G.
144th row Dec one st, P14[16] G, 33[35] B.
145th row Dec one st, K36[38] B, 7[9] G.
146th row Dec one st, P23[25] G, 19[21] B.
147th row Dec one st, K18[20] B, 23[25] G.
148th row Dec one st, P16[18] G, 12 D, 12[14] B.
149th row Dec one st, K11[13] B, 12 D, 16[18] G.
150th row Dec one st, P21[23] G, 9 D, 8[10] B.
151st row Dec one st, K6[8] B, 15 D, 16[18] G.
152nd row Dec one st, P15[17] G, 15 D, 6[8] B.
153rd row Dec one st, K11[13] B, 15 D, 9[11] G.
154th row Dec one st, P19[21] G, 15[17] D.
155th row Dec one st, K14[16] D, 19[21] G.
156th row Dec one st, P18[20] G, 14[16] D.
157th row Dec one st, K14[16] D, 17[19] G.
158th row Dec one st, P22[24] G, 8[10] D.
159th row Dec one st, K8[10] D, 21[23] G.
160th row Dec one st, P20[22] G, 8[10] D.
161st row Dec one st, K18[20] D, 9[11] G.
162nd row Dec one st, P8[10] G, 18[20] D. 26[30] sts.
36in size only
Cont to dec one st at beg of every row, rep 159th–162nd rows once more. 26 sts.
Both sizes
Next row K2 tog D, K18 D, 4 G, K2 tog G.
Next row P5 G, 19 D.
Next row K2 tog D, K18 D, 2 G, K2 tog G.
Next row P15 G, 7 D.
Next row K2 tog D, K5 D, K13 G, K2 tog G.
Next row P14 G, 6 D.
Next row K2 tog D, K10 D, 6 G, K2 tog G.
Next row P9 G, 9 D.
Next row K2 tog D, K8 D, K6 G, K2 tog G.
Next row P11 G, 5 D.
Next row K2 tog D, K8 D, 4 G, K2 tog G.
Next row P9 G, 5 D.
Next row K2 tog D, K7 D, 3 G, K2 tog G.
Next row P8 G, 4 D.
Next row K2 tog D, K4 D, 4 G, K2 tog G.
Next row P3 G, 7 D.
Cast off.

Back neckband
Using No.11 needles, A and with RS of work facing. K up 104 sts round back neck. Work 2in K2, P2 rib as given for back.
Next row *K2, P2 tog, rep from * to end.
Cast off in rib.

Front neckband
Using No.11 needles, A and with RS of work facing K up 76 sts down right side of neck, K up one st in centre and mark with coloured thread, K up 76 sts up left side of neck. Work 2in K2, P2

rib as given for back, dec one st at each side of centre st on every alt row.
Next row *K2, P2 tog, rep from * to end.
Cast off in rib.

To make up
Press each piece under a damp cloth with a warm iron, omitting ribbing. Join shoulder and neckband seams. Set in sleeves. Join side and sleeve seams. Press seams.

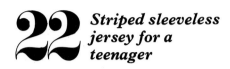

22 Striped sleeveless jersey for a teenager

Size
To fit 28/30in bust
Length to shoulder, 17in
Tension
$6\frac{1}{4}$ sts and 9 rows to 1in over st st worked on No. 10 needles
Materials
2 balls Sirdar Fontein Crepe 4 ply in main shade, A
2 balls each of contrast colours, B, C and D
One pair No.10 needles
One pair No.11 needles
Set of 4 No.11 needles pointed at both ends

Back
Using No.11 needles and A, cast on 99 sts.
1st row K1, *P1, K1, rep from * to end.
2nd row P1, *K1, P1, rep from * to end.
Rep these 2 rows for $1\frac{1}{2}$in, ending with 2nd row.
Change to No.10 needles and B. Beg with a K row, cont in st st working in stripe patt of 10 rows B, 10 rows C, 10 rows D, 10 rows A, until work measures 11in from beg, ending with a P row.
Shape armholes
Cont in stripe patt, casting off 5 sts at beg of next 2 rows, 3 sts at beg of foll 2 rows and 2 sts at beg of next 2 rows. Dec one st at each end of foll 2 rows. 75 sts.
Cont in striped st st without shaping until armholes measure 7in from beg, ending with a P row.
Shape neck
Next row K32, cast off next 11 sts, K to end. 32 sts. P 1 row.
Cast off 5 sts at neck edge on next and foll alt row.
Shape shoulder
Cast off 3 sts at armhole edge on next and foll 3 alt rows, *at the same time* cont to cast off 5 sts at neck edge on alt rows twice more. With WS of work facing, rejoin yarn to rem sts and complete to match first side, reversing shaping.

Front
Work as given for back until armhole shaping has been completed. 75 sts. Work 1in without shaping.
Shape neck
Next row K32, cast off next 11 sts, K to end. 32 sts. P 1 row.
Cast off 5 sts at beg of next row, 3 sts at beg of foll 2 alt rows and 2 sts at beg of next 2 alt rows. 17 sts. P 1 row. Dec one st at neck edge on foll 5 alt rows. 12 sts.
Cont without shaping until armhole measures same as back to shoulder, ending at armhole edge.
Shape shoulder
Cast off 3 sts at beg of next and foll 3 alt rows. With WS of work facing, rejoin yarn to rem sts and complete to match first side, reversing shaping.

To make up
Press each piece on WS under a damp cloth with a warm iron avoiding ribbing. Join shoulder and side seams. Press seams.
Armbands Using set of 4 No.11 needles, A

22 23,24

Happy-go-lucky striped sleeveless jersey for a teenager. Worked in wide bands of four colours.

Pullover in a striped and diamond pattern with a round neck. Sleeveless pullover worked in contrasting colours.

Knit
Size to fit 71.0|
76.0cm (28|30in)
bust

*

Knit
Sizes to fit 66.0
[71.0:76.0]cm
(26[28:30]in) chest

**

and with RS of work facing, beg at side seam and K up 106 sts evenly round armhole. Work ¾in in K1, P1 rib. Cast off in rib.

Neckband Using set of 4 No.11 needles, A and with RS of work facing, beg at left shoulder seam and K up 160 sts evenly round neck. Work ¾in in K1, P1 rib. Cast off in rib.

23 Diamond patterned pullover

Sizes

To fit 26[28:30]in chest
Length to shoulder, 15[16½:18]in
The figures in brackets [] refer to the 28 and 30in sizes respectively

Tension

6 sts and 8 rows to 1in over st st worked on No.9 needles

Materials

2[2:3] balls Sirdar Double Knitting in main shade, A
1[2:2] balls of contrast colour, B
1[2:2] balls of contrast colour, C
One pair No.9 needles
One pair No.11 needles
Set of 4 No.11 needles pointed at both ends

Note

To avoid breaking yarn at ends of rows and rejoining as required on patt rep, double pointed No.9 needles may be used to go back to the correct end of work to pick up yarn and complete row

Back

Using No.11 needles and A, cast on 85[91:97] sts.
1st row K1, *P1, K1, rep from * to end.
Break off A. Join in B.
2nd row P to end.
3rd row As 1st.
4th row P1, *K1, P1, rep from * to end.
Rep 3rd and 4th rows until work measures 2in, ending with a 4th row. Change to No.9 needles.
Beg with a K row cont in st st, working in patt as foll:
1 row A, 4 rows C, 1 row A, 3 rows B and 2 rows A.
12th row P3 A, *1 C, 5 A, rep from * to last 4 sts, 1 C, 3 A.
13th row K2 A, *3 C, 3 A, rep from * to last 5 sts, 3 C, 2 A.
14th row P1 A, *5 C, 1 A, rep from * to end.
15th row As 13th.
16th row As 12th.
Work 2 rows A, then 3 rows B.
These 21 rows form rep of patt, noting that on every alt rep it will be necessary to read K for P and P for K. Cont in patt until work measures 9½[10½:11½]in from beg, ending with a P row.

Shape armholes

Keeping patt correct throughout, cast off at beg of next and every row, 4 sts twice and 3[4:5] sts twice. 71[75:79] sts. Work 2 rows without shaping.
Cast on at beg of next and every row, 3[4:5] sts twice, 4 sts twice and 9[12:15] sts twice. 103[115: 127] sts. Mark each end of this row with coloured thread. Cont without shaping until work measures 12[13½:14½]in from beg, ending with a WS row.**

Shape shoulders and neck

Dec one st at each end of next and foll 4th row, then at each end of foll 4 alt rows, ending with a P row.
Next row Cast off 2 sts, K31[37:43], cast off 25 sts, K to end.
Complete this side first.
Cast off at armhole edge on next and every alt row, 2 sts 3 times, 3 sts 1[2:3] times, then 8 sts once, *at the same time* cast off at neck edge on every

alt row, 2 sts 3 times and one st 2[3:4] times.
Cast off rem 8[10:12] sts.
With WS of work facing, rejoin yarn to rem sts and complete to match first side, reversing shaping, noting that first 2 sts have already been cast off at armhole edge.

Front

Work as given for back to **.
Shape shoulders and neck
Next row K2 tog, K44[50:56], cast off 11 sts, K to last 2 sts, K2 tog.
Complete this side first. Shape shoulder as given for back, *at the same time* cast off at neck edge on next and every alt row, 2 sts 3 times and one st 9[10:11] times. Cast off rem 8[10:12] sts.
With WS of work facing, rejoin yarn to rem sts and complete to match first side, reversing shaping.

Neckband

Join shoulder seams from marked points. Using set of 4 No.11 needles, A and with RS of work facing, K up 116[124:132] sts round neck. Work ¾in K1, P1 rib. Cast off in rib.

Armbands

Using No.11 needles, A and with RS of work facing, K up 60[66:72] sts round armholes. Work ¾in K1, P1 rib. Cast off in rib.

To make up

Press each piece under a damp cloth with a warm iron. Join side seams. Press seams.

24 Striped pullover

Sizes

To fit 26[28:30]in chest
Length to shoulder, 15[16½:18]in
The figures in brackets [] refer to the 28 and 30in sizes respectively

Tension

6 sts and 8 rows to 1in over st st worked on No.9 needles

Materials

Sirdar Double Knitting
1[1:1] ball each of 8 colours, A, B, C, D, E, F, G and H
One pair No.9 needles
One pair No.11 needles
Set of 4 No.11 needles pointed at both ends

Back

Using No.11 needles and A, cast on 81[87:91] sts.
1st row K1, * P1, K1, rep from * to end.
2nd row P1, *K1, P1, rep from * to end.
Rep these 2 rows until work measures 1½in, ending with a 2nd row and inc one st at end of last row on 26 and 30in sizes only.
82[87:92] sts.
Change to No.9 needles.
Commence patt.
1st row Using B, K3, *sl 1, K4, rep from * to last 4 sts, sl 1, K3.
2nd row Using B, P3, *sl 1, P4, rep from * to last 4 sts, sl 1, P3.
3rd row Using B, K to end.
4th row Using C, as 2nd.
5th row Using C, as 1st.
6th row Using C, P to end.
These 6 rows form patt and are rep throughout, working 3 rows in each colour, i.e. D, E, F, G, H, A, B, C, etc.
Cont in patt until work measures 9½[10½:11½]in from beg, ending with a WS row.

Shape armholes

Keeping patt correct, cast off 4 sts at beg of

next 2 rows.
Dec one st at each end of next and foll 3[4:5] alt rows. 66[69:72] sts. Cont without shaping until armholes measure 5½[6:6½]in from beg, ending with a WS row.

Shape shoulder and neck

Next row Patt 22[23:24] sts, turn and leave rem sts on holder.
Complete this side first.
Next row Cast off 2 sts, patt to end.
Next row Cast off 6 sts, patt to end.
Rep these 2 rows once more. Work 1 row. Cast off rem 6[7:8] sts.
With RS side of work facing, sl first 22[23:24] sts on to holder and leave for centre back neck, rejoin yarn to rem sts and patt to end. Complete to match first side, reversing shaping.

Front

Work as given for back until armhole shaping is completed. Cont without shaping until armholes measure 3½[4:4½]in from beg, ending with a WS row.

Shape neck

Next row Patt 27[28:29] sts, turn and leave rem sts on holder.
Complete this side first.
Cast off at neck edge on next and every alt row, 2 sts 3 times and one st 3 times. Cont without shaping until armhole measures same as back to shoulder, ending with a WS row.

Shape shoulder

Cast off at beg of next and every alt row 6 sts twice and 6[7:8] sts once.
With RS of work facing, sl first 12[13:14] sts onto holder and leave for centre neck, rejoin yarn to rem sts and patt to end. Complete to match first side, reversing shaping.

Neckband

Join shoulder seams. Using set of 4 No.11 needles, A and with RS of work facing, K up 6 sts down right back neck, K across back neck sts on holder, K up 6 sts up left back neck and K up 30 sts down left front neck, K across front neck sts on holder and K up 30 sts up right front neck. 106[108:110] sts. Work in rounds of K1, P1 rib for ¾in. Cast off in rib.

Armbands

Using No.11 needles, A and with RS of work facing, K up 70[76:82] sts round armhole. Work in K1, P1 rib for ¾in.
Cast off in rib.

To make up

Press each piece under a damp cloth with a warm iron.
Join side seams.
Press seams.

25 Trouser suit with triangle patterns

Sizes

To fit 34 [36:38]in bust
36 [38:40]in hips
Jacket length to shoulder, 25 [26:27]in
Sleeve seam, 17 [17½:18]in
Trousers inside leg, 28½in, adjustable
The figures in brackets [] refer to the 36 and 38in sizes respectively

Tension

7 sts and 9 rows to 1in over reversed st st worked on No.10 needles

Materials

45[48:51] balls Lee Target New Duo Crepe Tricel Nylon 4 ply

One pair No.10 needles
Set of 4 No.12 needles pointed at both ends
Cable needle
6 buttons
Waist length of elastic

Trousers
Right front leg
Using No.10 needles cast on 77[80:83] sts. Beg with a P row cont in reversed st st until work measures 20in from beg, ending with a K row. Adjust leg length here, allowing for 1½in hem. Inc one st at beg of next and every foll 8th row until there are 89[92:95] sts. Cont without shaping until work measures 30in from beg, ending with a K row.

Shape crutch
Cast off at beg of next and every alt row 3 sts once, 2 sts once and one st 2[3:4] times. Dec one st at this edge on every 8th row 6 times in all, *at the same time* dec one st at end of 1st and every foll 10th row 6 times in all. 70[72:74] sts. Cont without shaping until work measures 11½in from beg of crutch shaping, ending with a K row. Cast off.

Left front leg
Work as given for right front leg, reversing shaping.

Right back leg
Using No.10 needles cast on 87[90:93] sts. Beg with a P row cont in reversed st st until work measures 20in from beg, or required length, ending with a P row.
Inc one st at beg of next and every foll 8th row until there are 99[102:105] sts. Cont without shaping until work measures same as right front leg to beg of crutch shaping, ending with a P row.

Shape crutch
Cast off at beg of next and every alt row 6 sts once, 3 sts once, 2 sts 4 times and one st 5[6:7] times. Dec one st at this edge on every 8th row 5 times in all, *at the same time* dec one st at end of 1st and every foll 10th row 6 times in all. 66[68:70] sts. Cont without shaping until work measures same as front legs, ending with a K row. Cast off.

Left back leg
Work as given for right back leg, reversing shaping.

To make up
Press each piece lightly under a dry cloth with a cool iron. Join front and back seams. Join leg and side seams. Make 2 darts in back waist 4in long. Turn 1in at waist to WS and sl st down. Thread elastic through waist. Turn up 1½in hem at lower edge of legs and sl st down. Press seams.

Jacket back
Using No.10 needles cast on 130[138:146] sts. Beg with a K row work in st st for 2in, ending with a P row. Beg with a P row work in reversed st st for 20 rows.
Shape sides
Dec one st at each end of next and every foll 8th row until 110[118:126] sts rem. Cont without shaping until work measures 14in from beg, ending with a K row. Inc one st at each end of next and every foll 6th row until there are 122[130:138] sts. Cont without shaping until work measures 19 [19½:20]in from beg, ending with a K row.
Shape armholes
Cast off at beg of next and every row 5 sts twice, 3 sts twice and 2 sts twice. P2 tog at each end of next and foll 0[1:2] alt rows. 100[106: 112] sts. Cont without shaping until armholes

measure 7 [7½:8]in from beg, ending with a K row.
Shape shoulders
Cast off at beg of next and every row 8[8:9] sts 4 times and 8[9:9] sts 4 times. Cast off rem 36[38:40] sts.

Jacket left front
Using No.10 needles cast on 68[72:76] sts. Beg with a K row work 2in st st, ending with a P row. Beg with a P row work 2 rows reversed st st. Commence patt.
1st row P30[32:34] sts, ybk, sl 1, yfwd, P to end.
2nd row K37[39:41] sts, P1, K to end.
Rep these 2 rows 10 times more but shape side by P2 tog at beg of 17th row.
23rd row P22[24:26] sts, K15 sts, P to end.
24th row K30[32:34] sts, P15 sts, K to end.
25th row P2 tog, P20[22:24] sts, sl next st on to cable needle and hold at front of work, P1 then sl 1 from cable needle – called C2L –, K11 sts, sl next st on to cable needle and hold at back of work, sl 1 then P1 from cable needle – called C2R –, P to end.
26th row K31[33:35] sts, P13 sts, K to end.
27th row P22[24:26] sts, C2L, K9 sts, C2R, P to end.
28th row K32[34:36] sts, P11 sts, K to end.
29th row P23[25:27] sts, C2L, K7 sts, C2R, P to end.
30th row K33[35:37] sts, P9 sts, K to end.
31st row P24[26:28] sts, C2L, K5 sts, C2R, P to end.
32nd row K34[36:38] sts, P7 sts, K to end.
33rd row P2 tog, P23[25:27] sts, C2L, K3 sts, C2R, P to end.
34th row K35[37:39] sts, P5 sts, K to end.
35th row P25[27:29] sts, C2L, K1, C2R, P to end.
36th row K36[38:40] sts, P3 sts, K to end.
37th row P26[28:30] sts, sl next st on cable needle and hold at front of work, P2 tog then sl 1 from cable needle, K up 1, P to end.
38th row K37[39:41] sts, P1, K to end.
Rep these 38 rows throughout, keeping patt in line, *at the same time* cont to dec at beg of every 8th row until 58[62:66] sts rem. Cont without shaping until work measures 14in from beg, ending with a WS row. Inc one st at beg of next and every foll 6th row until there are 64[68:72] sts. Cont without shaping until work measures same as back to underarm, ending with a WS row.
Shape armhole and front edge
Cast off at beg of next and every alt row 5 sts once, 3 sts once, 2 sts once, then dec one st at armhole edge on foll 1[2:3] alt rows, *at the same time* P2 tog at front edge on 3rd and every foll alt row until 32[34:36] sts rem. Cont without shaping until armhole measures same as back to shoulder, ending with a WS row.
Shape shoulder
Cast off at beg of next and every alt row 8[8:9] sts twice and 8[9:9] sts twice.

Jacket right front
Work as given for left front, reversing all shaping and position of patt, as foll:
1st row P37[39:41] sts, ybk, sl 1, yfwd, P to end.

Sleeves
Using No.10 needles cast on 53[57:61] sts. Beg with a K row work 2in st st, ending with a P row. Commence patt.
1st row P9[10:11] sts, *ybk, sl 1, yfwd, P16 [17:18] sts, rep from * once more, ybk, sl 1, yfwd, P9[10:11] sts.
2nd row K9[10:11] sts, *P1, K16[17:18] sts, rep from * once more, P1, K9[10:11] sts.
Rep these 2 rows 3 times more.
9th row P2[3:4] sts, *K15 sts, P2[3:4], rep from * twice more.

10th row K2[3:4] sts, *P15 sts, K2[3:4], rep from * twice more.
Cont to work these 3 groups of 15 sts in patt as given for front until 14 more rows have been worked to complete triangle, then cont in reversed st st only. *at the same time* inc one st at each end of next and every foll 6th row until there are 85[89:93] sts. Cont without shaping until sleeve measures 18 [18½:19]in from beg, ending with a K row.
Shape top
Cast off at beg of next and every row 3 sts twice and 2 sts 4[6:8] times. Dec one st at each end of next and foll 17 alt rows. Cast off 2 sts at beg of next 8 rows.
Cast off rem 19 sts.

Front band
Using set of 4 No.12 needles cast on 22 sts and work in rounds of st st for 3in.
Next round (buttonhole round) K4 sts, cast off 3 sts, K8 sts, cast off 3 sts, K4 sts.
Next round K4 sts, cast on 3 sts, K8 sts, cast on 3 sts, K4 sts.
Cont in rounds of st st, making 5 more buttonholes in this way at intervals of 3in measures from base of previous buttonhole, then cont until band is long enough to fit up right front edge, round neck and down left front edge. Cast off.

To make up
Press as given for trousers. Join shoulder seams. Set in sleeves. Join side and sleeve seams. Fold all hems in half to WS and sl st down leaving 1in hem in st st on the reversed st st side. Sew on front band. Press seams. Sew on buttons.

26 Midi-length cardigan

Sizes
To fit 32 [34:36]in bust
Length to shoulder, 43 [45:47]in
Sleeve seam, 17 [17½:18]in
The figures in brackets [] refer to the 34 and 36in sizes respectively
Tension
6 sts and 8 rows to 1in over st st worked on No.9 needles
Materials
36[38:40] balls Wendy Double Knitting Nylonised
One pair No.9 needles
One pair No.11 needles
8 buttons

Back
Using No.9 needles cast on 143[153:163] sts.
1st row K1, *P1, K1, rep from * to end.
2nd row P1, *K1, P1, rep from * to end.
Rep these 2 rows twice more.
Beg with a K row, cont in st st until work measures 2½in from beg, ending with a P row.
Shape darts
Next row K38[43:48] sts, sl 1, K1, psso, K63 sts, K2 tog, K to end.
Beg with a P row work 13 rows st st.
Next row K38[43:48] sts, sl 1, K1, psso, K61 sts, K2 tog, K to end.
Beg with a P row work 13 rows st st.
Cont to dec in this way on next and every foll 14th row until 117[127:137] sts rem. Cont without shaping until work measures 25½ [26: 26½]in from beg, ending with a P row.
Next row K8[7:8] sts, *K2 tog, K7[6:5] sts, rep from * 10[13:16] times more, K2 tog, K8[6:8] sts. 105[112:119] sts.
Change to No.11 needles. Beg with a 2nd row, cont in K1, P1 rib as given at beg for 7½in,

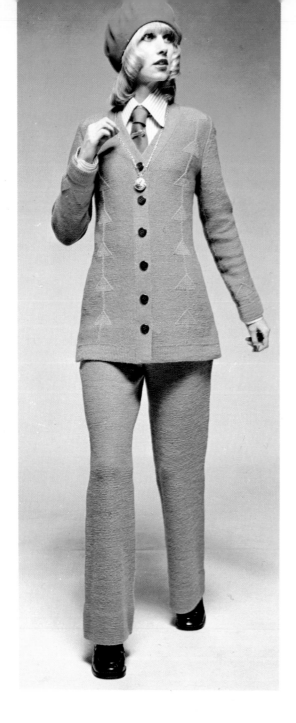

25 26

Smart fitted trouser
suit worked in
reversed stocking
stitch with triangle
pattern on fronts
and round cuffs.

Knit
Sizes to fit 86.5
[91.5:96.5]cm (34[36:
38]in) chest

**

Superbly styled
midi-length cardigan,
with shaped skirt, ribbed
waist and eyelet rib
pattern on bodice,
sleeves and pockets.

Knit
Sizes to fit 81.5
[86.5:91.5]cm (32[34:
36]in) bust

**

27

*Zipped jacket
in three colours*

Knit
*Sizes to fit 51.0
[56.0:61.0]cm
(32[34:36]in) chest*

*

28

*Sturdy playsuit for a
tomboy—shorts with bib
and braces front*

*Knit
Size to fit 61.0/66.0cm
(24/26in) chest*

*

29

*Practical pinafore dress with
contrast stripes of colour
on hem, neck, armholes and waist*

*Knit
Size to fit 66.0/71.0cm
(26/28in) chest*

*

ending with a WS row.
Change to No.9 needles.
Commence patt.
1st row (RS) P3, K1, P3, *yrn, P3, K1, P3, rep from * to end.
2nd row K3, *P1, K3, rep from * to end.
3rd row P2, P2 tog, P3, *K1, P2, P2 tog, P3, rep from * to end.
4th row K6, *P1, K6, rep from * to end.
5th row P3, yrn, P3, *K1, P3, yrn, P3, rep from * to end.
6th row As 2nd.
7th row P3, *K1, P2, P2 tog, P3, rep from * to last 4 sts, K1, P3.
8th row K3, *P1, K6, rep from * to last 4 sts, P1, K3.
These 8 rows form patt. Cont in patt until work measures 36 [37½:39]in from beg, ending with an 8th row and noting that the number of sts varies on different rows and that sts should be counted after an 8th patt row.

Shape armholes
Keeping patt correct, cast off at beg of next and every row 7 sts twice and 2 sts 4 times. Dec one st at each end of next and foll 4[5:6] alt rows. 73[78:83] sts. Cont without shaping until armholes measure 7 [7½:8]in from beg, ending with a WS row.

Shape shoulders
Cast off at beg of next and every row 6[7:7] sts 4 times and 6[6:8] sts twice. Cast off rem 37[38:39] sts.

Left front
Using No.9 needles cast on 77[83:87] sts. Work 6 rows K1, P1 rib as given for back, inc one st at end of last row on 32 and 36in sizes only. 78[83:88] sts.
Next row K to last 10 sts, (P1, K1) 5 times.
Next row (P1, K1) 5 times, P to end.
Rep last 2 rows until work measures 2½in from beg, ending with a WS row.

Shape dart
Next row K38[43:48] sts, sl 1, K1, psso, K to last 10 sts, rib to end.
Cont to dec in this way on every 14th row until 65[70:75] sts rem. Cont without shaping until work measures 25½ [26:26½]in from beg, ending with a WS row.
Next row K6[7:8] sts, *K2 tog, K7[6:5] sts, rep from * 4[5:6] times more, K2 tog, K2[3:6] sts, rib 10 sts. 59[63:67] sts.
Change to No.11 needles. Cont in K1, P1 rib for 7½in, ending with a WS row and inc one st at end of last row on 32in size only. 60[63:67] sts. Change to No.9 needles. Commence patt.
1st row P3, K1, P3, *yrn, P3, K1, P3, rep from * 4[4:5] times more, yrn, (P3, K1) 1[2:1] times, P4[3:4], rib 10 sts.
2nd row Rib 10 sts, *P1, K3, rep from * to end.
Keeping 10 sts at front edge in rib, cont in patt as now set until work measures 35 [36½:38]in from beg, ending with an 8th row.

Shape front edge
Next row Patt to last 12 sts, K2 tog, rib 10 sts.
Keeping patt correct, work 3 rows without shaping. Rep last 4 rows once more.

Shape armhole
Cont to dec at front edge on next and every foll 4th row, *at the same time* cast off at beg of next and every alt row 7 sts once and 2 sts twice. Dec one st at armhole edge on foll 5[6:7] alt rows, then cont to dec at front edge only on every 4th row until 29[31:33] sts rem. Cont without shaping until armhole measures same as back to shoulder, ending at armhole edge.

Shape shoulder
Cast off at beg of next and every alt row 6[7:7] sts twice and 6[6:8] sts once.

Neckband
Cont in rib on rem 11 sts until band reaches to centre back neck. Cast off in rib.

Mark positions for 8 buttons on left front, first to come ½in below beg of front shaping and last to come 11in above lower edge, with 6 more evenly spaced between.

Right front
Using No.9 needles cast on 77[83:87] sts. Work 6 rows rib as given for back, inc one st at beg of last row on 32 and 36in sizes only. 78[83:88] sts.
Next row (K1, P1) 5 times, K to end.
Next row P to last 10 sts, rib to end.
Complete to match left front, reversing all shaping and making buttonholes as markers are reached, as foll:
Next row (RS) Rib 5 sts, cast off 2 sts, patt to end.
Next row Patt to end, casting on 2 sts above those cast off in previous row.

Sleeves
Using No.11 needles cast on 55[55:63] sts. Work 4in K1, P1 rib as given for back, ending with a 2nd row and inc one st at end of last row on 32 and 34in sizes only. 56[56:63] sts. Change to No.9 needles. Cont in patt as given for back, inc one st at each end of 5th and every foll 10th row until there are 72[76:79] sts, noting that sts are counted after an 8th patt row. Cont without shaping until sleeve measures 17 [17½:18]in from beg, ending with a WS row.

Shape top
Cast off 7 sts at beg of next 2 rows. Dec one st at each end of next and every alt row until 30[30:29] sts rem, ending with a WS row. Cast off at beg of next and every row 2 sts 6 times and 3 sts twice.
Cast off rem 12[12:11] sts.

Pockets (make 2)
Using No.9 needles cast on 32 sts. K 2 rows.
Next row K2, P3, K1, P3, *yrn, P3, K1, P3, rep from * to last 2 sts, K2.
Next row K5, *P1, K3, rep from * to last 2 sts, K2.
Keeping 2 sts at each end in g st, cont in patt as now set until work measures 4in from beg, ending with an 8th row and inc one st in centre of last row. 33 sts.
Change to No.11 needles. Work ¾in K1, P1 rib as given for back. Cast off in rib.

To make up
Press each piece under a damp cloth with a warm iron. Join shoulder seams. Join ends of front bands and sew to back neck. Set in sleeves. Join side and sleeve seams. Sew on pockets. Press seams. Sew on buttons.

27 *Zipped jacket in three colours*

Sizes
To fit 20[22:24]in chest
Length to shoulder, 12[14:16]in, adjustable
Sleeve seam, 8[9½:11]in, adjustable
The figures in brackets [] refer to the 22 and 24in sizes respectively

Tension
7 sts and 9 rows to 1in over st st worked on No.10 needles

Materials
Sunbeam Hyland Superwash Wool 4 ply
3[3:4] balls in main shade, A
2[3:3] balls of contrast colour, B
1[1:2] balls of contrast colour, C
One pair No.10 needles
One pair No.12 needles
12[14:16]in open ended zip fastener

Back
Using No.12 needles and A, cast on 77[85:93] sts.
1st row K1, *P1, K1, rep from * to end.
2nd row P1, *K1, P1, rep from * to end.
Rep these 2 rows for 1½in, ending with a 2nd row. Break off A. Change to No.10 needles. Join in B. Beg with a K row cont in st st until work measures 8[9½:11]in from beg, or required length to underarm ending with a P row.

Shape armholes
Next row Cast off 5 sts, break off B and join in C, K to end.
Cont using C only. Cast off at beg of next and every row 5 sts once, 3 sts twice and 2 sts twice.
Dec one st at each end of next and foll 1[2:3] alt rows. 53[59:65] sts. Cont without shaping until armholes measure 4[4½:5]in from beg, ending with a P row.

Shape neck and shoulders
Next row Cast off 6[6:7] sts, K15[17:18] sts, turn and leave rem sts on holder.
Complete this side first.
Next row Cast off 2 sts, P to end.
Next row Cast off 6[6:7] sts, K to end.
Next row Cast off 2 sts, P to end.
Cast off rem 5[7:7] sts.
With RS of work facing, sl first 11[13:15] sts on to holder and leave for centre back neck, rejoin yarn to rem sts and K to end. Complete to match first side, reversing shaping.

Left front
Using No.12 needles and A, cast on 39[43:47] sts. Work as given for back until front measures same as back to underarm, ending with a P row.

Shape armhole
Next row Cast off 5 sts, break off B, join in C and K to end.
Cont using C only. P 1 row. Cast off at beg of next and foll alt row 3 sts once and 2 sts once. Dec one st at armhole edge on foll 2[3:4] alt rows. 27[30:33] sts. Cont without shaping until armhole measures 2[2½:3]in from beg, ending with a P row.

Shape neck
Next row K21[23:25] sts, turn and leave rem 6[7:8] sts on holder.
Dec one st at neck edge on foll 4 alt rows. Cont without shaping until armhole measures same as back to shoulder, ending with a P row.

Shape shoulder
Cast off at beg of next and every alt row 6[6:7] sts twice and 5[7:7] sts once.

Right front
Work as given for left front, reversing all shaping.

Sleeves
Using No.12 needles and A, cast on 41[43:45] sts. Work 1½in rib as given for back, ending with a 2nd row. Change to No.10 needles. Beg with a K row cont in st st, working in A throughout and inc one st at each end of 9th and every foll 8th row until there are 55[59:63] sts. Cont without shaping until sleeve measures 8[9½:11]in from beg, or required length to underarm ending with a P row.

Shape top
Cast off 5 sts at beg of next 2 rows. Dec one st at each end of next and every alt row until 21[23:25] sts rem, ending with a P row. Cast off at beg of next and every row 2 sts 4[4:6] times and 3 sts twice. Cast off rem 7[9:7] sts.

Collar
Join shoulder seams. Using No.12 needles, A and with RS of work facing, K across first 6[7:8] sts on holder for right front neck, K up 18 sts up right front neck and 6 sts down back neck, K across back neck sts on holder, K up 6 sts up back neck and 18 sts down left front neck and K across rem 6[7:8] sts on holder. 71[75:79] sts. Beg with a 2nd row work 4in rib as given for back. Cast off loosely in rib.

To make up
Press each piece under a damp cloth with a warm

iron. Set in sleeves. Join side and sleeve seams. Fold collar in half to RS and sl st down. Sew in zip. Press seams.

28 Playsuit

Size
To fit 24/26in chest
Length to waist at side, 12in
Tension
9 sts and 10 rows to 1in over rib patt worked on No.11 needles
Materials
7 balls Emu Machine Washable 4 ply
One pair No.11 needles
Set of 4 No.11 needles pointed at both ends

Back
Using No.11 needles cast on 71 sts for right leg.
1st row P1, *K1, P1, rep from * to end.
2nd row K1, *P1, K1, rep from * to end.
Rep these 2 rows for ¾in, ending with a 2nd row and inc one st in centre of last row. 72 sts.
Commence patt.
1st row (RS) P3 sts, *K1 tbl, P1, K1 tbl, P4, rep from * to last 6 sts, K1 tbl, P1, K1 tbl, P3.
2nd row K3 sts, *P1, K1, P1, K4, rep from * to last 6 sts, P1, K1, P1, K3.
These 2 rows form patt and are rep throughout.
Shape leg
Cont in patt, dec one st at end of next and foll 7 alt rows, *at the same time* dec one st at beg of 5th and every foll 10th row twice more, ending with 25th patt row. 61 sts. Break off yarn and leave sts for time being.
Left leg
Work to match right leg, reversing shaping and ending with 25th patt row. 61 sts.
Join legs
Next row Patt across 61 sts of left leg, cast on 14 sts, patt across 61 sts of right leg. 136 sts.
Cont in patt, dec one st at each end of every foll 10th row, counting from last dec row, until 118 sts rem. Cont without shaping until work measures 12in from beg, measured at side edge and ending with a WS row. **. Leave sts on holder.

Front
Work as given for back to **.
Shape bib
Cont in patt, cast off at beg of next and every row 3 sts 6 times and 2 sts 8 times. Dec one st at each end of next and foll 9 alt rows. 64 sts.
Cont without shaping until work measures 18½in from beg, ending with a WS row.
Shape neck
Next row Patt 28 sts, turn and leave rem sts on holder.
Complete this side first. Cast off at beg of next and every alt row 2 sts 3 times. Dec one st at neck edge on every alt row until 8 sts rem.
Strap
Cont in patt on these 8 sts until strap measures 12in, or required length to go over shoulder and down to back waist. Cast off.
With RS of work facing, sl first 8 sts onto holder and leave for centre neck, rejoin yarn to rem sts and patt to end. Complete to match first side, reversing shaping.

Back border
Join side seams. Using set of 4 No.11 needles and with RS of work facing, K up 196 sts along outer side of shoulder strap and front bib, work in K1, P1 rib across back sts on holder dec one st in centre and K up 196 sts along other side of front bib and shoulder strap. 509 sts. Working in rows and beg with a 2nd row, work 3 rows K1, P1 rib as given for back legs. Cast off in rib.

Front border
Using set of 4 No.11 needles and with RS of work facing, K up 160 sts along inner edge of shoulder strap, rib across front neck sts on holder dec one st in centre and K up 160 sts along other inner edge of shoulder strap. 327 sts. Work as given for back border.

Pockets (make 2)
Using No.11 needles cast on 37 sts. Work 4in patt as given for back, ending with a WS row. Beg with a 1st row work ¾in K1, P1 rib as given for back. Cast off in rib.

To make up
Press each piece under a damp cloth with a warm iron. Join gusset seam. Cross straps and sew to back waist. Sew on pockets to front. Press seams.

29 Pinafore dress

Size
To fit 26/28in chest
Length to shoulder, 24in
Tension
7½ sts and 10 rows to 1in over st st worked on No.11 needles
Materials
7 balls of Emu Machine Washable 4 ply in main shade, A
1 ball each of contrast colours, B and C
One pair No.11 needles
Set of 4 No.11 needles pointed at both ends

Back
Using No.11 needles and B, cast on 150 sts.
1st row K2, *P2, K2, rep from * to end.
2nd row P2, *K2, P2, rep from * to end.
3rd row As 1st. Break off B. Join in C.
4th row P to end.
5th row As 1st.
6th row As 2nd. Break off C. Join in A.
Beg with a K row work 10 rows st st. Cont using A only.
Shape skirt
Next row (dec row) K1, K2 tog, K30 sts, sl 1, K1, psso, K1, K2 tog, K74 sts, sl 1, K1, psso, K1, K2 tog, K30 sts, sl 1, K1, psso, K1.
Beg with a P row work 9 rows st st
Next row (dec row) K1, K2 tog, K28 sts, sl 1, K1, psso, K1, K2 tog, K72 sts, sl 1, K1, psso, K1, K2 tog, K28 sts, sl 1, K1, psso, K1.
Beg with a P row work 9 rows st st. Cont dec 6 sts in this way on next and every foll 10th row until 96 sts rem. Cont without shaping until work measures 10½in from beg, ending with a P row and dec one st at each end of last row.
Striped waistband
Join in B.
1st row K to end.
2nd row As 2nd rib row.
3rd row As 1st rib row.
4th row Join in C, P to end.
5th row As 1st rib row.
6th row As 2nd rib row.
7th row Using A, K to end.
8th row As 2nd rib row.
9th row As 1st rib row.
10th row Using B, P to end.
11th row As 1st rib row.
12th row As 2nd rib row.
13th row Using C, K to end.
14th row As 2nd rib row.
15th row As 1st rib row.
Using A only and beg with a P row, inc one st at each end of 1st row and cont in st st until work measures 13½in from beg, ending with a P row.
Shape armholes

Cast off at beg of next and every row 2 sts 8 times and one st 14 times. 66 sts. Cont without shaping until work measures 22in from beg, ending with a P row.
Shape neck and shoulders
Next row K18 sts, turn and leave rem sts on holder.
Complete this side first. Cast off at beg of next and every alt row 2 sts 3 times and one st 6 times. 6 sts. Cont without shaping until work measures 24in from beg, ending with a P row. Cast off.
With RS of work facing, rejoin yarn to rem sts, cast off first 30 sts, K to end. Complete to match first side, reversing shaping.

Front
Work as given for back until armhole shaping is completed. Work 4 rows without shaping ending with a P row.
Shape neck
Next row K33 sts, turn and leave rem sts on holder.
Complete this side first. Cast off at beg of next and every alt row 2 sts 4 times and one st 9 times. Dec one st at neck edge on every 4th row until 6 sts rem. Cont without shaping until work measures same as back to shoulder, ending with a P row. Cast off.
With RS of work facing, rejoin yarn to rem sts and K to end. Complete to match first side, reversing shaping.

Neckband
Join shoulder seams. Using set of 4 No.11 needles, C and with RS of work facing, K up 200 sts round neck.
1st round *K2, P2, rep from * to end.
2nd round As 1st, working 3 sts tog at centre front. 198 sts. Break off C. Join in B.
3rd round K to end.
4th round As 2nd. 196 sts.
Using B, cast off in rib.

Armbands
Using No.11 needles, C and with RS of work facing, K up 186 sts round armholes.
1st row P2, *K2, P2, rep from * to end.
2nd row K2, *P2, K2, rep from * to end. Break off C. Join in B.
3rd row P to end.
4th row As 2nd.
Using B, cast off in rib.

To make up
Press each piece under a damp cloth with a warm iron. Join side seams. Press seams.

30 Batwing jersey – for the experienced knitter

Size
To fit 34/36in bust
Length to shoulder, 25in
Tension
6 sts and 11 rows to 1in over g st worked on No. 9 needles
Materials
12 balls Hayfield Gaylon Double Knitting in main shade, A
6 balls of contrast colour, B
One pair No.9 needles
One pair No.11 needles

Jersey
Using No.11 needles and A, cast on 55 sts and beg at right sleeve edge.
1st row K1, *P1, K1, rep from * to end.
2nd row P1, *K1, P1, rep from * to end.
Rep these 2 rows for 3in, ending with a 2nd row and inc one st at end of last row. 56 sts. Change

30

*Striped batwing
jersey in garter stitch
—a design to
challenge the
experienced knitter*

*Knit
Size to fit 86.5|91.5cm
(34|36in) bust*

***

31

*Very elegant evening
pullover, worked in
a glitter yarn*

*Knit
Size to fit 81.5|
86.5cm (32|34in) bust*

***

to No.9 needles. Cont in g st, inc one st at each end of every 12th row until there are 74 sts, then at each end of every 3rd row until there are 98 sts, then at each end of every alt row until there are 116 sts. Commence striped patt, noting that a separate ball of yarn is used for each stripe and the colours are twisted at the back of the work where they join on every row.

Using B, cast on 7 sts at beg of next 2 rows, working centre 116 sts in A. Using A, cast on 5 sts at beg of next 2 rows. Rep the last 4 rows twice more, then first two of them again. 202 sts. Mark each end of last row with coloured thread, noting that the striped patt row now reads, (K7 B, K5 A) 3 times, K7 B, K116 A, (K7 B, K5 A) 3 times, K7 B. Cont in patt as now set until work measures 22½in from beg, ending with a WS row.

Divide for back neck

Next row K101 sts in patt, turn and leave rem sts on holder. Complete back first.

Next row Using B, cast on 23 sts for collar, then work to end in patt as set.

Cont back in patt as now set, *at the same time* on 23 collar sts work 13 more rows B, then (10 rows A, 14 rows B) twice, 10 rows A, 13 rows B, noting that the change of colour in the stripes on the collar must come on the opposite side to the rest of the back as the collar folds over to the outside.

Next row Work in patt to last 23 sts, using B, cast on these 23 sts. Break off yarn. Leave rem sts on holder until front neck is completed.

Place a second marker in the centre of the 2nd stripe in A of collar to show the centre of work. Using No.9 needles, A and with WS of work and RS of collar facing, K up 23 sts along cast on edge of collar sts, then K to end, working in patt as set. 124 sts. Working 23 collar sts in A work 9 rows patt, ending at upper edge.

Next row K24 B, K to end in patt.

Next row Patt to last 24 sts, K24 B.

Next row K25 B, K to end in patt.

Next row Patt to last 25 sts, K25 B.

Cont in this way working one more st in B at upper edge until there are 30 sts in B. Keeping collar sts in A, work 10 more rows patt.

Next row K46 B, turn and break off B.

Beg again at upper edge, using B, P81 sts, then K to end in patt. Keeping 43 sts in g st striped patt correct, *at the same time* keeping 81 sts in B in P throughout, work 18 rows.

Next row K43 sts in patt, using B, cast off 81 sts P-wise.

Using B, cast on 81 sts and work 18 rows in g st, then cont across all sts which were left. 124 sts. Cont in patt to match first half of front, reversing the shaping until the collar sts are cast off.

Join back and front

Cont across all sts of back and front without shaping until work measures same from centre marker to first 2 markers, then cont to shape left sleeve as for right sleeve, reversing all shaping by dec instead of inc. Dec one st at end of last row. 55 sts. Change to No.11 needles. Work 3in rib as given at beg. Cast off in rib.

To make up

Using No.11 needles, B and with RS of work facing, K up 111 sts along lower edge of back. Beg with a 2nd row work 5in rib as given for sleeves. Cast off in rib. Work along lower edge of front in same way. Join side and underarm seams. Join 2 cast off edges at left side of collar. Overlap the 18 sts in B of left front over those of right and sl st down. Press seams very lightly under a damp cloth with a warm iron.

Elegant evening pullover in glitter yarn

Sizes

To fit 32/34in bust

Length to shoulder, 22in

Tension

7 sts and 9 rows to 1in over st st worked on No.10 needles

Materials

4 balls Twilleys Goldfingering in main shade, A

3 balls of contrast colour, B

2 balls of contrast colour, C

One pair No.10 needles

One pair No.12 needles

Set of 4 No.12 needles pointed at both ends

Note

Use small separate balls of yarn for each colour, twisting yarns at back of work when changing colours

Back

Using No.12 needles and A, cast on 113 sts.

1st row K1, *P1, K1, rep from * to end.

2nd row P1, *K1, P1, rep from * to end.

Rep these 2 rows for 5in, ending with a 2nd row and inc one st at each end of last row. 115 sts. Change to No.10 needles. Join in B and C. Commence patt.

1st row K2 B, (15 C, 1 B, 15 A, 1 B) 3 times, 15 C, 2 B.

2nd row P as 1st row.

3rd row Using B, K1, K up 1, K1, (using C, sl 1, K1, psso, K11, K2 tog, using B, K1, P1, K1, all into next st – called K3 from 1 –, using A, sl 1, K1, psso, K11, K2 tog, using B, K3 from 1) 3 times, using C, sl 1, K1, psso, K11, K2 tog, using B, K1, K up 1, K1.

4th row P3 B, (13 C, 3 B, 13 A, 3 B) 3 times, 13 C, 3 B.

5th row Using B, K2, K up 1, K1, (using C, sl 1, K1, psso, K9, K2 tog, using B, K1, K up 1, K1, K up 1, K1, using A, sl 1, K1, psso, K9, K2 tog, using B, K1, K up 1, K1, K up 1, K1) 3 times, using C, sl 1, K1, psso, K9, K2 tog, using B, K1, K up 1, K2.

6th row P4 B, (11 C, 5 B, 11 A, 5 B) 3 times, 11 C, 4 B.

7th row Using B, K3, K up 1, K1, (using C, sl 1, K1, psso, K7, K2 tog, using B, K1, K up 1, K3, K up 1, K1, using A, sl 1, K1, psso, K7, K2 tog, using B, K1, K up 1, K3, K up 1, K1) 3 times, using C, sl 1, K1, psso, K7, Kw tog, using B, K1, K up 1, K3.

8th row P5 B, (9 C, 7 B, 9 A, 7 B) 3 times, 9 C, 5 B.

9th row Using B, K4, K up 1, K1, (using C, sl 1, K1, psso, K5, K2 tog, using B, K1, K up 1, K5, K up 1, K1, using A, sl 1, K1, psso, K5, K2 tog, using B, K1, K up 1, K5, K up 1, K1) 3 times, using C, sl 1, K1, psso, K5, K2 tog, using B, K1, K up 1, K4.

10th row P sts as now set, and on every foll alt row.

11th row Using B, K5, K up 1, K1, (using C, sl 1, K1, psso, K3, K2 tog, using B, K1, K up 1, K7, K up 1, K1, using A, sl 1, K1, psso, K3, K2 tog, using B, K1, K up 1, K7, K up 1, K1) 3 times, using C, sl 1, K1, psso, K3, K2 tog, using B, K1, K up 1, K5.

12th row P as now set.

13th row Using B, K6, K up 1, K1, (using C, sl 1, K1, psso, K1, K2 tog, using B, K1, K up 1, K9, K up 1, K1, using A, sl 1, K1, psso, K1, K2 tog, using B, K1, K up 1, K9, K up 1, K1) 3 times, using C, sl 1, K1, psso, K1, K2 tog, using B, K1, K up 1, K6.

14th row P as now set.

15th row Using B, K7, K up 1, K1, (using C, sl 1, K2 tog, psso, using B, K1, K up 1, K11, K up 1, K1, using A, sl 1, K1) 3 times, using A, sl 1, K2 tog, psso, using B, K1, K up 1, K11, K up 1, K1, using C, sl 1, K 2 tog, psso, using B, K1, K up 1, K7.

16th row P as now set.

17th row Using B, K7, K2 tog, (using C, K3 from 1, using B, sl 1, K1, psso, K11, K2 tog, using A, K3 from 1, using B, sl 1, K1, psso, K11, K2 tog) 3 times, using C, K3 from 1, using B, sl 1, K1, psso, K7.

19th row Using B, K6, K2 tog, (using C, K1, K up 1, K1, K up 1, K1, using B, sl 1, K1, psso, K9, K2 tog, using A, K1, K up 1, K1, K up 1, K1, using B, sl 1, K1, psso, K9, K2 tog) 3 times, using C, K1, K up 1, K1, K up 1, K1, using B, sl 1, K1, psso, K6.

21st row Using B, K5, K2 tog, (using C, K1, K up 1, K3, K up 1, K1, using B, sl 1, K1, psso, K7, K2 tog, using A, K1, K up 1, K3, K up 1, K1, using B, sl 1, K1, psso, K7, K2 tog) 3 times, using C, K1, K up 1, K3, K up 1, K1, using B, sl 1, K1, psso, K5.

23rd row Using B, K4, K2 tog, (using C, K1, K up 1, K5, K up 1, K1, using B, sl 1, K1, psso, K5, K2 tog, using A, K1, K up 1, K5, K up 1, K1, using B, sl 1, K1, psso, K5, K2 tog) 3 times, using C, K1, K up 1, K5, K up 1, K1, using B, sl 1, K1, psso, K4.

25th row Using B, K3, K2 tog, (using C, K1, K up 1, K7, K up 1, K1, using B, sl 1, K1, psso, K3, K2 tog, using A, K1, K up 1, K7, K up 1, K1, using B, sl 1, K1, psso, K3, K2 tog) 3 times, using C, K1, K up 1, K7, K up 1, K1, using B, sl 1, K1, psso, K3.

27th row Using B, K2, K2 tog, (using C, K1, K up 1, K9, K up 1, K1, using B, sl 1, K1, psso, K1, K2 tog, using A, K1, K up 1, K9, K up 1, K1, using B, sl 1, K1, psso, K1, K2 tog) 3 times, using C, K1, K up 1, K9, K up 1, K1, using B, sl 1, K1, psso, K2.

29th row Using B, K1, K2 tog, (using C, K1, K up 1, K11, K up 1, K1, using B, sl 1, K2 tog, psso, using A, K1, K up 1, K11, K up 1, K1, using B, sl 1, K2 tog, psso) 3 times, using C, K1, K up 1, K11, K up 1, K1, using B, sl 1, K1, psso, K1.

30th row As 2nd row.

Rep 3rd–30th rows throughout, *at the same time* inc one st at each end of next and every foll 12th row until there are 121 sts. Work 9 rows more, ending with a 4th patt row. 88 rows in patt.

Shape armholes

Keeping patt correct, cast off at beg of next and every row 5 sts twice, 3 sts twice, 2 sts 4 times and one st 14 times. 83 sts. Cont without shaping until armholes measure 7in from beg, ending with a P row.

Shape neck

Next row Patt 24 sts, turn and leave rem sts on holder.

Complete this side first. Cast off 4 sts at beg of next and foll 2 alt rows, ending at armhole edge. Cast off rem 12 sts.

With RS of work facing, sl first 35 sts on to holder for centre back neck, rejoin yarn to rem sts and patt to end. Complete to match first side, reversing shaping.

Front

Work as given for back until armhole shaping is completed. Work 4 rows, ending with a 30th patt row.

Shape neck

Next row Patt 34, turn and leave rem sts on holder.

Complete this side first.

Next row Patt to end.

Next row Patt to last 3 sts, K2 tog, K1.

Rep last 2 rows until 12 sts rem, noting that last neck edge st is worked in same colour as dec st. Cont without shaping until armhole measures same as back to shoulder, ending at armhole edge. Cast off.

With RS of work facing, sl first 15 sts on to holder for centre front neck, rejoin C to rem sts, using C, K1, sl 1, K1, psso, K11, K2 tog, using B, K3 from 1, using A, sl 1, K1, psso, K11, K2 tog, using B, K1, K up 1, K1.

Next row Patt to end.

Next row K1, sl 1, K1, psso, patt to end.

Complete to match first side, reversing shaping.

Neckband

Join shoulder seams. Using set of 4 No.12 needles.

A and with RS of work facing, K up 15 sts down right back neck, K across back neck sts, K up 15 sts up left back neck and 42 sts down left front neck, K across front neck sts, then K up 42 sts up right front neck 164 sts. Work ¾in K1, P1 rib round neck. Cast off in rib.

Armbands
Using No.12 needles, A and with RS of work facing, K up 127 sts round armhole. Beg with a 2nd row, work ¾in rib as given for back. Cast off in rib.

To make up
Press each piece under a damp cloth with a cool iron. Join side seams. Press seams.

32 Sleeveless dress

Sizes
To fit 26[28:30]in chest
Length to shoulder, 23[26:29]in, adjustable
The figures in brackets [] refer to the 28 and 30in sizes respectively

Tension
7½ sts and 9½ rows to 1in over st st worked on No.11 needles

Materials
9[10:11] balls Emu Scotch 4-ply
One pair No.11 needles
One pair No.12 needles

Back
Using No.12 needles cast on 131[141:151] sts. Beg with a K row work 15 rows st st.
Next row K all sts tbl to form hemline.
Change to No.11 needles. Beg with a K row cont in st st, dec one st at each end of 21st and every foll 8th row until 107[115:123] sts rem. Cont without shaping until work measures 12[14:16]in from hemline, or required length to waist, ending with a P row. Commence bodice patt.
1st row K2, *yfwd, K3, yfwd, K1, rep from * to last st, K1, noting that yfwd is not counted as a st.
2nd row P to end.
3rd row K3, *sl 1, K2 tog, psso, K3, rep from * to end.
4th row P to end.
These 4 rows form patt. Cont in patt until work measures 17½[20:22½]in from hemline, or required length to underarm, ending with a P row.

Shape armholes
Keeping patt correct, cast off at beg of next and every row 5 sts twice, 3 sts twice and 2 sts twice. Dec one st at each end of next and foll 4[5:6] alt rows. 77[83:89] sts. Cont without shaping until armholes measure 5½[6:6½]in from beg, ending with a P row.

Shape neck and shoulders
Next row Cast off 4[4:5] sts, patt 27[29:30], turn and leave rem sts on holder.
Complete this side first.
Next row Cast off 5 sts, P to end.
Next row Cast off 4[4:5] sts, patt to end.
Rep last 2 rows once more then first of them again.
Cast off rem 4[6:5] sts.
With RS of work facing, sl first 15[17:19] sts onto holder, rejoin yarn to rem sts and patt to end. Complete to match first side, reversing shaping.

Front
Work as given for back until armhole shaping is completed. Cont without shaping until armholes measure 3[3½:4]in from beg, ending with a P row.
Shape neck
Next row Patt 34[36:38], turn and leave rem sts on holder.
Complete this side first. Cast off at beg of next and every alt row 5 sts once, 3 sts twice and

2 sts once. Dec one st at neck edge on every alt row until 16[18:20] sts rem. Cont without shaping until armhole measures same as back to shoulder, ending at armhole edge.

Shape shoulder
Cast off at beg of next and every alt row 4[4:5] sts 3 times and 4[6:5] sts once.
With RS of work facing, sl first 9[11:13] sts onto holder for centre neck, rejoin yarn to rem sts and patt to end. Complete to match first side, reversing shaping.

Neckband
Join right shoulder seam. Using No.12 needles and with RS of work facing, K up 30 sts down left front neck, K across front neck sts, K up 30 sts up right front neck and 18 sts down right back neck, K across back neck sts, then K up 18 sts up left back neck. 120[124:128] sts. Beg with a P row work ¾in st st.
Cast off loosely.

Armbands
Join left shoulder seam. Using No.12 needles and with RS of work facing, K up 88[96:104] sts round armholes. Work as given for neckband. Cast off loosely.

To make up
Press each piece under a damp cloth with a warm iron. Join side seams. Fold neck and armbands in half to WS and sl st down. Using 6 strands of yarn make a twisted cord 48[54:58]in long and thread through first row of holes in patt at waist. Knot ends and ease out into small tassels. Turn up hem at lower edge and sl st down.

33 Cardigan for mother and daughter

Sizes
To fit 28 [30:32:34:36:38]in chest/bust
Length to shoulder, 17 [18½:20:21½:22½:23½]in
Sleeve seam, 12 [14:16:17:17½:18]in
The figures in brackets [] refer to the 30, 32, 34, 36 and 38in sizes respectively

Tension
5 sts and 7 rows to 1in over st st worked on No.8 needles

Materials
8 [9:10:12:12:13] x 40 grm balls of Pingouin Mohair for high buttoned version
7[7:8:8:9:9] balls for low buttoned version
One pair No.8 needles
One pair No.10 needles
5[5:5:7:7:7] buttons for high buttoned version
4[4:4:5:5:5] buttons for low buttoned version
Cable needle

Back
Using No.10 needles cast on 75[79:85:89:95:99] sts.
1st row K1, * P1, K1, rep from * to end.
2nd row P1, *K1, P1, rep from * to end.
Rep these 2 rows 3[3:3:4:4:4] times more, inc one st in centre of last row on 30, 34 and 38in sizes only. 75[80:85:90:95:100] sts. Change to No.8 needles. Beg with a K row cont in st st until work measures 11 [12:13:14:14½:15]in from beg, ending with a P row.

Shape armholes
Cast off 5 sts at beg of next 2 rows.
Next row K3 sts, K2 tog, K to last 5 sts, sl 1, K1, psso, K3 sts.
Next row P to end.
Rep last 2 rows until 23[24:25:26:27:28] sts rem, ending with a P row. Leave sts on holder for high buttoned version and cast off for low buttoned version.

Left front
Using No.8 needles cast on 21[21:21:27:27:27] sts for pocket lining. Beg with a K row work 16[16:16:24:24:24] rows st st.
Next row K4[4:4:7:7:7] sts, P2, (K4, P2) twice, K3[3:3:6:6:6] sts.
Next row P3[3:3:6:6:6] sts, K2, (P4, K2) twice, P4[4:4:7:7:7] sts.
Rep last 2 rows once more, then first of them again, ending with a RS row. Leave sts on holder.
Using No.10 needles cast on 43[45:47:53:55:57] sts. Work 8[8:8:10:10:10] rows rib as given for back, inc one st at end of last row on 30, 32 and 38in sizes only. 43[46:48:53:55:58] sts. Change to No.8 needles. Commence patt.
Next row K11[12:13:15:16:17] sts, P2, (K4, P2) twice, K10[12:13:14:15:17] sts, turn and leave rem sts on holder for front band.
Next row P10[12:13:14:15:17] sts, K2, (P4, K2) twice, P11[12:13:15:16:17] sts.
Work 4 more rows as now set.
Next row K11[12:13:15:16:17] sts, P2, sl next 2 sts on to cable needle and hold at back of work, K2 then K2 from cable needle – called C4B –, P2, C4B, P2, K to end.
Work 9[9:9:17:17:17] more rows patt as now set, working C4B on every 8th row.
Place pocket
Next row K7[8:9:8:9:10] sts, (P1, K1) 10[10:10:13:13:13] times, P1, K to end.
Next row P7[9:10:8:9:11] sts, (K1, P1) 10[10:10:13:13:13] times, K1, P to end.
Next row K7[8:9:8:9:10] sts, cast off 21[21:21:27:27:27] sts in rib, K to end.
Next row P7[9:10:8:9:11] sts, patt across sts of pocket lining, P to end.
Cont in patt as now set, working C4B on every 8th row, until work measures same as back to underarm ending with a WS row.
Low buttoned version only
Shape armhole
Cast off 5 sts at beg of next row.
Next row Patt to end.
Next row K3 sts, K2 tog, patt to last 2 sts, K2 tog.
Cont to dec at front edge on every 5th row 6[7:7:8:8:9] times more, *at the same time* cont to dec at armhole edge on every alt row until 4 sts rem, ending with a P row and noting that when working raglan dec over patt, always end WS rows with P4.
Next row K2 sts, K2 tog.
Next row P3 sts.
Next row K1, K2 tog.
Next row P2 tog. Fasten off.
High buttoned version only
Shape armhole
Cast off 5 sts at beg of next row.
Next row Patt to end.
Next row K3 sts, K2 tog, patt to end.
Rep last 2 rows until 16[17:17:19:19:20] sts rem, ending with a WS row and noting that when working raglan dec over patt, always end WS rows with P4.
Shape neck
Next row K3 sts, K2 tog, patt 8[8:8:10:10:10] sts, turn and leave rem 3[4:4:4:4:5] sts on holder.
Next row Patt to end.
Next row K3 sts, K2 tog, patt to last 2 sts, K2 tog.
Rep last 2 rows until 4 sts rem, ending with a WS row.
Next row K2 sts, K2 tog.
Next row P3 sts.
Next row K1, K2 tog.
Next row P2 tog. Fasten off.

Right front
Using No.8 needles cast on 21[21:21:27:27:27] sts for pocket lining. Beg with a K row work 16[16:16:24:24:24] rows st st.
Next row K3[3:3:6:6:6] sts, P2, (K4, P2)

32

Sleeveless dress
for summer or
parties.

Knit
Sizes to fit 66.0
[71.0:76]cm (26
[28:30]in) chest

**

33

Gossamer light mohair
cardigan.

Knit
Sizes to fit 71.0 [76.0:
81.5:86.5:91.5:96.5]cm
28[30:32:34:36:38]in)
chest/bust

**

34

Snug snow suits with jacket,
trousers, cap and mitts

Knit
Sizes to fit 51.0 [56.0:
61.0]cm (20[22:24]in) chest

*

twice, K4[4:4:7:7:7] sts.
Next row P4[4:4:7:7:7] sts, K2, (P4, K2) twice, P3[3:3:6:6:6] sts.
Rep last 2 rows once more, then first of them again. Leave sts on holder.
Using No.10 needles cast on 43[45:47:53:55:57] sts. Work 4 rows rib as given for back.
Next row (buttonhole row) Rib 3[3:3:4:4:4] sts, cast off 3 sts, rib to end.
Next row Rib to end, casting on 3 sts above those cast off in previous row.
Work 2[2:2:4:4:4] more rows rib, inc one st at beg of last row on 30, 32 and 38in sizes only. 43[46:48:53:55:58] sts.
Next row Rib 8[8:8:10:10:10] sts and leave on holder for front band, change to No.8 needles, K10[12:13:14:15:17] sts, P2, (K4, P2) twice, K11[12:13:15:16:17] sts.
Complete to match left front, reversing all shaping.

Sleeves
Using No.10 needles cast on 37[39:43:45:49:51] sts. Work 12[12:12:16:16:16] rows rib as given for back. Change to No.8 needles. Beg with a K row cont in st st, inc one st at each end of 7th and every foll 8th row until there are 51[55:61:65:71:75] sts. Cont without shaping until sleeve measures 12 [14:16:17:17½:18]in from beg, ending with a K row.
Mark this point with coloured thread. Work a further 7 rows.
Shape top
Next row K3 sts, K2 tog, K to last 5 sts, sl 1, K1, psso, K3 sts.
Next row P to end.
Rep last 2 rows until 9[9:11:11:13:13] sts rem, ending with a P row. Leave sts on holder for high buttoned version. Cast off for low buttoned version.

Left front band
Sl sts from holder on to No.10 needle, with RS of work facing, inc in first st, rib to end. Cont in rib until band reaches to centre back neck for low buttoned version, or to front neck for high buttoned version, ending with a WS row. Leave sts on holder.
Tack band in position.
Low buttoned version only
Mark positions for 4[4:4:5:5:5] buttons on left front band, first to come on 5th row of welt and last to come ½in below beg of front shaping with 2[2:2:3:3:3] more evenly spaced between.
High buttoned version only
Mark positions for 5[5:5:7:7:7] buttons on left front band, first to come on 5th row of welt and last to come in neckband, with 3[3:3:5:5:5] more evenly spaced between.

Right front band
Sl sts from holder on to No.10 needle, with WS of work facing, inc in first st, rib to end. Complete to match left front band, making buttonholes as before as markers are reached.

Neckband for high buttoned version
Using No.10 needles and with RS of work facing, rib across 8[8:8:10:10:10] sts of right front band, K next st tog with first st of front neck, K rem 2[3:3:3:3:4] front neck sts, K up 12[12:12:14:14:14] sts up side of neck, K across sts of right sleeve, back neck and left sleeve, K 2 tog at each back raglan seam on all sizes and inc one st in centre of back neck on 30, 34 and 38in sizes only, K up 12[12:12:14:14:14] sts down side of neck, K2[3:3:3:3:4] sts of left front neck, K next st tog with first st of front band and rib across rem front band sts. 85[89:93:103:107:111] sts. Cont in rib for 5[5:5:9:9:9] rows, making buttonhole as before on 2nd [2nd:2nd:4th:4th:4th] row.
Cast off in rib.

To make up
Press each piece very lightly under a damp cloth with a warm iron. Join raglan seams, sewing last 7 rows of sleeves from marked point to underarm. Join side and sleeve seams. Sew on front bands, joining band at centre back neck for low buttoned version. Sew down pocket linings. Press all seams. Sew on buttons.

34 Snow suit, cap and mittens

Sizes
To fit 20[22:24]in chest
Jacket length to shoulder, 14[15½:17]in
Sleeve seam, 8[9:10]in
Trousers inside leg length, 9[10½:12]in
The figures in brackets [] refer to the 22 and 24in sizes respectively
Tension
5½ sts and 7½ rows to 1in over st st worked on No.7 needles
Materials
18[20:22] balls of Sunbeam Super Nylon Double Knitting
One pair No.7 needles
One pair No.9 needles
One cable needle
14[16:16]in open ended zip fastener
Waist length of elastic

Jacket back
Using No.9 needles cast on 62[66:74] sts.
1st row K2, *P2, K2, rep from * to end.
2nd row P2, *K2, P2, rep from * to end.
Rep these 2 rows 4 times more, inc one st at each end of last row on 22in size only. 62[68:74] sts.
Change to No.7 needles. Beg with a K row cont in st st until work measures 9[10:11]in from beg, ending with a P row.
Shape armholes
Cast off 4 sts at beg of next 2 rows.
Next row K2 sts, K2 tog, K to last 4 sts, K2 tog tbl, K2 sts.
Next row P to end.
Rep last 2 rows until 18[20:22] sts rem, ending with a P row. Leave sts on holder for centre back neck.

Jacket left front
Using No.9 needles cast on 30[34:38] sts. Work 10 rows rib as given for back, inc one st in centre of last row on 20in size only. 31[34:38] sts. **.
Change to No.7 needles. Commence patt.
1st row K5[5:7] sts, P2, K4, P2, K5[8:8] sts, P2, K4, P2, K4[4:6] sts, K into front then into back of

To make up
Press each piece under a damp cloth with a cool iron.
Join side and sleeve seams. Fold neckband in half to RS and sl st down. Sew in zip. Press seams.

Trousers right leg
Using No.9 needles cast on 42[46:50] sts. Work ¼in rib as given for jacket back, ending with a 2nd row.
Change to No.7 needles.
Shape leg
1st row K11[12:13] sts, sl 1, K18[20:22] sts, sl 1, K11[12:13] sts.
2nd row P to end.
Rep last 2 rows once more.
Next row K3 sts, K up 1, K8[9:10] sts, sl 1, K8[9:10] sts, K up 1, K2, K up 1, K8[9:10] sts, sl 1, K8[9:10] sts, K up 1, K3. 46[50:54] sts.
Keeping sl st correct, work 7 rows st st.
Next row K3 sts, K up 1, K9[10:11] sts, sl 1, K9[10:11] sts, K up 1, K2, K up 1, K9[10:11] sts,

sl 1, K9[10:11] sts, K up 1, K3.
Keeping sl st correct, work 7 rows st st.
Cont inc in this way on next and every foll 8th row until there are 70[78:86] sts. Cont without shaping until work measures 9[10½:12]in from beg, or required leg length, ending with a P row.
Shape crutch
Cast off 4 sts at front edge at beg of next row and 3 sts at back edge at beg of foll row.
Next row K1, K2 tog, K to last 3 sts, K2 tog tbl, K1.
Beg with a P row work 3 rows. Dec one st at beg of next and every foll 8th row 3 times in all, *at the same time* dec one st at end of next and every foll 4th row 4[6:8] times in all. 54[60:66] sts.
Cont without shaping until work measures 7[7½:8]in from beg of crutch shaping, ending with a K row.
Shape back
Next row P44[48:52] sts, turn and patt to end.
Next row P33[36:39] sts, turn and patt to end.
Cont working 11[12:13] sts less on every alt row twice more, then P to end dec one st at each end of last row on 22in size only. 54[58:66] sts. Change to No.9 needles. Beg with a 1st row work 1½in rib as given at beg.
Cast off in rib.

Trousers left leg
Work as given for right leg, reversing all shaping.

To make up
Press as given for jacket. Join back, front and leg seams. Press seams.
Sew elastic inside waistband using casing st.
If required, sew elastic across bottom of legs as underfoot strap.

Cap
Using No.9 needles cast on 98[98] sts. Work 10 rows rib as given for jacket back. Change to No.7 needles.
Commence patt.
1st row K5 sts, *P2, K4, P2, K8[K4, K up 1, K4], rep from * 4 times more, P2, K4, P2, K5[K4, K up 1, K1]. 98[104] sts.
2nd row P5[6] sts, *K2, P4, K2, P8[9] sts, rep from * 4 times more, K2, P4, K2, P5.
Cont in patt as now set, working C4B on 11th and every foll 16th row, until work measures 5½[6¼]in from beg, ending with a WS row.
Shape top
1st row K4 sts, *sl 1, K1, psso, K2 tog, K2, sl 1, K1, psso, K2 tog, K6[7] sts, rep from * 4 times more, sl 1, K1, psso, K2 tog, K2, sl 1, K1, psso, K2 tog, K4[5] sts. 74[80] sts.
2nd row P to end.
3rd row K3 sts, *K2 tog, K4, rep from * to last 5 sts, K2 tog, K3. 62[67] sts.
4th row P to end.
5th row K2, *K2 tog, K3, rep from * to end. 50[54] sts.
6th row P to end.
7th row K1, *K2 tog, K2, rep from * to last st, K1. 38[41] sts.
8th row P to end.
9th row K0[1], *K2 tog, rep from * to end. 19[21] sts.
10th row P to end.
11th row K1, *K2 tog, rep from * to end. 10[11] sts.
Break off yarn, thread through rem sts, draw up and fasten off.

To make up
Press as given for jacket.
Join seam. Press seam.
Make pompon and sew to top.

Left mitten
Using No.7 needles cast on 46[50] sts. Commence

patt.

1st row K4[5] sts, *P2, K4, P2, K7[8] sts, rep from * once more, P2, K4, P2, K4[5] sts.

2nd row P4[5] sts, *K2, P4, K2, P7[8] sts, rep from * once more, K2, P4, K2, P4[5] sts.

Rep these 2 rows 3 times more.

9th row K2[3] sts, K2 tog, *P2, K4, P2, sl 1, K1, psso, K3[4] sts, K2 tog, rep from * once more, P2, K4, P2, sl 1, K1, psso, K2[3] sts.

10th row P3[4] sts, *K2, P4, K2, P5[6] sts, rep from * once more, K2, P4, K2, P3[4] sts.

11th row K3[4] sts, *P2, C4B, P2, K5[6] sts, rep from * once more, P2, C4B, P2, K3[4] sts.

12th row As 10th.

Work 4 more rows as now set.

17th row K1[2] sts, K2 tog, *P2, K4, P2, sl 1, K1, psso, K1[2] sts, K2 tog, rep from * once more, P2, K4, P2, sl 1, K1, psso, K1[2] sts. 34[38] sts.

Work 5 rows patt as now set.

23rd row As set, working C4B in cable panels.

24th row As 18th.

Change to No.9 needles. Work 8 rows rib as given for jacket back.

Change to No.7 needles. Beg with a K row work 12[14] rows st st.

Shape thumb

Next row K16[18] sts, turn and cast on 6[7] sts.

Next row P12[14] sts, turn.

Cont on these sts for 8[10] more rows, ending with a P row.

Next row *K2 tog, rep from * to end.

Break off yarn, thread through rem sts, draw up and fasten off.

With RS of work facing, rejoin yarn and K up 6[7] sts from cast on sts at base of thumb, K to end.

Beg with a P row, cont in st st until work measures 3½[4]in from beg of st st, ending with a P row.

Shape top

Next row K1, K2 tog, K11[13] sts, K2 tog tbl, K2, K2 tog, K11[13] sts, K2 tog tbl, K1.

Next row P to end.

Next row K1, K2 tog, K9[11] sts, K2 tog tbl, K2, K2 tog, K9[11] sts, K2 tog tbl, K1.

Next row P to end.

Cont dec in this way on next and every alt row until 14 sts rem, ending with a dec row.

Next row P7 sts, turn, fold work in half and graft sts tog.

Right mitten

Work as given for left mitten, reversing position of thumb as foll:

Next row K24[27] sts, turn.

Next row P6[7] sts, turn and cast on 6[7] sts.

To make up

Press as given for jacket. Join seams. Press seams.

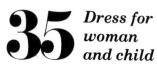

Dress for woman and child

Sizes

Woman's dress to fit 32[34:36]in bust
Length to shoulder, 33[33½:34]in
Sleeve seam, 17[17½:18]in
Child's dress to fit 22[24:26]in chest
Length to shoulder, 16[17½:19]in
Sleeve seam, 9[10:11]in
The figures in brackets [] refer to the 34 and 36in Woman's sizes respectively and the 24 and 26in Child's sizes respectively

Tension

4 sts and 5 rows to 1in over st st worked on No.6 needles

Materials

Woman's dress 16[17:18] balls Emu Filigree in main shade, A
1[1:2] balls of contrast colour, B

Child's dress 8[9:10] balls in main shade, A
1[1:1] ball of contrast colour, B
One pair No.6 needles
One pair No.8 needles

Woman's dress back

Using No.8 needles and A, cast on 82[86:90] sts.
Work 1½in st st, ending with a P row. Change to No.6 needles.

Shape side

Cont in st st, dec one st at each end of 7th and every foll 8th row until 60[64:68] sts rem. Cont without shaping until work measures 21½in from beg, ending with a P row. Cont in st st, inc one st at each end of next and every 10th row until there are 66[70:74] sts. Work 3 rows st st, ending with a P row. Commence striped patt. Join in B.

1st row Using B, K to end.

2nd row Using B, K to end.

3rd row Using A, K to end.

4th row Using A, P to end.

These 4 rows form striped patt. Rep 1st and 2nd rows once more.

Shape armholes

Keeping patt correct, cast off 4 sts at beg of next 2 rows. Rep patt 3 times more, *at the same time* dec one st at each end of next and foll 3[4:5] alt rows. 50[52:54] sts. Break off B. Using A only, cont in st st without shaping until armholes measure 7[7½:8]in from beg, ending with a P row.

Shape neck and shoulders

Next row K17[18:19] sts, turn and leave rem sts on holder.

Complete this side first.

Next row Cast off 3 sts, P to end.

Next row Cast off 4[4:5] sts, K to end.

Next row Cast off 2 sts, P to end.

Next row Cast off 4[4:5] sts, K to end.

Next row P to end.

Cast off rem 4[5:4] sts.

With RS of work facing, sl first 16 sts on to holder for back neck, rejoin yarn to rem sts and K to end. Complete to match first side, reversing shaping.

Woman's dress front

Work as given for back until armhole shaping is completed. Cont without shaping until armholes measure 5[5½:6]in from beg, ending with a P row.

Shape neck

Next row K21[22:23] sts, turn and leave rem sts on holder.

Complete this side first. Cast off at beg of next and every alt row 2 sts 3 times. Dec one st at neck edge on next and foll 2 alt rows, ending with a P row.

Shape shoulder

Cast off at beg of next and every alt row 4[4:5] sts twice and 4[5:4] sts once.

With RS of work facing, sl first 8 sts on to holder for front neck, rejoin yarn to rem sts and K to end. Complete to match first side, reversing shaping.

Sleeves

Using No.8 needles and A, cast on 29[31:33] sts.

1st row K1, *P1, K1, rep from * to end.

2nd row P1, *K1, P1, rep from * to end.

Rep these 2 rows for 2in, ending with a 2nd row. Change to No.6 needles. Beg with a K row cont in st st, inc one st at each end of every 8th row until there are 43[45:47] sts. Cont without shaping until work measures 17[17½:18]in from beg, ending with a P row.

Shape top

Cast off 4 sts at beg of next 2 rows. Dec one st at each end of next and every alt row twice, ending with a P row. 31[33:35] sts. Join in B. Commence striped patt as given for back, *at the same time* dec one st at each end of next and every alt row until 11 sts rem. Cast off at beg of next and every row 2 sts 3 times and 5 sts once.

Neckband

Join right shoulder seam. Using No.8 needles, A and with RS of work facing, K up 19 sts down left front neck, K across front neck sts, K up 18 sts up right front neck and 7 sts down right back neck, K across back neck sts, then K up 7 sts up left back neck. 75 sts.

Beg with a 2nd row, work 2in rib as given for sleeves. Change to No.6 needles. Cont in rib for a further 5in. Cast off in rib.

To make up

Press each piece under a damp cloth with a warm iron. Join left shoulder seam and neckband, folding neckband to outside. Set in sleeves. Join side and sleeve seams. Turn 1½in hem up at lower edge to WS and sl st down. Press seams.

Child's dress back

Using No.8 needles and A, cast on 58[64:70] sts. Beg with a K row work 1in st st. Change to No.6 needles.

Shape side

Cont in st st, dec one st at each end of every 6th row until 44[48:52] sts rem. Cont without shaping until work measures 11[12:13]in from beg, ending with a P row. Join in B. Work striped patt as given for Woman's dress 3 times.

Shape armholes

Keeping striped patt correct for 8 more rows, then cont in st st using A only, cast off 3 sts at beg of next 2 rows. Dec one st at each end of next and foll 2[3:4] alt rows. 32[34:36] sts. Cont without shaping until armholes measure 4½[5:5½]in from beg, ending with a P row.

Shape neck and shoulders

Next row K9[10:11]sts, turn and leave rem sts on holder.

Complete this side first. Cast off at beg of next and foll row 3[3:3] sts once and 3[4:4] sts once. Work 1 row. Cast off rem 3[4:4] sts.

With RS of work facing, sl first 6 sts on to holder for back neck, rejoin yarn to rem sts and K to end. Complete to match first side, reversing shaping.

Child's dress front

Work as given for back until armhole shaping is completed. Cont without shaping until armholes measure 3[3½:4]in from beg, ending with a P row.

Shape neck

Next row K9[10:11] sts, turn and leave rem sts on holder.

Complete this side first. Cast off 2 sts at beg of next row then dec one st at beg of foll alt row. Cont without shaping until armhole measures same as back to shoulder, ending with a P row.

Shape shoulder

Cast off at beg of next and foll alt row 3[3:4] sts once and 3[4:4] sts once..

With RS of work facing, sl first 6 sts on to holder for front neck, rejoin yarn to rem sts and K to end. Complete to match first side, reversing shaping.

Sleeves

Using No.8 needles and A, cast on 23[25:27] sts. Work 1½in rib as given for sleeves on Woman's dress, ending with a 2nd row. Change to No.6 needles. Beg with a K row cont in st st, inc one st at each end of 3rd and every foll 8th row until there are 33[35:37] sts. Cont without shaping until work measures 9[10:11]in from beg, ending with a P row.

Shape top

Cast off 3 sts at beg of next 2 rows. Dec one st at each end of next and foll alt row. Join in B. Work 18 rows striped patt as given for Woman's dress, *at the same time* dec one st at each end of 1st and every foll alt row. 5 sts. Cast off 5 sts.

Neckband

Join right shoulder seam. Using No.8 needles, A and with RS of work facing, K up 11 sts down left

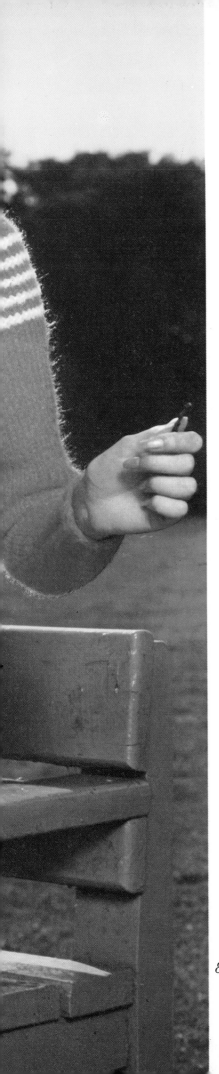

35

Soft, feminine mohair dresses for a woman and child with contrast bands of stripes on the yoke.

Knit
Sizes : woman's dress to fit 81.5[86.5: 91.5]cm (32[34:36]in) bust. Child's dress to fit 56.0[61.0:66.0] cm (22[34:26]in) chest

*

36

Chic, well-shaped jumper suit with a buttoned skirt and a neat ribbed shirt top.

Knit
Sizes to fit 81.5 [86.5:91.5:96.5: 101.5]cm (32[34:36: 38:40]in) bust and 86.5[91.5:96.5:101.5: 107.0]cm (34[36:38: 40:42]in) hips

**

front neck, K across front neck sts, inc 3 sts evenly across them, K up 10 sts up right front neck and 5 sts down right back neck, K across back neck sts, inc 3 sts evenly across them, then K up 5 sts up left back neck. 49 sts. Beg with a 2nd row work 1in rib as given for sleeves. Change to No.6 needles. Cont in rib for a further 2½in. Cast off in rib.

To make up
Press as given for Woman's dress. Make up as given for Woman's dress, noting that there is only a 1in hem.

36 Jumper suit with buttoned skirt and shirt top

Sizes
To fit 32[34:36:38:40]in bust
      34[36:38:40:42]in hips
Jersey length to shoulder, 21[21½:22:22½:23]in
Sleeve seam, 14½[15:15½:16:16½]in
Skirt length to waist, 23in
The figures in brackets [] refer to the 34, 36, 38 and 40in bust sizes respectively

Tension
6 sts and 8 rows to 1in over st st worked on No.9 needles

Materials
Jersey 15[16:17:18:19] balls Robin Roulette in main shade, A
2[2:2:2:2] balls of contrast colour, B
Skirt 14[15:16:17:18] balls in main shade, A
Oddment of contrast colour, B
One pair No.9 needles
One pair No.11 needles
5 buttons for jersey
8 buttons for skirt
Waist length of elastic

Jersey back
Using No.11 needles and A, cast on 104[110:116:122:128] sts.
1st row (RS) P2, *K1, P2, rep from * to end.
2nd row K2, *P1, K2, rep from * to end.
Rep these 2 rows for 2in. Change to No.9 needles.
Cont in rib as now set until work measures 14½in from beg, ending with a WS row.
Shape armholes
Cast off at beg of next and every row 4 sts twice and 2[2:3:3:4] sts 4 times. Dec one st at each end of next and foll 3[4:4:5:5] alt rows. 80[84:86:90:92] sts. Cont without shaping until armholes measure 6½[7:7½:8:8½]in from beg, ending with a WS row.
Shape neck and shoulders
Next row Rib 28[29:30:31:32] sts, turn and leave rem sts on holder.
Complete this side first.
Next row Cast off 2 sts, rib to end.
Next row Cast off 6[6:6:7:7] sts, rib to end.
Rep last 2 rows twice more. Work 1 row. Cast off rem 4[5:6:4:5] sts.
With RS of work facing, sl first 24[26:26:28:28] sts on to holder for back neck, rejoin yarn to rem sts and rib to end. Complete to match first side, reversing shaping.

Front
Work as given for back until work measures 2in less than back to underarm, ending with a RS row.
Divide for neck
Next row Rib 49[52:55:58:61] sts, cast off 6 sts, rib to end.
Complete this side first. Cont without shaping until work measures same as back to underarm, ending with a WS row.

Shape armhole
Cast off at beg of next and every foll alt row 4 sts once and 2[2:3:3:4] sts twice. Dec one st at beg of foll 4[5:5:6:6] alt rows. 37[39:40:42:43] sts. Cont without shaping until armhole measures 4½[5:5½:6:6½]in from beg, ending with a WS row.
Shape neck
Next row Rib 27[28:29:30:31] sts, turn and leave rem 10[11:11:12:12] sts on holder for front neck. Cast off 2 sts at beg of next row. Dec one st at neck edge on next and foll 2 alt rows. Cont without shaping until armhole measures same as back to shoulder, ending with a WS row.
Shape shoulder
Cast off at beg of next and every alt row 6[6:6:7:7] sts 3 times, and 4[5:6:4:5] sts once.
With RS of work facing, rejoin yarn to rem 49[52:55:58:61] sts and rib to end. Complete to match first side, reversing shaping.

Sleeves
Using No.11 needles and B, cast on 50[53:53:56:56] sts. Work 8 rows rib as given for back. Break off B. Join in A. Change to No.9 needles.
Next row K to end.
Beg with a 2nd row, cont in rib as given for back, inc one st at each end of every 8th row until there are 68[71:75:78:82] sts. Cont without shaping until sleeve measures 14½[15:15½:16:16½]in from beg, ending with a WS row.
Shape top
Cast off 4 sts at beg of next 2 rows. Dec one st at each end of next and every alt row until 32[33:33:34:34] sts rem, ending with a WS row. Cast off at beg of next and every row 2 sts 8 times, 3 sts twice, and 10[11:11:12:12] sts once.

Front borders
Using No.11 needles, A and with RS of work facing, K up 54[57:60:63:66] sts down left front edge.
Next row K1, *P1, K2, rep from * to last 2 sts, P1, K1.
Work 6 rows more as now set. Cast off in rib.
Using No.11 needles, A and with RS of work facing, K up 54[57:60:63:66] sts up right front edge. Work 3 rows rib as given for left front edge.
Next row (buttonhole row) Rib 6[7:5:7:6] sts, *cast off 3 sts, rib 9[10:11:11:12] sts, rep from * 3 times more.
Next row Rib to end, casting on 3 sts above those cast off in previous row.
Rib 2 rows more. Cast off in rib.

Neckband
Join shoulder seams. Using No.11 needles, B and with RS of work facing, K up 8 sts along top of right front border, rib across front neck sts, K up 23[24:24:25:25] sts up right front neck and 9 sts down left back neck, rib across back neck sts, K up 9 sts up left back neck and K up 23[24:24:25:25] sts down left front neck, rib across front neck sts, K up 8 sts along top of left front border. 124[130:130:136:136] sts.
Next row P1, *K2, P1, rep from * to end.
Rib 2 rows more as now set.
Next row Rib 3 sts, cast off 3 sts, rib to end.
Next row Rib to end, casting on 3 sts above those cast off on previous row.
Rib 2 rows more. Cast off in rib.

Pocket (make 1)
Using No.9 needles and A, cast on 17 sts. Work 2¼in rib as given for back, ending with a WS row. Break off A. Join in B. Change to No.11 needles.
Next row K to end.
Rib 7 rows. Cast off in rib.

To make up
Do not press. Set in sleeves. Join side and sleeve seams. Sew down ends of front border to cast off sts at centre front. Sew on pocket to left side of front with bottom edge level with front opening.

Press seams lightly under a damp cloth with a warm iron.

Skirt back
Using No.11 needles and A, cast on 133[139:145:151:157] sts. Beg with a K row, work 1½in st st, ending with a K row.
Next row (hemline) K to end.
Change to No.9 needles. Beg with a K row, cont in st st for 5in, or required length before side shaping, ending with a P row.
Shape sides
Next row K1, K2 tog, K39[41:43:45:47] sts, K2 tog, K45[47:49:51:53] sts, sl 1, K1, psso, K39[41:43:45:47] sts, sl 1, K1, psso, K1.
Beg with a P row, work 9 rows st st.
Next row K1, K2 tog, K38[40:42:44:46] sts, K2 tog, K43[45:47:49:51] sts, sl 1, K1, psso, K38[40:42:44:46] sts, sl 1, K1, psso, K1.
Cont dec in this way on every foll 10th row until 77[83:89:95:101] sts rem. Cont without shaping until work measures 22in from hemline, ending with a P row. Change to No.11 needles.
Waistband
Next row K1, *P1, K1, rep from * to end.
Next row P1, *K1, P1, rep from * to end.
Rep last 2 rows for 1¼in. Cast off in rib.

Left front
Using No.11 needles and A, cast on 69[73:75:78:81] sts. Beg with a K row work 1½in st st, ending with a K row.
Next row (hemline) Cast on 2 sts, K to end.
Change to No.9 needles.
Next row K to end.
Next row K3 sts, P to end.
Keeping 3 sts at front edge in g st throughout, cont without shaping until work measures 5in from hemline, or same as back to side shaping, ending with a WS row.
Shape side
Next row K1, K2 tog, K to last 15 sts, K2 tog, K to end.
Cont dec in this way on every foll 10th row until 43[46:49:52:55] sts rem. Cont without shaping until work measures same as back to beg of waist, ending with a WS row, dec 0[1:0:1:0] st at end of last row. 43[45:49:51:55] sts.
Waistband
Change to No.11 needles. Keeping 3 sts at front edge in g st, work 1¼in rib as given for waistband on back. Cast off in rib.
Mark positions for 8 buttons on front, 1st to come 2in above hemline and last to come in centre of waistband, with 6 more evenly spaced between.

Right front
Work as given for left front, reversing all shaping, noting that dec rows will read, K13, sl 1, K1, psso, K to last 3 sts, sl 1, K1, psso, K1, and making buttonholes as markers are reached as foll:
Next row (RS) K7, cast off 3 sts, K to end.
Next row P to end, casting on 3 sts above those cast off in previous row.

Pockets (make 2)
Using No.9 needles and A, cast on 26 sts. Work 4¼in patt as given for Jersey back, ending with a 2nd row. Break off A. Join in B. Change to No.11 needles.
Next row K to end.
Rib 7 rows. Cast off in rib.

To make up
Press each piece under a damp cloth with a warm iron. Join side seams. Fold in 3 g st edge at each front to WS and sl st down. Turn up hem at lower edge to WS and sl st down. Sew on pockets in centre of each front between 2nd and 4th buttonholes from waist. Press seams. Sew elastic inside waistband using casting st. Sew on buttons.